ARTIST DESCENDING A TYPEWRITER

NINE ESSAYS ON CONTEMPORARY ART

ARTIST DESCENDING A TYPEWRITER
NINE ESSAYS ON CONTEMPORARY ART

MICHAEL PAUL HOGAN

SHANTI ARTS PUBLISHING

BRUNSWICK, MAINE

ARTIST DESCENDING A TYPEWRITER
NINE ESSAYS ON CONTEMPORARY ART

Published by Shanti Arts Publishing

Designed by Shanti Arts Designs

Shanti Arts LLC
193 Hillside Road
Brunswick, Maine 04011
shantiarts.com

Cover image is by Toti O'Brien and used with her permission:
As in Aria, mixed media, 2022.

Artists discussed herein have given permission to print quoted conversation as well as their artwork.

Printed in the United States of America / United Kingdom

ISBN: 978-1-956056-87-7 (softcover)

Library of Congress Control Number: 2023910508

for Susan

The creative act is not performed by the artist alone;
the spectator brings the work in contact with the external
world by deciphering and interpreting its inner qualifications
and thus adds his contribution to the creative act.

—Marcel Duchamp

CONTENTS

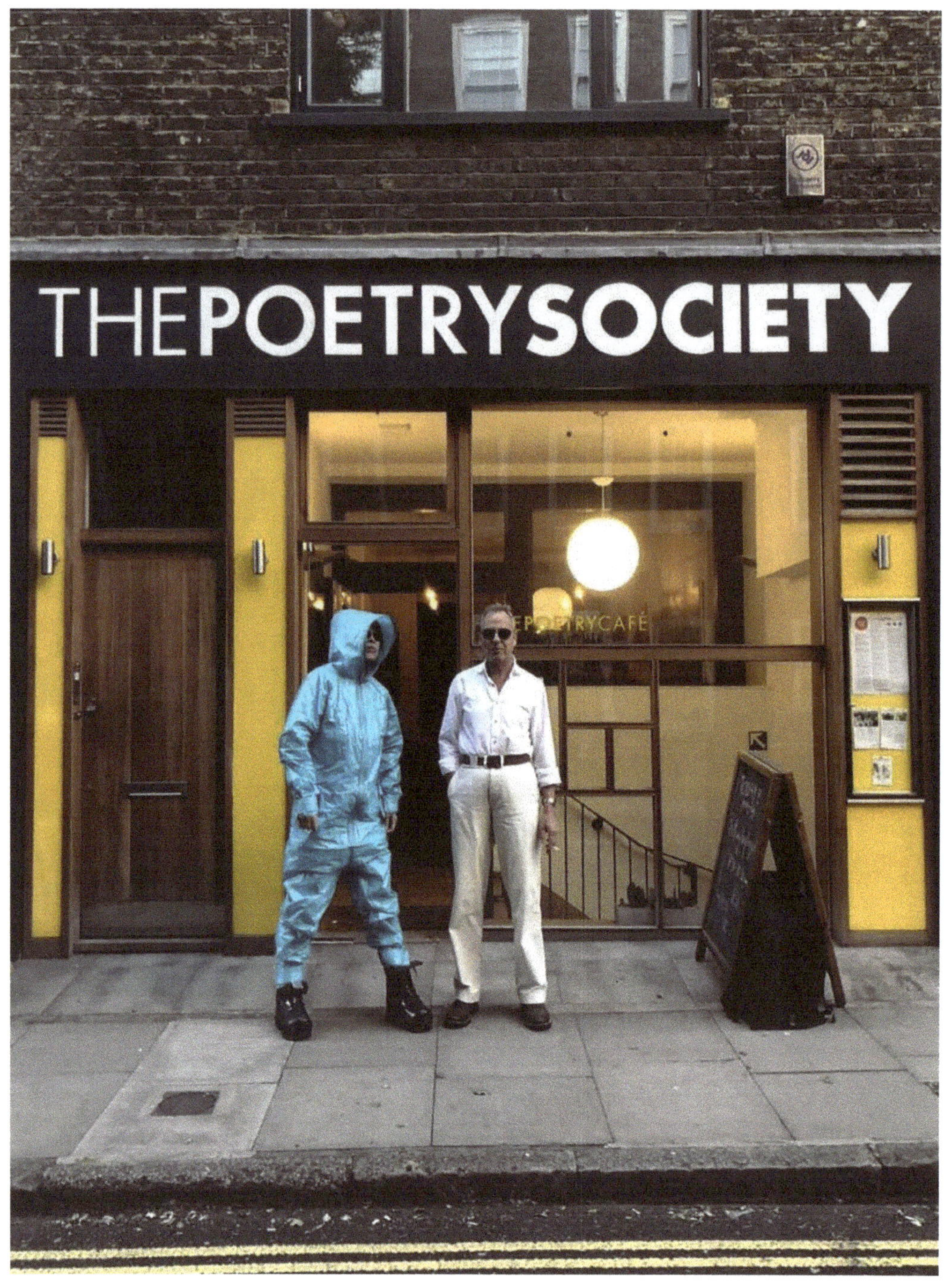

Artist Kong Ning with the author, Michael Paul Hogan, Covent Garden, London, 2018

INTRODUCTION

In 1991 I published my first book, a collection of poems titled ***Ahab's Dead***. It was brought out by a small independent press called Making Waves in simultaneous hard and soft cover editions, both of which were printed on high-grade paper and both of which were supposed to have illustrations to accompany the text. I can't remember the name of the artist—I'd never heard of him previously—but after designing the cover, he had a nervous breakdown, and so the book came out text-only. It was, as you might say, an inauspicious start.

The following year I found myself in Key West and decided to stay for a while. I got myself an interim job waiting tables and washing dishes at a restaurant on Whitehead Street, rented a room with a shared bathroom and kitchen on Varela Street, and located the offices of a weekly paper called ***Island Life*** at the top end of Duval. I figured Monday morning at 9:00 would be a suitably businesslike time to pay a call on the editor. It was a mistake that was to have near-epic consequences for me as a writer, providing me with an accidental break rather like those you hear about in old-time Hollywood, where the unemployed actor is cleaning a famous film director's swimming pool and happens to look exactly like the director's conception of the romantic lead opposite Joan Crawford or Lana Turner in his next picture. The editor's name was Dick Epler, and Monday was never a good time for anything. Monday was hangover day.

It never even occurred to me to make an appointment; I just showed up. Back then they didn't have a reception area; you just walked up the stairs, pushed open a door that was already ajar, and entered the compositing room. A nice-looking lady cutting and pasting with a pair of scissors and a tube of glue, a lady who, I later learned when we became good friends, was juggling two simultaneous engagements—to a naval officer and a commercial fisherman, rarely in town at the same time—heard my request to speak to the editor with slender amusement and indicated a door with EDITOR stenciled on the woodwork. I knocked and went in.

Now the whole point of my being there at all was merely this: I intended to introduce myself, tell the editor I had recently published a collection of poems, and ask if he might be interested in giving it a small review. I thought it would be cool to be able to say that my book had been taken note of in Key West. However, within a few minutes it became clear that we were totally at cross-purposes. Mr. Epler, not really concentrating properly, not even *focusing* properly, assumed I had come looking for a job and, no doubt the sooner to get rid of me, offered me my own bi-weekly column that would be called "Books & Writers." I was speechless. Interpreting my astonishment as disappointment, he upped the offer by suggesting I write features on subjects of my choice in the alternating weeks. I thanked him as best I could and got out of there before he woke up and changed his mind. The lady compositor gave me a lovely smile. I think she must've twigged what it was all about.

Now that I was a professional Key West journalist I needed to act like one, so I went straight into Sloppy Joe's for a beer. Sloppy Joe's, along with a few other of the real old-style fishermen's bars, closed at 3:00 a.m. and reopened at 8:00. I then went to the office supply shop on Simonton Street to buy a typewriter and a ream of paper. It seems hard to believe now, but thirty years ago it was still perfectly normal to type your copy. The office supply shop was large and airy, and arranged on a shelf up near the ceiling, about the same height as the ceiling fan, was a row of beautiful old vintage typewriters. I asked the proprietor how much they were and was told that, no, they were not for sale, they were just a decorative feature. We got talking. I said that I needed a typewriter for my new job as a features writer and columnist for ***Island Life***. That clinched it. He went and got a stepladder from somewhere out back and told me I could choose any of those vintage typewriters I liked and it was mine for ten dollars. Put a kid in a toy store and tell him to take his pick, and you have an idea of me right then. After half an hour of going up and down the ladder, trying out different machines, I settled on a near-perfect condition 1928 Royal Portable. Anyone who understands anything about typewriters will appreciate what a beautiful piece of work that is. It's the same make and model that Hemingway used. It won't make you write like Hemingway, but you just know it'll make you write the best you can.

My landlord was a carpenter. He found me a couple of orange crates and a plank of wood and—voila!—I had a desk. Within a few days of my first piece for the paper appearing, I was accepted as one of the team; within a few weeks people started to know who I was. I liked it that bartenders and waitresses and fishermen and truck drivers read and enjoyed my stuff. I liked it when I was told by the owner of the paper that people were grabbing the latest issue to read my column first. Fame, even fame on an island four-and-a-half miles long and one-and-a-half miles wide, was exciting for an English kid with only previously a small book of poems to his name. It opened doors—literally. I spent the day in Philip Burton's house, drinking sherry in his kitchen and hearing first-hand the well-honed tales of how he adopted a marvelous boy named Richard Jenkins. I remember a line from the piece I subsequently wrote (my first cover story): "In the cultural demi-monde of Key

West, it is rather fascinating to spend the day with a man whose greatest dilemma is what to give Elizabeth Taylor for Christmas." He even showed me the red cashmere sweater Elizabeth Taylor had given *him* for his birthday. I met Budd Schulberg and James Dickey and Joy Williams and Richard Wilbur and James Merrill. I got invited to join a bunch of ***Miami Post*** journalists on an illegal trip to Havana on a covertly chartered fishing boat. I got invited to great parties. I got a fan letter from a high-profile lawyer in Washington, D.C. There was nothing not to like about it. It was eighteen months of rollercoaster fun on a small island in the subtropics. I eventually quit because I wanted to be someone small in somewhere big, and ended up in India—which was very, very big and where I was very, very small indeed.

But the legacy of my year and a half in Key West was the realization that, even with only the slender reputation that a published book of poems and a regular opportunity to demonstrate my flair for literary journalism conferred, I was accepted into a higher stratum of the art world than I would have otherwise been. I also realized, rather to my credit I think, that fame, real fame, in either poetry or literary journalism, was as unlikely as winning the lottery with a single ticket—to say nothing of being ephemeral, irrelevant and downright petit-bourgeois. What mattered was that armed with only a moderate degree of commercial success backed up with the aura of artistic integrity that this implies, I was able to meet people whose work I admired on a more or less equal social footing; that with only the lightest dusting of fame myself, doors have opened to me that might to others have remained closed; that I have been, and am, in a privileged position, not just with writers but with artists in the broadest sense of the term; that this book would not have been written unless I actually knew each of the subjects, several of whom have become personal friends. I am neither scholar nor archivist; I would have no idea how to even begin a biography of Modigliani or a critique of Raphael—and frankly have little interest in trying. My knowledge of painting has been gained far more in the painters' studios than in the galleries that exhibit them; far more in drinking with them than researching them; far more, as one might say, in the street rather than in the salon. And not just painting, of course, but photography, mixed media, assemblage and performance art too.

But now let us be more specific and talk about the book you are holding in your hand and, hopefully, about to read.

It might seem strange, perhaps even condescending, to start by defining "contemporary," as in our subtitle, ***Nine Essays on Contemporary Art***, but it is an important distinction, as well as potentially ambiguous, and needs to be clarified sooner rather than later. So here goes:

By contemporary I mean artists who are currently producing new work in the sense that it extends their oeuvre rather than merely adding to it or reflecting back on it. To an only slightly lesser extent, it at least implies that the artists be of approximately my own generation rather than that of my parents or even grandparents. I can't say that age is exactly an issue, and refuse to make it so, but I am unlikely to consider as contemporary anybody who, despite being still alive (at least at time of writing), became famous in the 1950s and 1960s; for example, Jasper Johns, b. 1930; Bridget Riley, b. 1931; Frank Auerbach, b. 1931; Gerhard Richter, b. 1932; Frank Bowling, b. 1934; Woody Allen, b. 1935; David Hockney, b. 1937; Allen Jones, b. 1937; David Bailey, b. 1938; Gilbert & George, b. 1943 & 1942. Actually, what I find rather wonderful is that these people, despite being nearly legendary, are still alive. We all, I think, want to live in an age of celebrity; to hope that one day, in a restaurant in London or Paris or New York, we might glimpse among the crowded tables an artist or writer or filmmaker whose work we have admired since childhood, eating the same food and breathing the same air as ourselves. But however alive they may be, they are not in any meaningful sense contemporary. They and their work already seem to belong to a bygone era; in fact, they are usually written or spoken about in the (totally past tense) context of Twentieth-Century Art.

But, when selecting artists to appear in this book, an equally important criterion has been, and absolutely must have been, the quality of their work. My position as author would be untenable if I did not trust my own opinion, but that opinion is backed up by the fact that each of the artists between these covers could, if asked, provide you with a sheaf of reviews, critiques, exhibition posters and an extensive list of public galleries and private collectors in over twenty countries across four continents to back up their right to inclusion.

So what it comes down to is this: (a) I am only interested in writing about artists I know personally; artists whom I can write to, call up on the telephone, or drink a cup of coffee with and gain insights into their work first-hand rather than relying on secondary sources, and (b) I will not write about anybody whose work I would not be prepared to hang on my own walls, and I mean most specifically on the walls of my writing room, my studio, my atelier, where even the pencils in the pencil jars have to be of a specific brand and optimum sharpness to be allowed admittance and where are hung photographs by Michael Woods and Paul Polydorou, drawings by Kong Ning, and paintings by Erika Capobianco, Toti O'Brien and Li Bin, although we, I mean my wife and myself, have further Li Bins hanging in nearly every room of our rather abbreviated flat, and Kong Ning's amazing larger than life-size portrait of my wife hangs in our bedroom—a gift delivered from Paris that you will read about in a later chapter of this book. In the meantime, our apartment faces exactly east; the sun rises above the center of our bed with the implacable mathematical precision of a plumbline; however, we have crumb-foraging friends to lessen the glare at our window every morning, courtesy of a net curtain embroidered with sparrows, a wedding anniversary present to Susan and myself from the aforementioned Toti O'Brien, a painter and collagist whose work, I am proud to say, was once published next to mine in a literary art journal. *Grazie mille, Toti. Ho bisogno della bellezza dei tuoi passeri sul davanzale della mia prosa indifferente.*

Before I conclude, a word about the way I have written this book. It was always my intention to vary the style, the *approach*, of each individual chapter or essay; to try and find a way of making the construction of each piece appropriate to the artist being discussed. Like the artists themselves, I have experimented with collage, pastiche and assemblage, as well as more traditional variations on literary journalism, direct-quote interview and first-person narrative. I cannot say I have always been successful, but at least it means there is not just variety in the illustrations but also in the prose that they illustrate.

One thing that genuinely surprised even myself when I had finalized the contents of this book was the sheer breadth of media that would be represented in its pages. Perhaps because I am so close to these people, I had somehow taken their talents for granted and underestimated their exceptional range. What it does mean is that you, the reader, are about to be in the company of not just painters (using oils, acrylic, gouache and Chinese ink) and photographers, but also collagists, installation artists, performance artists, mixed media artists, illustrators, makers of boxes and assemblages, surrealists, costume designers, as well as actors, filmmakers, poets and musicians. When I was in my teens I thought that Jean Cocteau was the most amazingly multi-talented artist imaginable; nowadays to exhibit fluidity in crossing and blurring artistic boundaries is almost the norm. It is my sincere belief that we, who were born in the twentieth century and make our futures in the twenty-first, live in an exceptional era for the arts. And if this new millennium has not so far produced a titan, a Picasso, for example, a Man Ray or, indeed, a Cocteau, it presents just as broad a range of talent as any period in the celebrated past; perhaps more so. Well—history will be the better judge of that. In the meantime, it is my sincere honor and pleasure to be sufficiently respected by a handful of this generation, these contemporaries, to have had their enthusiastic cooperation in the making of this book. It needs hardly be said that any inadequacies in the writing of it are mine; all the success I hope it achieves belongs to the artists whose work it contains.

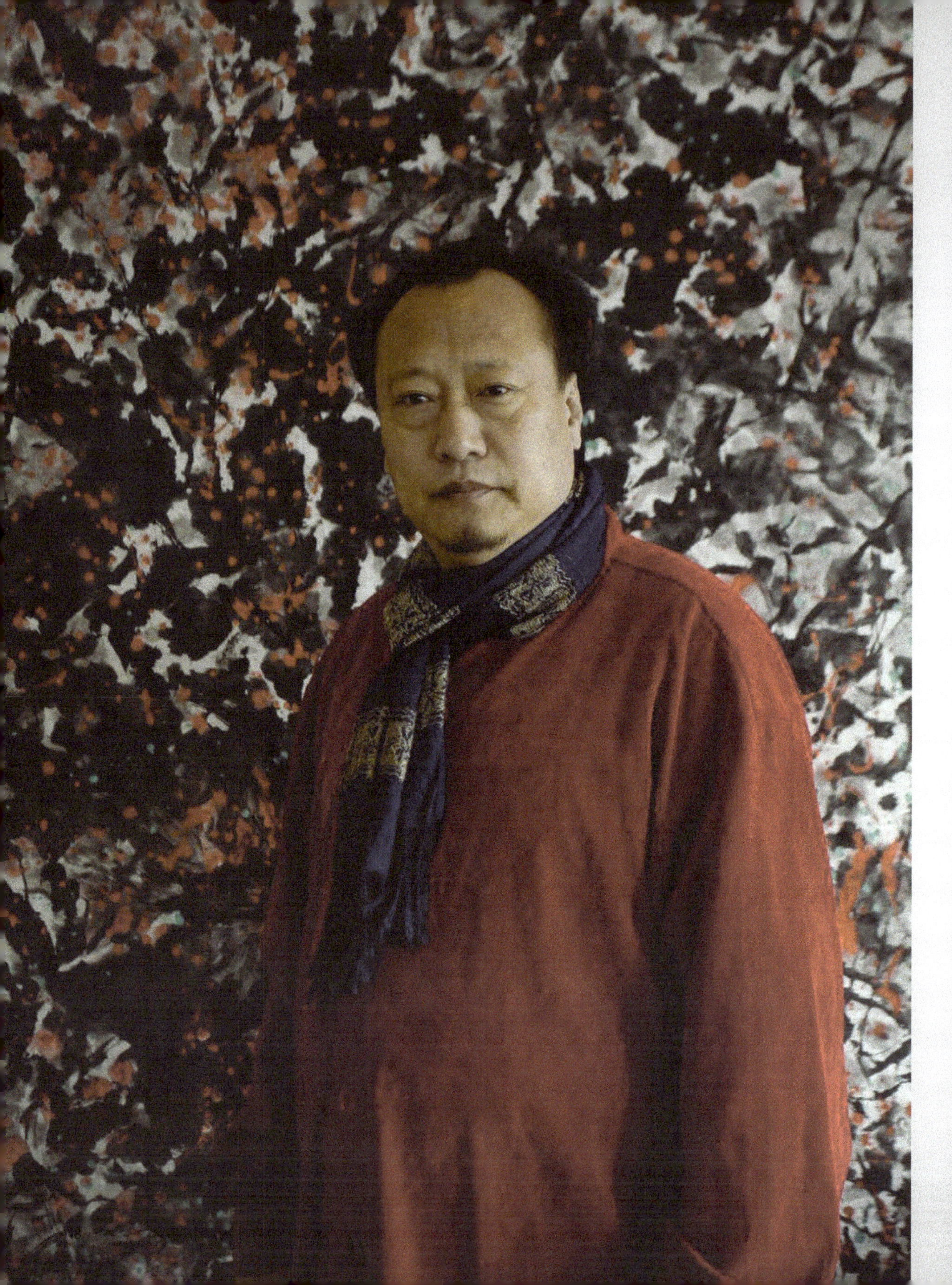

LI BIN

"In the winter it was so cold, my hands would swell up until the skin split across the knuckles. They were constantly bleeding. And in the summer I was so hungry I used to catch dragonflies and eat them. That is not the history of the Cultural Revolution. That is the memory of it."

Li Bin was born in Dalian, a coastal city in Northeast China, in 1964. At the age of six he and his parents were forced out of their comfortable middle-class home by Mao Zedong's Cultural Revolutionary Red Guards and put on a boat to Shandong, a rural province across the Bohai Sea, there to be politically "re-educated" as farmers.

"Neither of my parents knew anything about farming. It was a constant and terrible struggle for survival. The predominant memory is of being left alone and having nothing to eat. They were out in the fields from dawn to dusk every day. We—by which I mean myself and the other village children—used to forage for any food we could find. I can still remember once finding a piece of old corn bread and heating it up on a stick over a fire. Looking back, I've no idea how we even managed to survive for those seven years, let alone stay healthy both mentally and physically."

But survive he did (although countless others did not), and in 1977, the Cultural Revolution having effectively ended with the death of Mao Zedong the previous September and the subsequent arrest of the Gang of Four, the family decided it might be safe to return home. There was, however, no certainty as to whether they even had a home to return to as many so-called "bourgeois" residences had been ransacked, burned, or turned over to Communist Party members.

"But even so, we left our village secretly in the middle of the night. Just stole away with what we could carry. And somehow made our way back across the Bohai Sea to Dalian."

However, they returned safely to find that the political climate had changed in their favor. Victims of the Cultural Revolution with no affiliations to the Red Guards were not just allowed to return to normal life but were, Li Bin recalls, respected for their sacrifices. His parents resumed their former occupations—his father an executive for the local gas company, his mother a teacher—and their son was enrolled in middle school.

"Paper! A school with real paper! I couldn't believe it. How wonderful! For seven years the only paper I saw was revolutionary posters stuck up on walls. We wrote in the dust with sticks and wiped our noses or whatever else needed wiping with leaves."

After graduating from high school, Li Bin studied art at Liaoning Normal University and subsequently taught drawing and painting at both the high school and university level, also working for a while at an advertising agency. In his midtwenties he began to paint seriously for himself, and it was those hard, lonely years of the Cultural Revolution that provided him with a theme not just for his early paintings, in fact, but for the majority of a rich and varied career.

This career can be divided into three quite distinct periods, the first of which, with Li Bin's approval, I refer to as his MAGIC REALIST PERIOD. These paintings, all done in oils, have as their inspiration the scenes of his childhood, shot through with surrealist flashes, as though seen through an imaginative boy's eyes. The hardship and fatigue are brilliantly captured in the slumped shoulders of the men, the resigned faces of the women, the angular rib-revealing leanness of the livestock, often rendered in a surprisingly expressive muted palette of browns and grays. In one striking composition, a woman stands abased in front of a brutish husband. But the contempt on his face is mirrored in hers, just as her finger mimics his cigarette. The cow, ironically, has more personality than either, demanding its share of the frame. But these are not just passive figures in a monotonous landscape. There is, for example, a disturbingly satanic quality in the slaughter of a goat; the half-naked executioners with their shaved heads and brutalized faces seem to take a sadistic pleasure in the

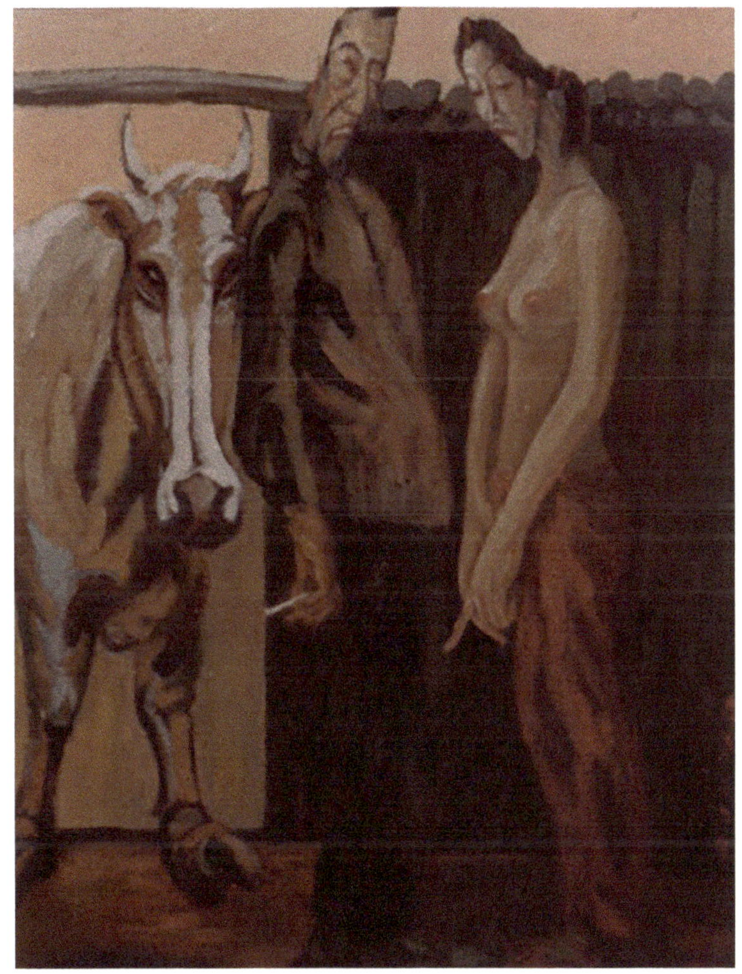

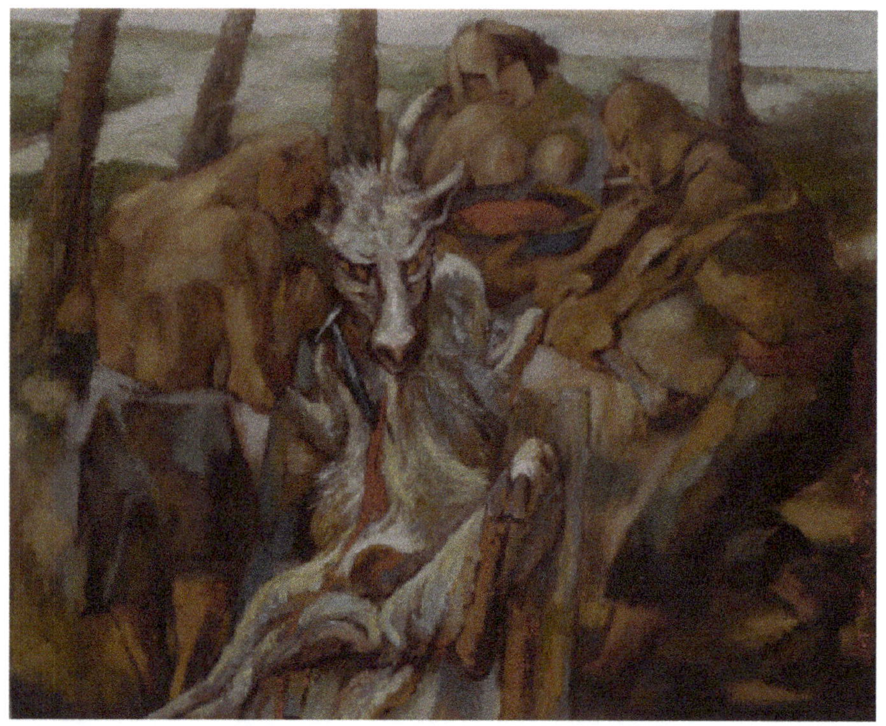

sacrifice; the goat, in another glorious piece of composition, is painted white against a predominantly brown background, and seems to project from the foreground of the canvas, although if you look carefully you will see that the arm of the man on the left is actually closer to the viewer than the head of the goat. A woman completes the composition. As semi-naked as the men, she holds beneath her breasts a bowl of blood. The violence that underpinned the whole of Chinese society during the Cultural Revolution is turned into a chilling metaphor.

But there is joy here, too, as well as hardship, for Li Bin is a consummate humanist, well aware that the harsher the environment, the more a simple pleasure needs to be celebrated. The simple pleasure, for example, of a stolen kiss between two

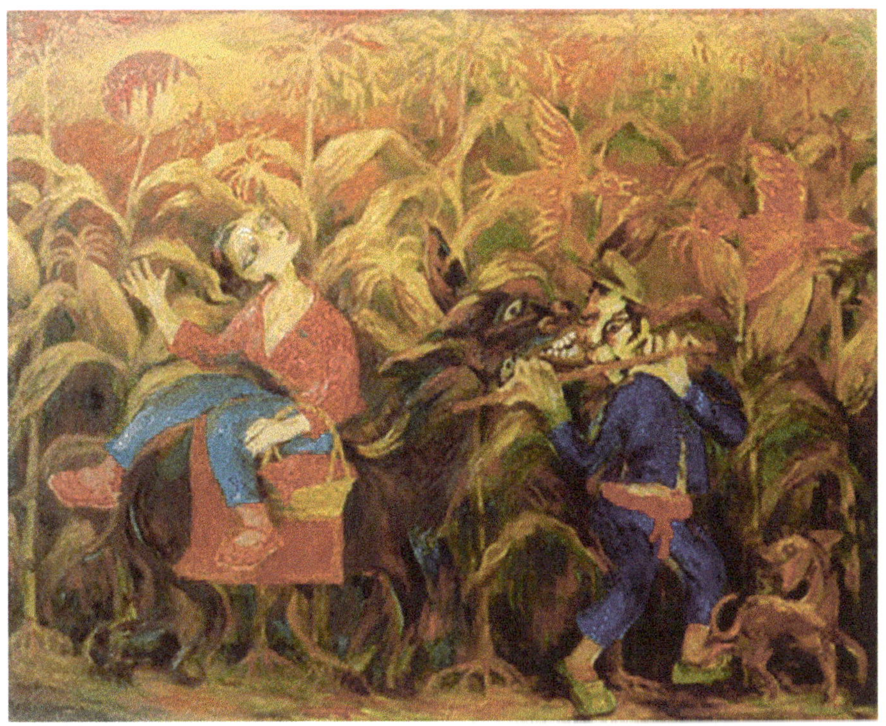

lovers in the middle of plowing a field or a young man playing an improvised flute to his girl. A village wedding provides a wonderfully welcome splash of color, the bride radiant in her bright red dress, her hair adorned with flowers and leaves; the groom's bashful smile transcends the Mao-style tunic he is forced to wear and which he has left unbuttoned sufficiently to reveal a corresponding red posy tucked into the waistband of his trousers—a delightful touch. And although sometimes deliberately naïf, there is a wonderful sophistication in the compositions and a sly humor in the way that cattle are given the same prominence as their human masters. This was, after all, an era of completely non-mechanized farming, when a man's cow was as important as any member of his family.

But to completely come to terms with the impact of the Cultural Revolution, something much more overtly political, much grander in scope was required. So it was that in 2000 Li Bin embarked on a unified project that would take eight years and span 149 canvases, each of which is either 200 or 248 centimeters high and 124 centimeters wide. This series, comprising his **Cultural Revolution Period**, is a unified whole, and despite being offered tens of thousands of dollars by American collectors for individual canvases, Li Bin has steadfastly refused to allow the sequence to be broken. It is probably the most significant artistic response we will ever see to the darkest period of postrevolutionary China.

Executed with Chinese watercolor (the nearest Western equivalent would be gouache) and collage, the pieces combine contemporary posters and photographs of, among others, Mao, Lenin, Stalin, and Marx with demons from Chinese mythology, cartoons of murderous violence, and elements of graffiti. Seen "life-size" they possess the same angry power and sheer overwhelming force as Picasso's ***Guernica***—another overtly political work—and have the collective effect of a nightmare from which the sleeper cannot awaken. Red, yellow, and blue, the principal colors, are used symbolically. Red represents violence, revolution, and bloodshed,

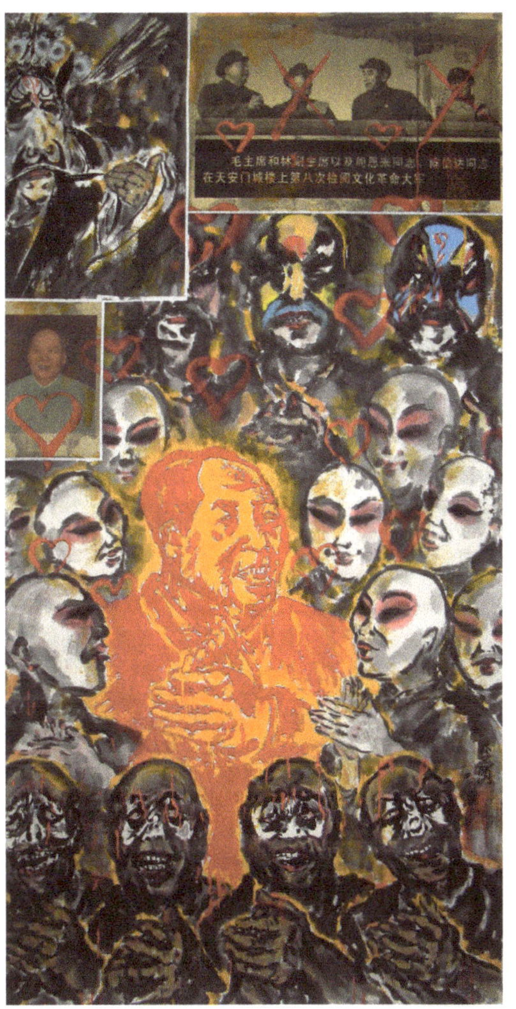
毛主席和林副主席以及周恩来同志、陈伯达同志
在天安门城楼上第八次检阅文化革命大军

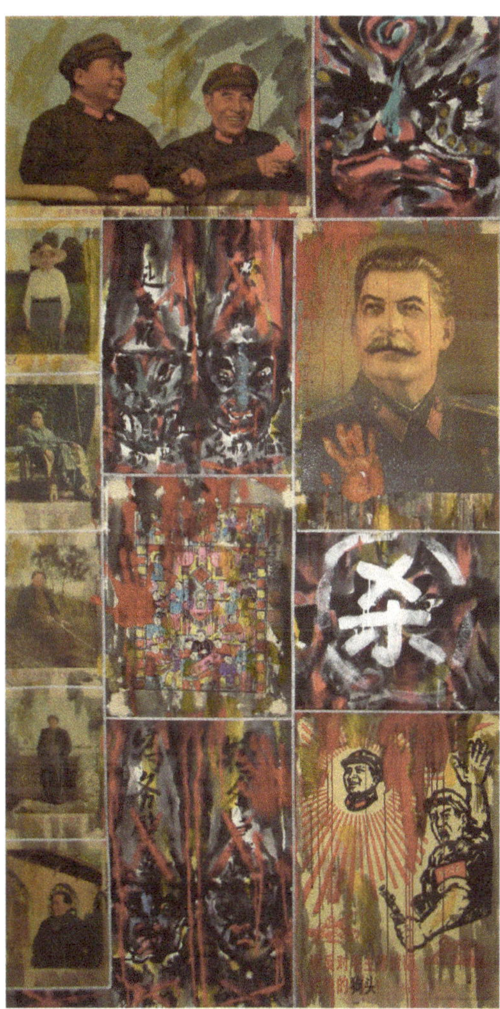
杀

as well as being the color of the Chinese flag. Yellow was the color of the imperial court in the Dynastic era. It is used ironically, for Mao Zedong was as powerful and ruthless a dictator as any emperor. It is also used to symbolize the insularity of China at that time. Blue is uncompromising. It represents the stupidity of the ordinary people who became Red Guards, who were given uniforms and guns and power beyond their intelligence to use them, and without whom the Cultural Revolution could not have happened. If the early paintings promoted cattle to the level of humans, these later works demote people to the level of cattle. "If the government told them to kill, they killed," says Li Bin. "They didn't ask why. They are responsible too."

Why spend eight years producing what is, in effect, a single work?

"For me, as an artist, I have a social responsibility. I want people to remember this ten-year period. Writers can write books; historians can record history. I have only painting. This is my way to commemorate what happened."

Later, sitting down specifically to write this essay, I asked Li Bin to elucidate certain paintings I might use to illustrate it. He thought about it, shook his head, and said:

"Each one represents a ten-thousand-word story. According to even official records, that's one painting for every ten thousand who died. No essay is long enough. Just show people the paintings."

A reaction to the horror and violence of the Cultural Revolution canvases, plus the necessity of respite after their intellectual and technical rigors was perhaps inevitable, and Li Bin's third, or **Beijing Opera Period**, is the result. These paintings, with their graceful (but deceptive) simplicity and easily accessible charm,

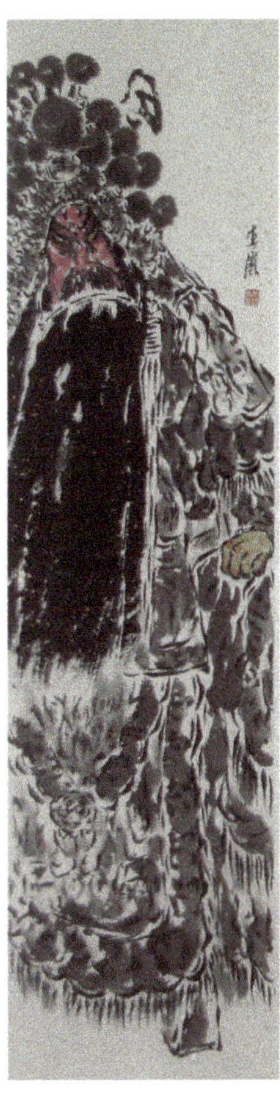
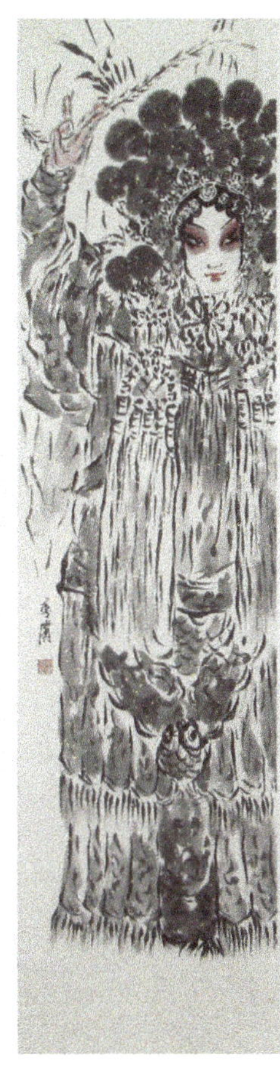
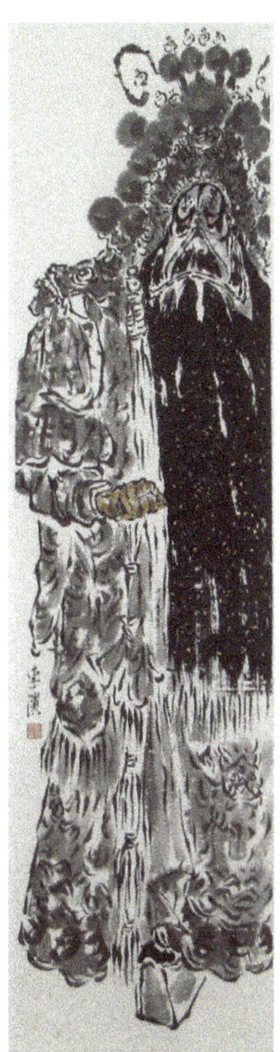
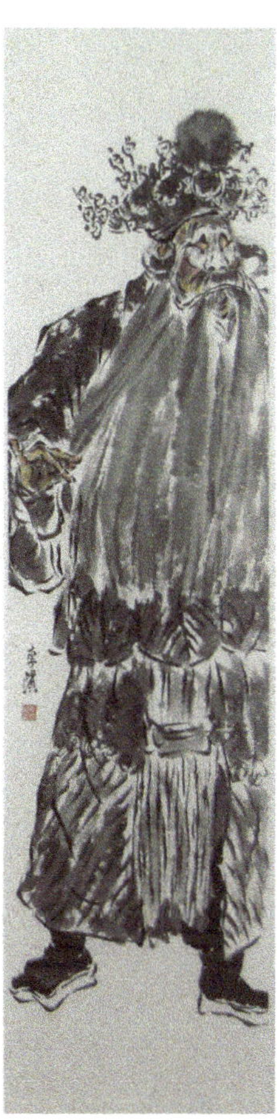

have become his most popular works, although the irony is that they, too, owe their genesis to the Cultural Revolution.

"During that time, traditional Chinese theatre was the only entertainment that ordinary people were allowed, so I grew up with Beijing Opera. There was nothing else. I even hoped I might become a singer myself when I was older. So these are not just paintings. They represent an important part of my childhood."

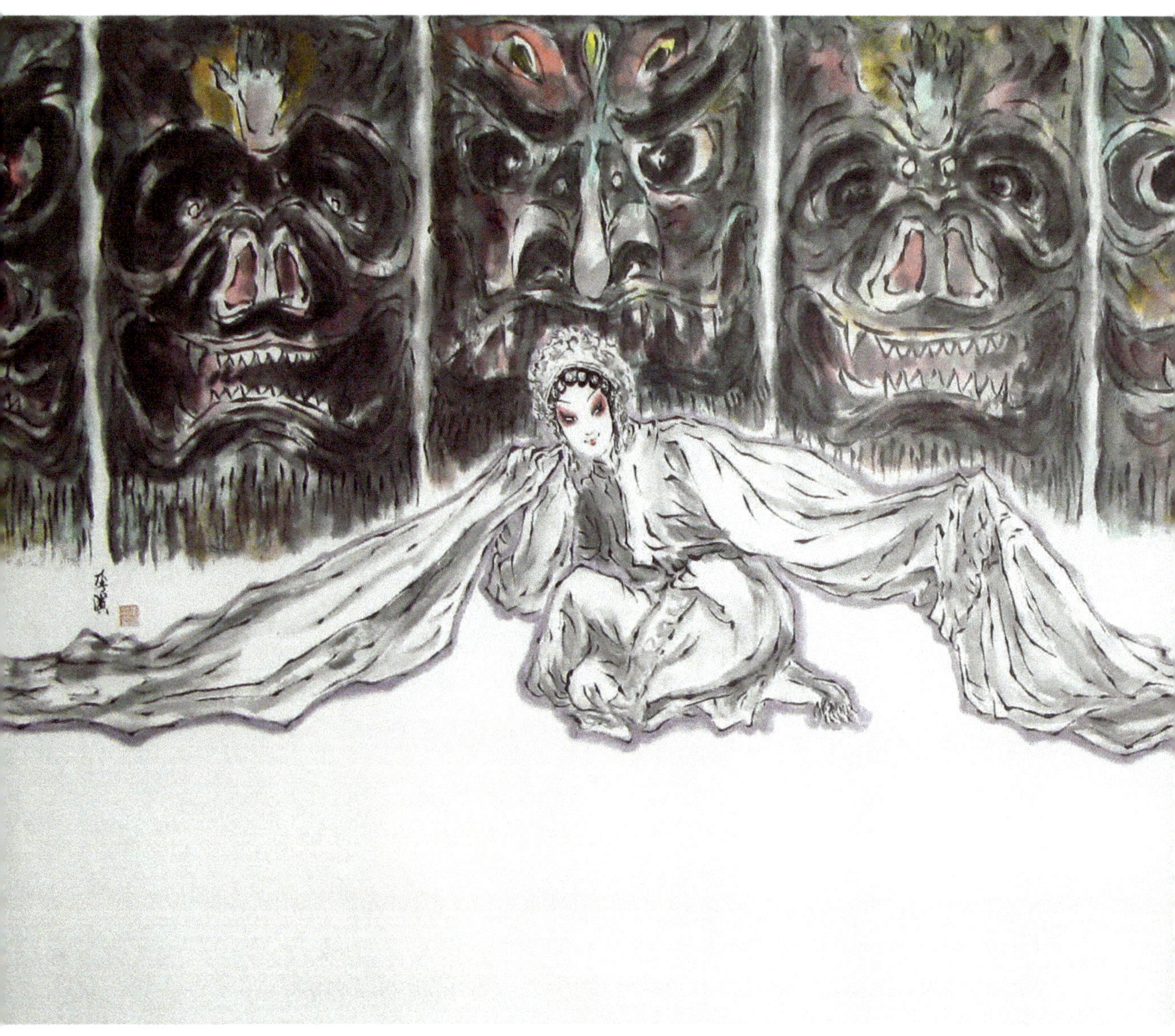

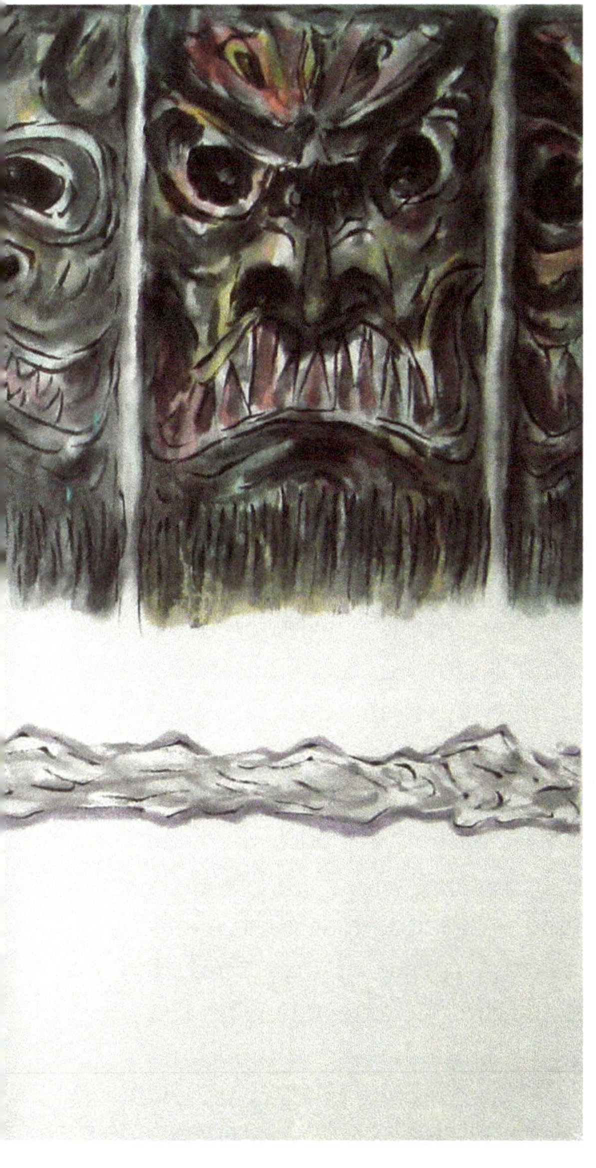

After the muted tones of the Magic Realism Period and the symbolic primary colors of the Cultural Revolution paintings, here we see a delicacy, a wholly unanticipated gracefulness combined with the same unerring eye for composition that characterized the earlier oils. Color is kept to a minimum in many of the pieces—although in others it is used with the same abundance as it is on the traditional stage—and it is in these, where the color is most sparing, that Li Bin's technical ability is most on display. The medium is black ink wash with touches of gouache. No more red or blue than can fit on the tip of a brush gives personality to the eyes, a bursting sex appeal to the lips. Beijing Opera is a very strict, very classical form of theatre, with each character clearly delineated. Think of the ballet of Tchaikovsky's era as a Western equivalent, or perhaps Italian *commedia dell'arte,* and these paintings match it for a classical and restrained simplicity of style. It is also worth noting that each character depicted on one of Li Bin's many canvases of this period is strictly accurate in respect of costume, makeup, headdress, and physical posture. But the important thing is that, under his hands, they live; they perform for us, charm us, and delight us each time we enter a gallery where they are exhibited.

I seem to have spoken at some length about the paintings. Perhaps now I should turn my attention, albeit briefly, to the man himself. Growing up, even after the Cultural Revolution, in a China very much insulated from the West, his style, his superb eye for composition is all the more remarkable for not having been influenced by the masters of European art. If pressed, he expresses an admiration for van Gogh, but in fact he far more resembles Gauguin. A big man both in respect of personality and physical size, he drinks wine by the bottle, not the glass, orders six dishes a time at a restaurant, and has an infectious laugh that he delivers with his head thrown back for the sheer joy of sharing his happiness. He is immensely disciplined, arriving at his studio at nine o'clock every morning, putting on a pot of coffee, and working till four in the afternoon. After four in the afternoon, he lets rip. He despises hypocrisy, sycophants, liars, and fools, and would sooner go without a meal than tolerate fake artists and fake art, but I have never seen him angry or petty or jealous of another's success, and he would sacrifice his most precious commodity—time alone in his studio—to help a struggling artist if he thought that artist was genuine and needed help.

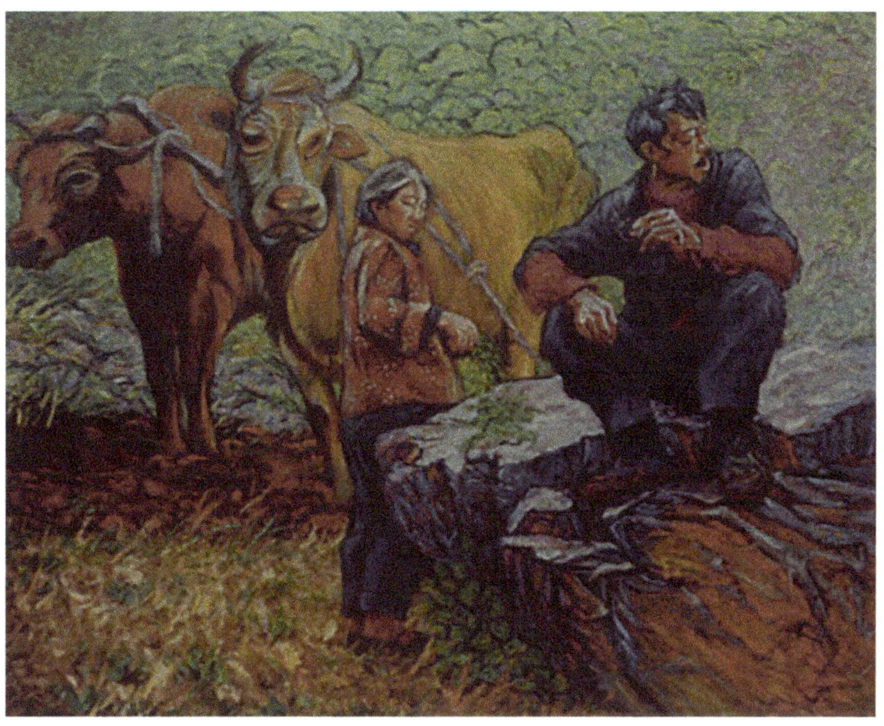

A few years ago, desiring a change of scene and wanting to paint plein-air, he rented a small farmhouse on the rural outskirts of Beijing and set up a trestle table in the courtyard, painting every day by natural sunlight and living on local vegetables and turtle soup. Work progressed well, to say nothing of the fact that, wearing only a pair of shorts, he developed a terrific (and very un-Chinese) tan. Then an artist-admirer discovered his whereabouts and paid a call. One visitor led to two, then three, then four.

"I didn't have the heart to turn them away. Then every night it was *baijiu* (Chinese alcohol) and turtle soup and talking about art until 4:00 am. They were really respectful and really wanted to learn about painting. Trouble was, they really didn't want to learn about washing the dishes afterward!"

I spoke earlier of three periods; in fact, there are four. In January 2013 Li Bin was finally granted an exit visa, having been invited to France by the French government's Department of Culture. He traveled with a selection of Beijing Opera paintings and almost immediately gave a one-man exhibition at Le Havre. It was a critical and popular success and led to him staying on for six months, renting his own studio in the attractive French coastal town. At the end of that year, he achieved his (and most painters') lifetime ambition—an exhibition in Paris. Since then, having been deemed of sufficient cultural importance by the French government to be granted an indefinite entry visa, he has been able to come and go between China and France, and something in this physical freedom has been transformed into a new phase of his art.

When I first saw his abstracts in his Dalian studio, I could hardly believe my eyes. A riot of color and form that, after the sheer painstaking exactitude of the Beijing Opera pictures, was like opening the window of an elegant black and white drawing room and seeing the sky explode with fireworks outside. But there to be seen, was the same unerring eye for composition, the same pinpoint accuracy of brushwork that had always characterized his style.

Which inevitably raises the question: What of the future? Are we about to see a whole new facet, even a complete aesthetic reinvention of China's greatest living painter? Li Bin thinks for a few moments before he answers.

"Now I just want to paint 'Art,' pure art, not with any political or philosophical meaning. Yes, my French paintings are more abstract. But, whatever. Art goes on for life. An artist never stops reinventing himself and his material. He cannot stop. Why should he? And I now realize, too, that culture does not have nationalities or boundaries. In the last two or three years I have invited artists from Germany, France, Switzerland, and Ireland to share my exhibitions with me. The walls of these galleries are big; there's room for all of us. Having said that, next year I will have solo retrospectives in France and Taiwan. But I think I've done everything I can in respect of my duty to society—Chinese society, the period of the Cultural Revolution. Now it's up to the public to study my paintings, to know for themselves, and for themselves to judge."

现在我只想画画

Now I just want to paint.

Coda: Requiem for a Painter

On the evening of November 2, 2019, we were dressing for dinner at the country hotel where we were staying for the weekend in the south of England when my wife decided to check her phone. I think she was expecting a call from her sister. Something, anyway, perfectly routine. I distinctly remember knotting my tie in the bathroom mirror and hearing a sudden cry of "Oh, no." That was when we got the news that Li Bin was dead.

The following day we learned the details in a text message from his wife in Dalian. He had been in a restaurant and had suffered a massive and almost instantaneously fatal stroke, no doubt with a brimming glassful of *baijiu* in his right hand. It was grimly appropriate but agonizingly premature. He was fifty-five years old.

After the initial refusal to believe it's true, memories come crowding back in a wonderful and random collage. For eight years Li Bin had been one of our closest friends. My wife, Susan, was his confidant and muse; she was the first person he called when he was offered a solo exhibition in France, and even when we left China to come and live in England, they spoke on the phone every couple of weeks. Li Bin! We had a seriously spacious apartment in Chunliu, one of the working-class districts on the edge of Dalian, and Li Bin was a constant guest. On his first visit to Paris, having had his exhibition in Le Havre and giving a lecture on contemporary Chinese art, he bought a pair of suede boots, of which he was inordinately proud. Apart from some Winsor & Newton paints and brushes, I think they were the only souvenir he brought back from his trip. Shortly after his return to China, he came to our apartment where we drank whiskey and champagne and Beaujolais and got ridiculously, wonderfully drunk together. And at the end of the evening, because he was unable to stand up and bend down at the same time, I had to lace his precious shoes for him. How he safely got down three flights of concrete stairs I'll never know.

For several years he had a studio in the Sanhuan Hotel, a posh façade situated near the beach, the studio actually a converted suite and adjacent room complete with bedroom and two bathrooms. He painted, as traditionally-trained Chinese painters do, horizontally on a large trestle table rather than at an easel, eventually tacking his paintings to the wall so he could come along later and stand before it to apply the final touches. His routine was impeccable.

However late he had been out the night before, however much *baijiao* or red wine had been consumed, he would arrive at nine o'clock in the morning, make a large pot of coffee, and work until four in the afternoon. He might have had the larger-than-life personality of a Gauguin or a Diego Rivera, but, as I have said before, he was the most extraordinarily disciplined artist I have ever known.

Do you remember, Susan? That time in December, the sidewalks piled with ice and slush, a heavy snow already falling in the late afternoon dark, and as our taxi slished to the curbside in Sanba Square, there was Li Bin standing on the sidewalk, waiting for a taxi himself, the sheer coincidence of that in a city of five million people, our respective destinations forgotten as we headed to the nearest restaurant for noodles and beer.

On November 2, 2019, suitably and elegantly attired, we went down to dinner and ate whatever we ate and drank the no doubt appropriate wine and never by so much as a word or a glance referred to the news we had just heard. Later we went to the cabaret and danced to the resident band, and shortly before midnight I excused myself and strolled out onto the terrace for a cigarette. It was a beautiful early winter's night, icy cold, the promise of a heavy frost, the air as sharp as a new spade. There was not a cloud in a perfectly clear sky and yet, by some perfectly explicable meteorological phenomenon, there was not a star to be seen. How very strange! And then, quite suddenly, one star appeared, directly opposite where I was standing, at an angle of about sixty degrees to the horizontal, one star only, and extremely bright, in an otherwise uninterrupted sky. I finished my cigarette, smiled at the star, and went back to the cabaret to dance with my wife.

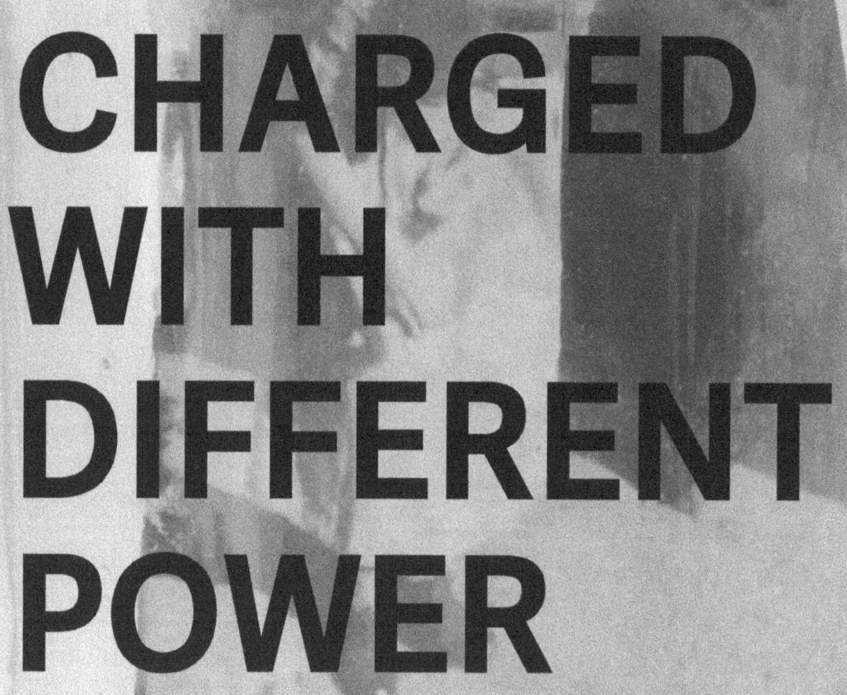

CHARGED WITH DIFFERENT POWER

The Extraordinary Art of Helen Ivory

1

"Working with ready-mades, as I so often do, is a little like working with words. A telephone as an object and the word *telephone* will each bring their own denotation and connotation with them. I actually get a buzz out of every assemblage I see; there is something magical—and fetishistic—about objects. And when they are taken out of their usual context and made strange, they are charged with different power."

In the extraordinary art of Helen Ivory, images and objects, words and photographs can be swiftly transformed through the twin alchemies of symbolism and surrealism into the substance of (rather wonderful) alternative worlds in which birds are juxtaposed with telephones, an antique doll has the wings of a crow, and a cow grazes serenely on the mountains of the moon.

Ivory is that *rara avis*, an artist of equal stature in the worlds of both poetry and the visual arts, and although it is as a visual artist that she is being featured here, it would be an omission of the greatest disservice both to her and to yourselves, the readers, not to establish from the outset that she has published seven volumes of highly regarded poetry, several of which have photographs of her assemblages as cover designs, and one of which, ***Hear What the Moon Told Me***, is a work of "found" poetry and collage and, indeed, a work of such visual brilliance and aesthetic integrity that I will consider it separately in the second part of this essay. As if this were not enough, there has also been a new (2016) version of the major arcana of the Tarot deck—a collaboration with the British multimedia artist Tom de Freston that breathes fresh life into a tradition at least six hundred years old. But for now, let us concentrate on Helen Ivory, the creator of figures and assemblages, and open, however briefly, a door into the *wunderkammer* of her art and mind.

𝔚

Helen was born in Luton, a large town in the southeast of England, in 1969, and although coming from the kind of working-class background that traditionally gives little or no encouragement to those who aspire to a career in the creative arts, she was fortunate to find progressive teachers at high school.

"I originally did A-level art where I studied the work of Howard Hodgkin and then went on to make some shadow theatre versions of his paintings because they already looked to me like they were stage sets."

In fact, it was a career in theatre design that at first seemed most likely, but "somehow I knew I wanted to do something with words." She went on to read for a BA in cultural studies at Norwich University College of the Arts, where she was mentored by the celebrated Anglo-Hungarian poet George Szirtes, and the books and the reputation and the prizes soon followed.

"I graduated in 1997 and then concentrated mainly on poetry because I didn't have any space to make art, and I thought I had nothing to say. Or perhaps I just didn't find myself as a visual artist until I had worked out who I was in poetry."

Be that as it may, and even with the inevitable benefit of hindsight, there can be no doubt that the poems laid down the themes that would recur in Helen's visual work, perhaps standing in relation to it as the architect's drawing, however beautiful in itself, might stand in relation to the sheer actual *thereness* of the completed building.

A Diversion on the Theme of Alice

Imagine if Helen Ivory, established poet and (potential) artist, had drunk from a bottle labeled DRINK ME and shrunk sufficiently to be able to live inside a doll's house, and then eaten a cake with EAT ME written on it (in currants) and expanded back to human size, squeezed within the now absurdly small four walls. Might that at least begin to explain her extraordinary faculty of being a part and apart, the observer and the observed, the child who possesses the doll's house and the doll who observes the enormous sunlike eye of the child?

Helen Ivory's visual works can be approximately divided into four categories, and although these may be somewhat false or at best rather over-simplified distinctions, they do at least enable us to better focus on the several aspects of her art.

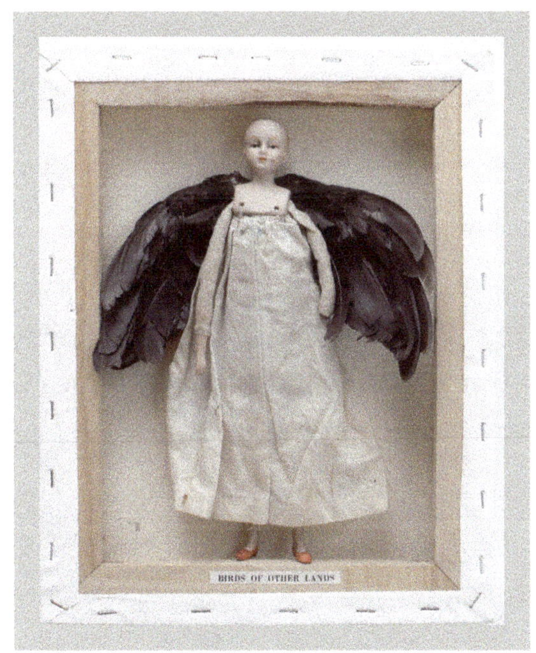

First, and perhaps most importantly, there is the **DOLL MOTIF** (see, for example, ***Birds of Other Lands***), a recurring feature not just of her assemblages but also of her poetry. In fact, it is this motif that most closely ties her poetry and her visual art together, and it is impossible to read . . .

There's always someone to do your dirty work,
always someone
with plucked-out eye,
with snapped-off hands...

in the junkshop window,
they have all lost their names.

from ***The Breakfast Machine*** (2010)

...without thinking of her strangely disturbing, strangely symbolic (but of what?) disembodied doll torsos and amputated doll limbs. This is not the erotic perversion of a Hans Bellmer; rather, it is some kind of parody of an anatomical textbook, and when we remember that traditionally doctors were men and that their female patients (indeed, their females) were passive objects in their hands, the image of a medical training manual makes psychological and political sense.

But the doll itself is only one aspect; even more important, I think, is the ever-recurring motif of the doll's house, one that goes back to the beginning of Helen's artistic ambitions:

"I have always been interested in miniature stage sets—I originally wanted to be a theatre designer—so I like the doll's house motif as a little set for big dreams."

If the doll is symbolic of a woman's body, then the doll's house is doubly symbolic—firstly, of a woman's place; secondly, that of which the frame or the box or the jar in which the art is displayed is itself symbolic, a sort of symbolism in reverse. But in the meantime, however important the doll's house, there must have been the doll:

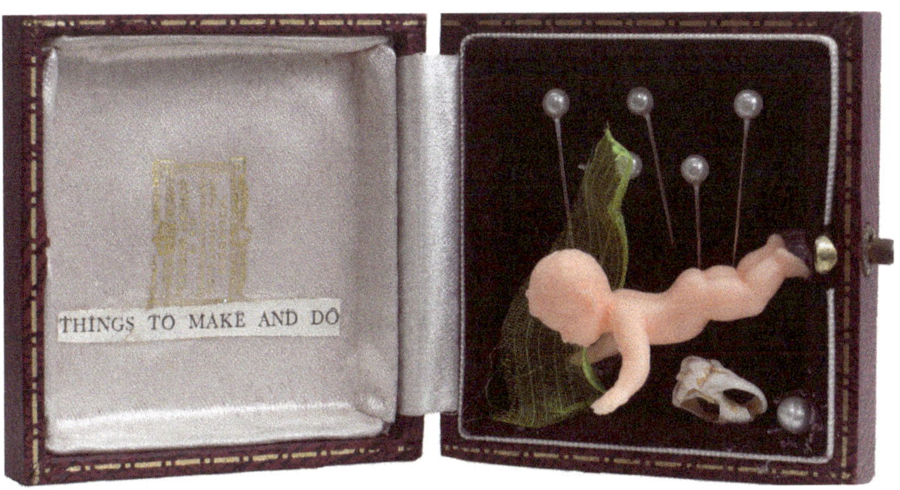

"I think dolls were part of my inner childhood landscape rather than an adult-learned influence. All little girls of my generation were given dolls, so I've always been around these little semblances of humans. The life we give them stems from our imaginations; we can make them act in certain ways by how we pose them and how we ventriloquize. Culturally and historically, dolls have a lot of responsibility placed on their shoulders. People seem to adore them or be terrified by them in equal measure."

One category will inevitably segue into the next, and now we have what I might call **Box or Frame Assemblages**, to which several of the doll artworks belong, and the one featuring a doll's torso topped with a bird's skull sitting next to a telephone on a plinth (***The Waiting***) rather wonderfully (and surrealistically!) is all about . . .

"... waiting for news that will never come. The bird has no arms to answer the phone (do birds have arms anyway?!) and the phone is clearly not connected to anything. So it's a kind of futile, empty-headed eternity!"

However, if I may be allowed a personal favorite among Helen's works within that frame category, it must be ***The Arthur Mee Series***, a set of boxed/framed assemblages based on (ironic?) quotations from the celebrated children's encyclopedia.

A Diversion on the Theme of Arthur Mee

Arthur Mee (1875–1943) was an English journalist and educator whose ten-volume *Children's Encyclopedia*, first published in 1922, the same year as *The Waste Land* and *Ulysses*, is, regardless of all its limitations in respect of time and place, a sheer masterpiece of education. The superbly chosen illustrations (which, when I was a child, introduced me to some wonderful painters, including the pre-Raphaelites) are worth the admission fee alone.

Consider ***Earth and Its Neighbors***—we are here presented with content and composition, intelligence and wit. The spatial representation is millimeter-perfect; the texture is even more three-dimensional than the actual dimensions of the objects used to create it. This is not a *wunderkammer* (another of Helen's consistent, in both poetry and art, motifs); rather it is, to coin a phrase, a *wunderfenster*: a window into the doll's house, the poet's house, but so beautifully presented as to be an end in itself. Look again at the (real) shell, the (toy) cow. Neither could have been placed anywhere else and each rather mischievously echoes the shape of the other. Yes, there is symbolism at work here, but there is also the simple beauty of spatial perfection, of an aesthetic made true.

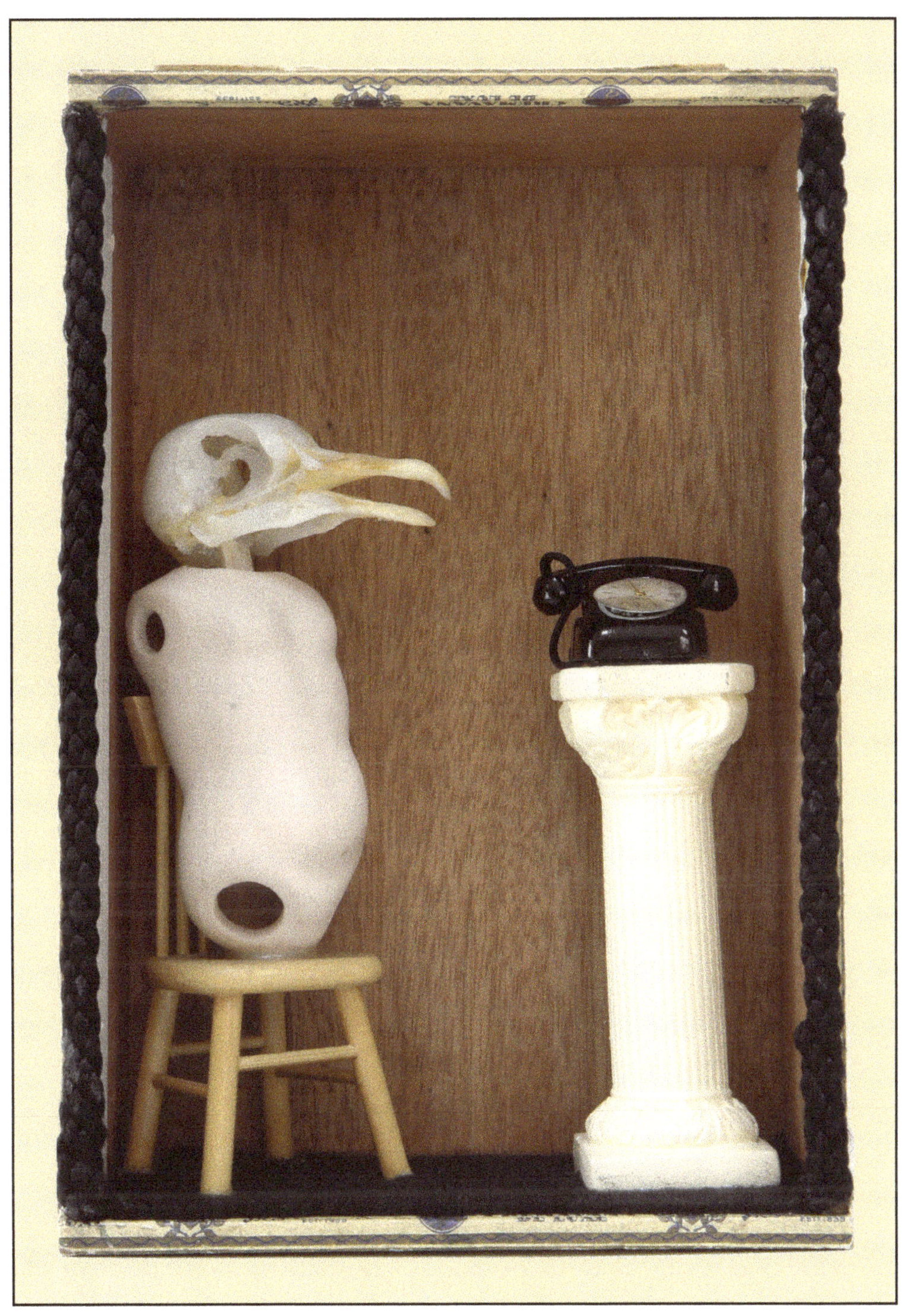

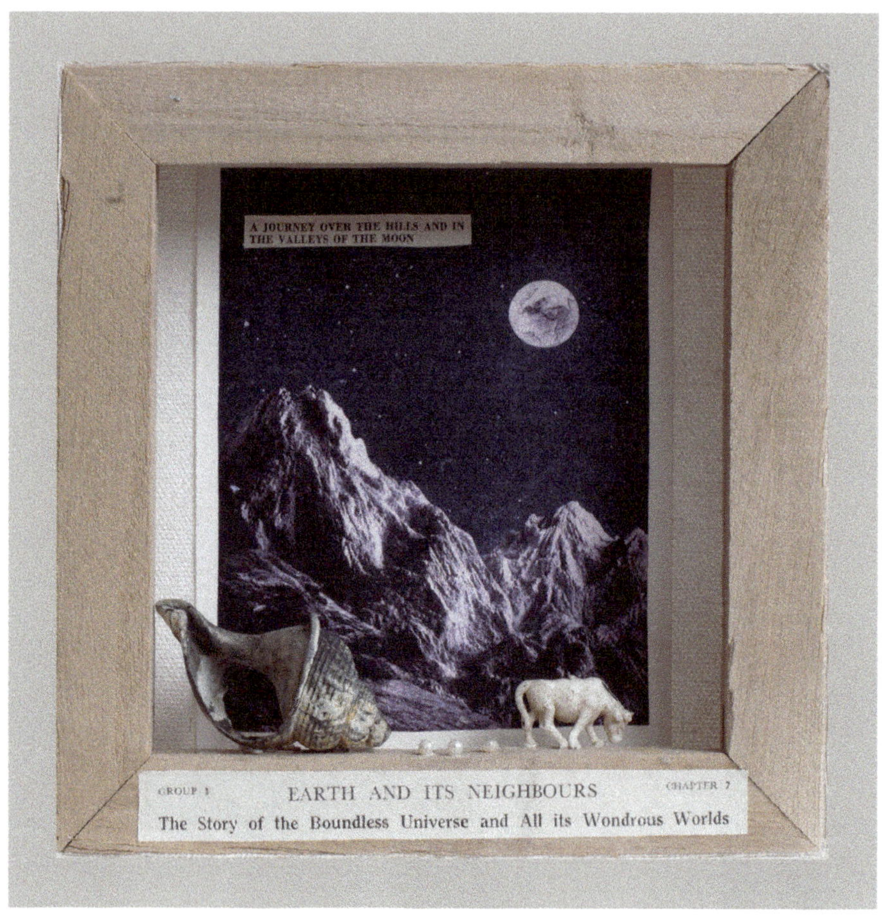

When is a box not a box? Well, maybe when it's a jar. The third aspect of Helen's art is the use of **GLASS JARS**—jars that might once have held jam or marmalade—in order to preserve items of memorabilia, of nostalgia, and present them differently to a modern audience. The most significant example, ironically, is not as a gallery work of art, but the cover of her 2013 poetry collection ***Waiting for Bluebeard***. But is there a more-than-obvious difference between a box, a two-dimensional frame, and a jar? The answer is hers:

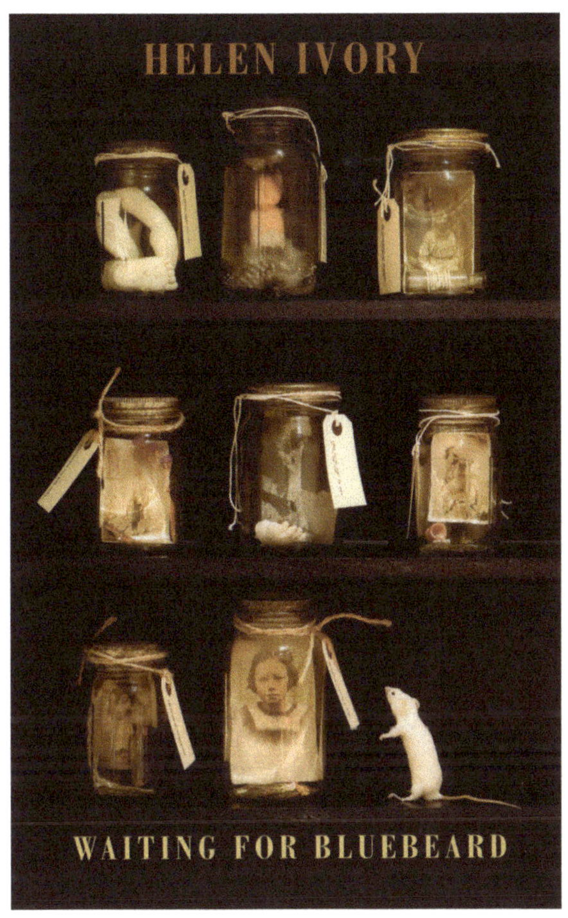

"I guess the glass jar suggests three-dimensional sculpture, whereas the box is more of an elevated two-dimensional relief. I used glass jars for the cover image of ***Waiting for Bluebeard*** as puns. The jars themselves are on a shelf, so they are only seen from the front. I have called this series ***Preserves*** because they are photographs and objects in Kilner jars, which are usually used for, well, preserves."

Often the jars contain old photographs, giving these jars a most curious double-aspect: firstly (as she herself says), of a past preserved, but secondly (and to me much more vividly), of a past captured, in the sense of imprisoned, and with a little imagination one can almost hear the characters in these photographs crying out with tiny voices, begging to be set free. Which rather begs the question of who these characters are:

"The pictures that I buy from flea markets are largely of women captured at the time of their wedding or posing in a photographer's booth on their own or with children, or sometimes children on their own. Roland Barthes talked about the punctum—the thing about an image that pierces you and speaks directly to you. Looking through some of the images I have now, I think it's probably to do with the subject's vulnerability and how they choose to present themselves to the camera."

> This time the door wasn't locked
> so she saw the room's plunder
> floating in the dark liquid
> of neatly labeled jars—
> fingernails, tangles of hair,
> an unborn child.
>
> from ***Waiting for Bluebeard*** (2013)

And finally, we come to our fourth category—the **COLLAGE**, of all visual arts surely the one that comes closest to poetry itself and which, when created by an artist who is also a poet, necessarily takes on a special significance. Combining cut-out (usually vintage) images with poems created from "found" texts, these exquisite (and often exquisitely profound) works, of which ***Lay the Heart*** is a very good example, have the added advantage of speaking so

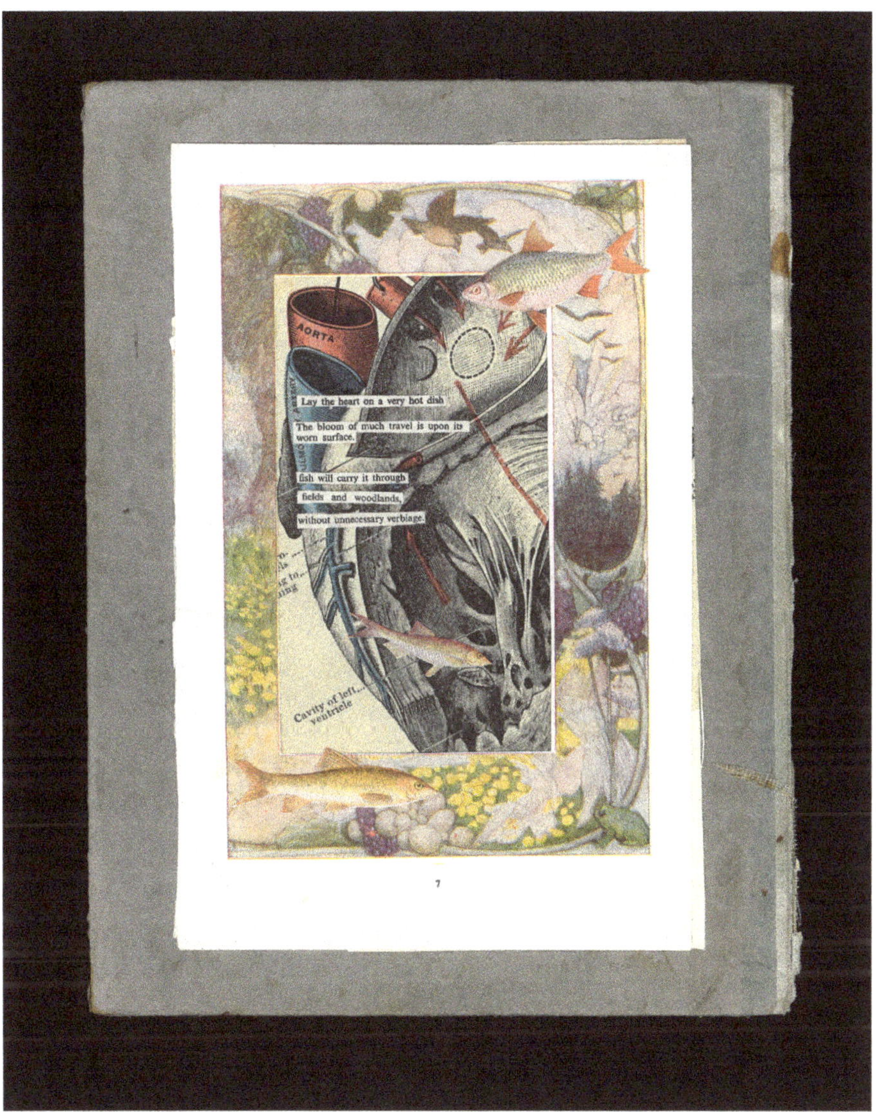

clearly for themselves that they obviate the necessity of critical interpretation. One point, however, should be made. The poems (themselves cut-outs) are so perfectly "placed" that they become part of the visual experience, transcending their literal meaning.

In other words, someone with no knowledge of English could still gain a complete aesthetic satisfaction from the overall work.

The extraordinary world of Helen Ivory, whether entered by eating a cake marked POETRY or by drinking from a bottle labeled VISUAL ART, is truly Alice-like in its sense of wonder, its sense of logical construction, its sense of logical deconstruction, its sense of sheer logical madness reflected in the looking glass of the illogically sane. It also possesses a sense of not just originality but artistic freedom, as Helen Ivory is one of those fortunate few who have the self-confidence—and the skill—to absolutely and fearlessly create the art they wish to create. There have been influences, sure, not least among them Angela Carter, Jan Svankmajer, Alexander Calder, Joseph Cornell, Vasko Popa, Leonora Carrington, Tim Burton, and the Brothers Quay ("Dark fairytale and surrealism!"). But the result is that which all artists, in whatever medium, aspire to—a look, a style, a sense of fresh perspective on a familiar theme that could only possibly have been the work of themselves.

What happens next is your choice
though the moon that I've painted

has calm seas,
warm enough to dive into.

If you come with me,
I will show you the earth wound up

in a neat little ball.
I will tell you my name.

from ***The Breakfast Machine*** (2010)

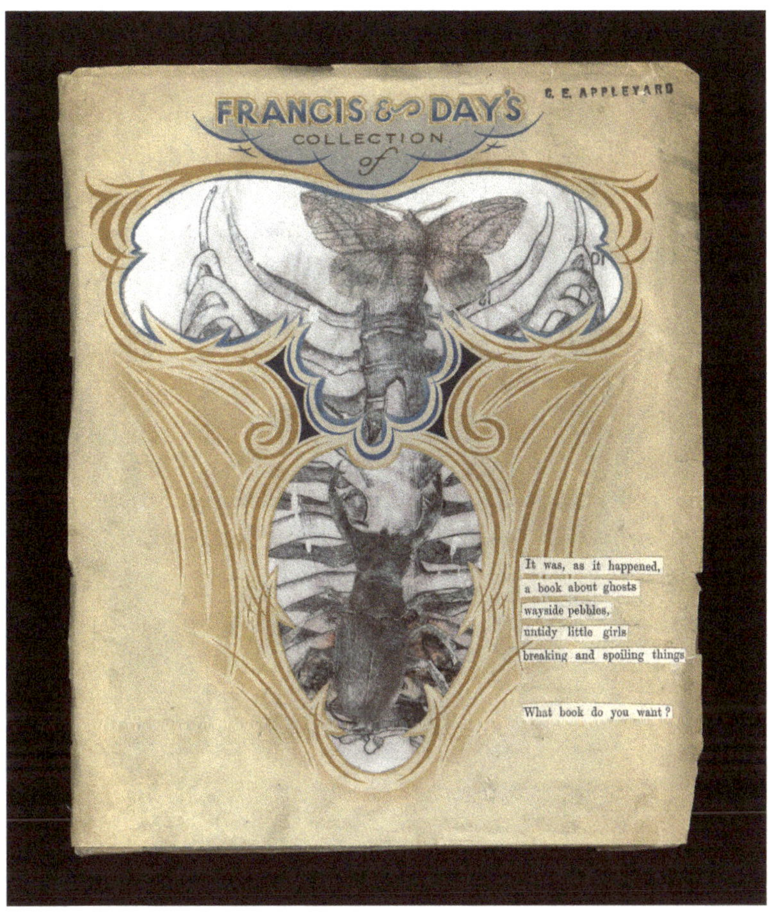

2

"Most of my practice involves play. I am interested in the way words and images dance with each other and shift their meanings and connotations. One of my main concerns as a practitioner is giving new life to discarded things, and the foraged materials here are sliced and patched from flea-market finds. I have always loved Bagpuss and would happily be one of his imagining, singing mice, stitching new stories from cast away threads."

In 2016 the experimental Knives Forks and Spoons Press published ***Hear What the Moon Told Me***, Helen Ivory's brilliant and almost unclassifiable book of collage/mixed media/cut-ups/acrylic-painted found poems that manages, in its forty-five pages, to reinvent several genres and to create a landscape that one might describe as retro-modern, and has the strangeness yet satisfying beauty of a 1950s advertisement for a trip to Mars. But before we go any further . . .

A Diversion on the Theme of Bagpuss

Bagpuss is a children's television program that ran for thirteen episodes on the BBC in 1974 and has since become a cult classic for people of all ages, especially adults. Each episode begins with a series of sepia Victorian/Edwardian photographs introducing a little girl called Emily who owns a shop to which she brings lost or abandoned or broken objects and places them in the window so that the original owners may be reunited with them. Each day, before she goes out, Emily wakes up her favorite toy, "a saggy old cloth cat, baggy and a bit loose at the seams," called Bagpuss who in turn wakes up his friends, Gabriel the toad, Madeleine the rag doll, Professor Yaffle the woodpecker (who is really a bookend), and the mice on the mouse organ. Together they set about identifying and restoring various items that Emily can place in the shop window when she returns home, by which time they themselves have reverted to being inanimate toys and pieces of furniture.

To coincide with the book's publication Helen Ivory issued an Artist's Statement, the first paragraph of which I quoted above and the rest of which runs as follows:

"The poems are made in the play of word and image. Materials are sourced from flea-market-foraged photographs bought for a song; from women's magazines of the 40s, 50s, and 60s—their drudgery and pragmatic glamour; from the magic and innocence of vintage fairy tale books and from the marvel at the glory of the world found in the 1950s Arthur Mee children's encyclopaedias.

"Nothing is arbitrary here; a logic is created and then stuck down with glue, sometimes dream logic rich in metaphor and symbolism. ***Hear What the Moon Told Me*** grows from the same family tree as the assemblages of Joseph Cornell and the imagining, singing mice who live with Bagpuss, stitching new stories from discarded threads.

"Meanings and connotations are shifted in the juxtaposition of tone, by the wit and mischievous imagination of placing them into the arena of a contemporary reading. They are far more than a simple ironic take on an earlier age; they inform where we (and women in particular) find ourselves now by digging deep. There is heartbreak in the innocence of their dreams; beauty and strength in the weight and imbalance of societal expectation. They are also songs to remind us of wonder: the habits of bees and small crawling creatures; electricity and other sorcery."

A Diversion on the Theme of Joseph Cornell

Joseph Cornell (1903–1972) was a New York-born artist who became famous for his boxed assemblages in which he combined a variety of seemingly random objects often discovered in bric-a-brac shops alongside Victorian photographs and plates from old books. He also made a number of short experimental films, of which the most famous is Rose Hobart, a nineteen-minute surrealist masterpiece that even managed to elicit the jealous rage of Salvador Dali.

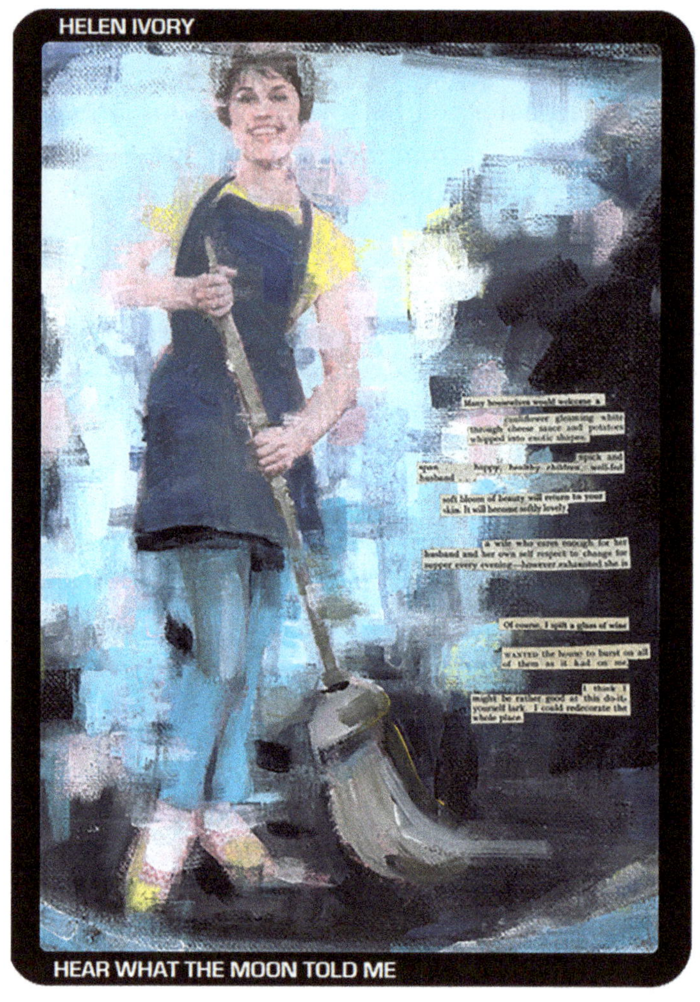

These last three paragraphs are worth reading twice, not just for the creative insight into an artist's work, which is always fascinating, but for their cool detachment. Although not exactly written in the third person, they certainly give that impression. I rather like that. Not enough critics seem to remember that the ultimate authority on any work of art in any medium is the artist herself.

The process of the book's construction is easier to describe than its aesthetic achievement and is actually very similar, at least to begin with, to the process by which Helen creates her boxes. Firstly, she finds a background and then builds onto it. With collages, she uses old book board covers as a ground or base, but this can sometimes become part of the finished work if the texture/words are interesting enough.

"I sometimes use frames from things like vintage copies of *National Geographic* or music score books to hold a composition in place. And yes, in answer to your question, the images do come first and then the words. The images present themselves quite quickly, as they are often the reason I selected or foraged the book from a flea market or second-hand shop in the first place."

And the words?

"The words take a little longer, and I think I am working both at making sense of the images and disrupting the reading of them. I often make myself laugh at the juxtapositions suggested to me in my word / phrase search. I don't think anything is random and that we are sense-making, story-making, logic-finding beasts. No matter how wild our stories, if there is a convincing enough thread, somebody will hold onto it!

"The materials I use are things like the Arthur Mee children's encyclopaedias, women's magazines from the 50s and fairy-tale books. I tend to like older stock books and ephemera because the quality of ink and paper is often a little degraded, foxed, and it's not quite as slick as modern printing, so it seems more human. Also, the idea that humans have touched and read these things before adds to the life story of the objects themselves. I use a scalpel (with the same scalpel handle I bought when I was nineteen for my Foundation Art and Design course!) but no ruler, so the edges are ragged and look like what they are—words cut from other sources. Older paper cuts differently—it's more pulpy—and sometimes you will have a ripped-edge effect no matter how neat you try to cut your lines. I am a bit of a materials fetishist, as you may have gathered!"

The experience of looking through ***Hear What the Moon Told Me*** is a curious combination of opposites: a multi-sensual reaction to the interplay of image and color and texture, as well as words, and a single aesthetic response to each page because there is not an image, not a color, not a strip of text (I mean physically, independent of meaning) out of place. Each concept is perfectly realized, and the unification of each separate element is made even more remarkable by the seeming randomness of it all. It is a straightforward and fairly commonplace thing to say of a work of art that it exists on multiple levels; the statement usually implies a sense of metaphor. But here it takes on an almost literal meaning; the marriage of text and texture produces a unique and simultaneous response that is both sensual and aesthetic, childlike and profound.

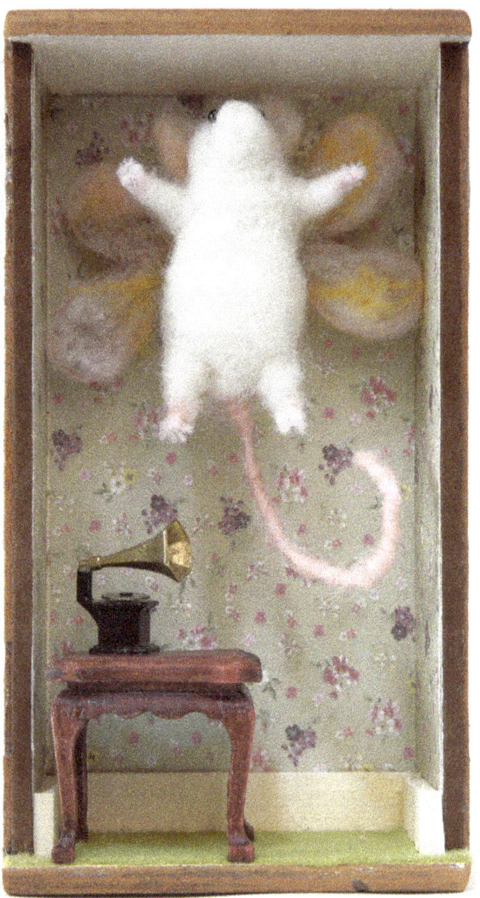

But let us not forgot, in conclusion, that just as for every extraordinary gown featured in *Harper's*

Bazaar or *Vogue* there is a seamstress with pins in her mouth and chalk dust under her fingernails, so we see Helen Ivory in her studio, the artisan behind the artist, the flesh and blood woman behind the hauntingly beautiful art:

"When I am happy with everything, I will begin sticking it down. It can take a couple of days, so I am lucky enough to have somewhere to work that is not frequented by drafts and other people. Paper is notoriously flighty. Just as an end note—I have no idea in my head about what is going to happen when I set off—I just go where the materials (that I have preselected, so nothing is random really!) take me."

People are pebbles
and windows are mirrors.

When the moon is pushed
down the chimney's throat,

the music begins.
So the pebbles dance

a formal little dance,
learned through generations.

Looking out the window
they see their reflection.

They think the whole world
is dancing.

from ***The Breakfast Machine*** (2010)

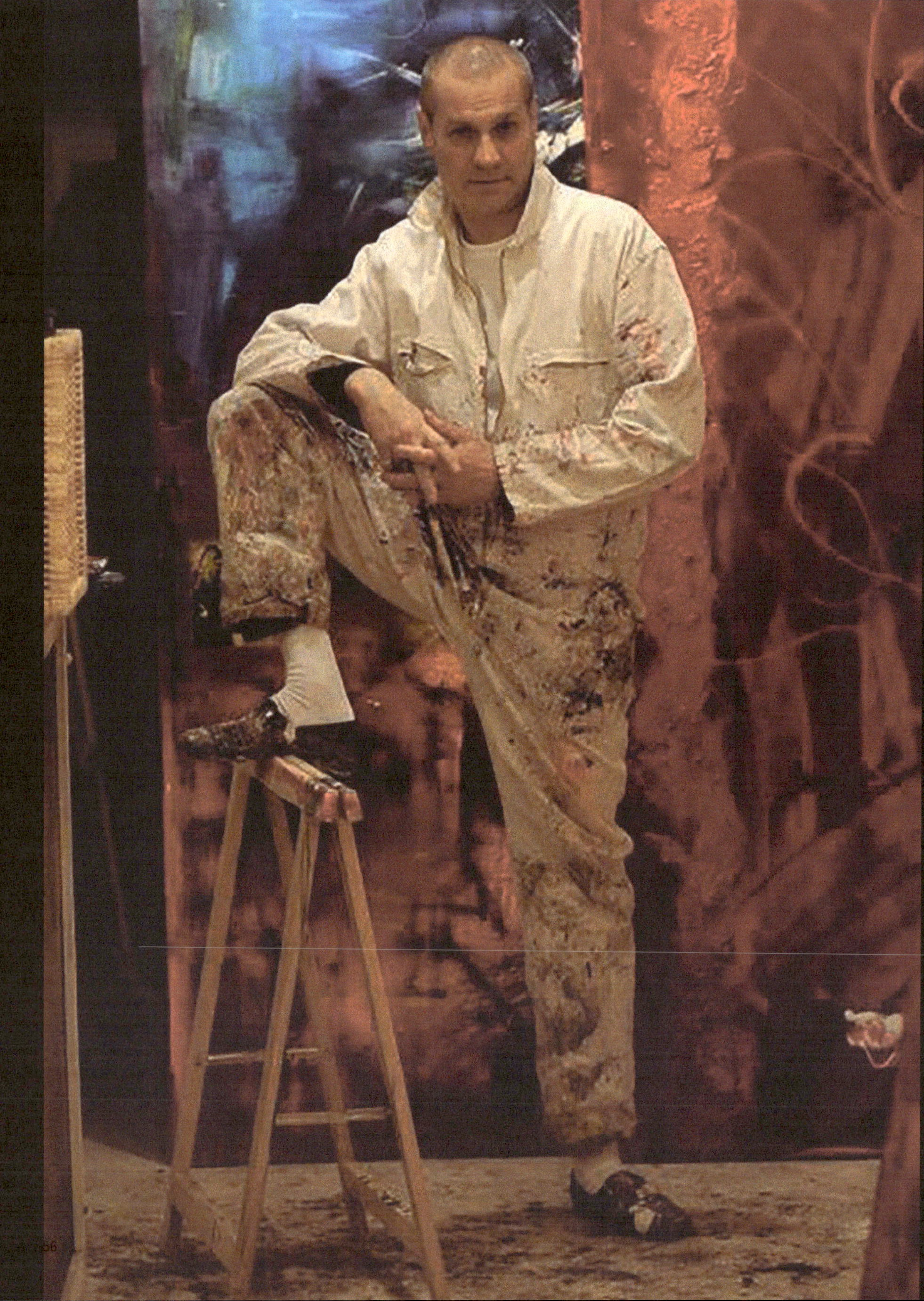

JEAN DOLANDE

COLOR, FORM, AND GESTURE

L'Atelier (2004)

Un film de Francois Rochal

Écrit et narré par Jean Dolande

"My work is above all emotional rather than intellectual. To affect the subconsciousness not the consciousness—that's most important. I was an actor. I experienced the word, then the gesture of the mime. Painting is made of color, form and gesture. The emotion is the same with a different aim.

"I first painted and then went to the Beaux Artes to reassure the others. I thought it won't be the word nor the gesture, but color and form. Life nurses me, goes through myself, life guides me.

"I realize that color is so important. Each one is linked to a musical note in terms of vibration. For example, red corresponds to DO, orange to RE, yellow to MI, green to FA, blue to SO, indigo to LA, purple to TI. Each color also corresponds to a specific part of the human body.

"Color, sound and material act in harmony. Each ingredient vibrates at a specific frequency. So, what I mean: the difference between us—material, atom and number—is in fact the quantity of electrons and their speed.

"I am traveling in an astral plain to select colors and forms. My work is as universe, in perpetual motion. Even when the canvas is hung, it is beyond my control.

"A painting should vibrate as music.

"I agree that people touch my painting. It is so important to touch; something happens between the work and the buyer. It's a feeling in molecular plan called molecular memory. Touching becomes important in painting.

"You feel in harmony, perhaps you understand, or you recognize a deep and strange feeling. Sometimes in life, when you meet people for the first time, you get the feeling you recognize them. It is a love story, a meeting, love at first sight."

This seven-minute film gives us a priceless insight into the mind and working methods of Jean Dolande. Available to watch free on YouTube, I suggest it as an almost necessary extension of the essay you are about to read.

Press Conference • Paris, March 6, 2022

II Monsieur Dolande, *s'il vous plait,* how old were you when you decided to become an artist?

JD Intuitively, I always thought that I had this artistic fiber, with a deep emotional feeling and a need for freedom.

II You are an actor, a painter and a performance artist. Which, if any, came first?

JD Firstly, I was an actor. It was the actor who then nurtured me as a painter and performer.

II Where, when, how did you study in each of these disciplines?

JD As an actor with Jack Waltzer, who himself studied with Lee Strasberg at the Actors Studio. I have always liked to share creative experiences with other painters and sculptors. Subsequently, I did different internships, including some at the Beaux-Arts.

II When and how did you make the breakthrough from "I want to be an artist" to "I am an artist"? What role did your family, your teachers play in your artistic development?

JD From the age of sixteen I evolved over the course of meetings with many interesting personalities and intellects. That's how I built up my freedom of life.

II Monsieur! Which artists did you most admire as a young man?

JD Marlon Brando, Al Pacino . . .

II They help you or influence you at all?

JD Life, encounters, and my intuition have influenced my life and my work as an artist. *Merci!*

ꟺ

Picture this: A man wearing a boiler suit, his face entirely (and chillingly) hidden behind a featureless white mask, stands in a room filled with toilet pans in which have been placed representations of all the evils of the world. Here we see the torso of an androgynous figure, reminiscent of the shop-window dummies one sees in high-end Parisian boutiques, except that this one wears a noose slung like a necklace around its shoulders; over there are skulls, firearms, leafless branches, a blue and red globe of the earth, and an obscene assemblage of plastic doll-children, trapped in the mess of their own destruction, waiting to be flushed away like so much useless shit. Each toilet is set against the backdrop of a large abstract oil painting in which the dominant color is red. Indeed, red is the dominant color of the entire exhibition, for the toilets (and the major part of their contents) are painted red also. This exhibition is called, appropriately, ***Red Line*** has been performed at least fifteen times in Paris, Germany, London, Japan, South Korea, Hong Kong, and Shanghai. But before we get to the performance itself, let us take a look at the official press release that introduces the work:

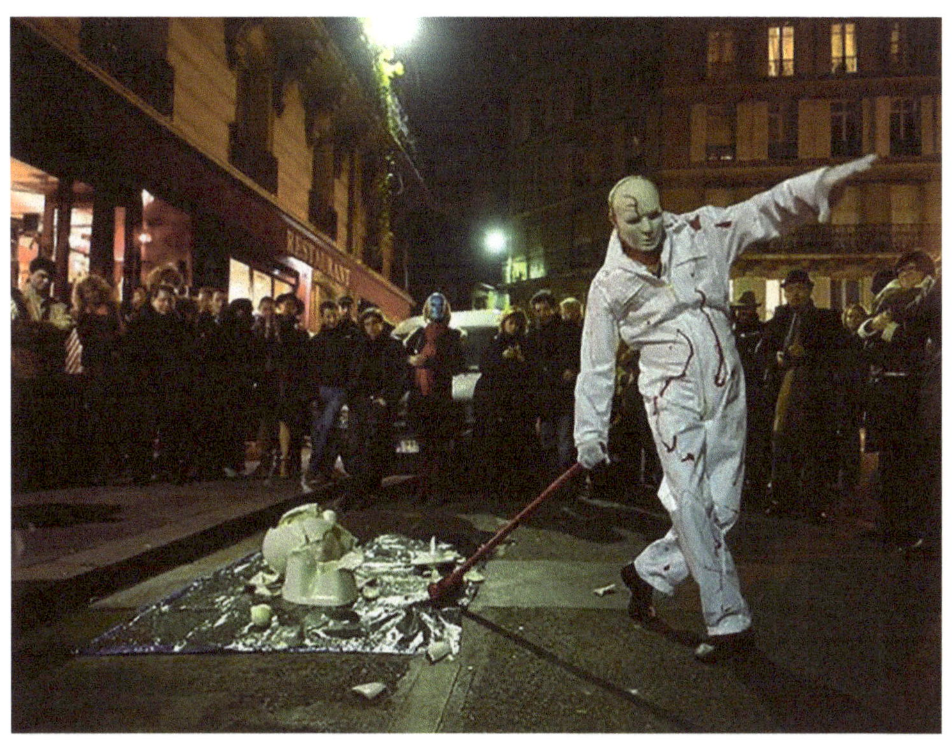
RESTAURANT

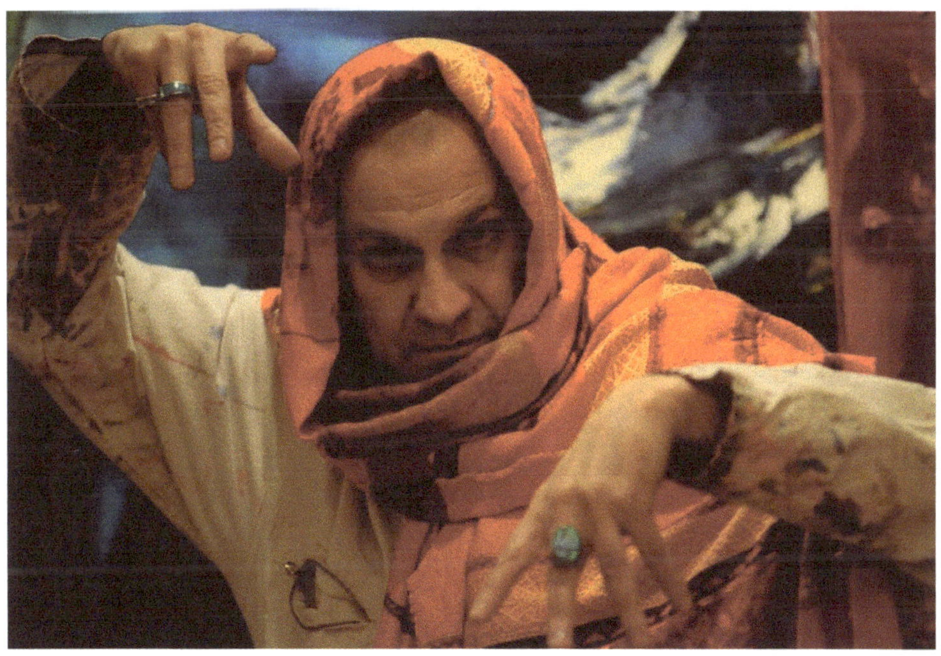

Jean Dolande

Red Line

THE ARTIST ABSORBS REALITIES AND SENSES OUR FUTURE

Jean Dolande, like a transcendental alchemist, expresses his faith in Beauty, Emotion, and Love. Through this event, Red Line, he wishes to call upon each one of us, whether as an individual, a consumer, member of a company, of an association, of an administration or a government, to think about the state of our planet. He is not being an alarmist, but he does think it's necessary that we become more globally aware in order to view the next twenty years with both a long- and medium-term vision.

Jean Dolande depicts a scene representing twelve insufferable realities:

Genocide	**Paedophilia**	**Terrorism**
Pollution	**Starvation**	**Antipersonnel Mines**
Human Pride	**Global warming**	**Organ Trading**
Deforestation	**Drugs**	**Nuclear Weapons**

Illustrated by red toilets from which these themes come out.

Man, through modern techniques associated with this new consciousness, can resolve worldly disequilibria, which he himself generated with his short-term actions and lack of vision.

Jean Dolande illustrates the destructive action of Mankind upon Life, through a "happening" with a scene in which the artist, still wearing his painting smock stained with red and holding a red mallet, smashes into pieces a thirteenth white toilet filled with white balls representing molecules, therefore expressing Life.

The shattered debris of this performance will be left on the ground for the duration of the exhibition as a continuing expression of the destructive actions of Man to this day, specifically as "Human Pride" and "Starvation" sculptures.

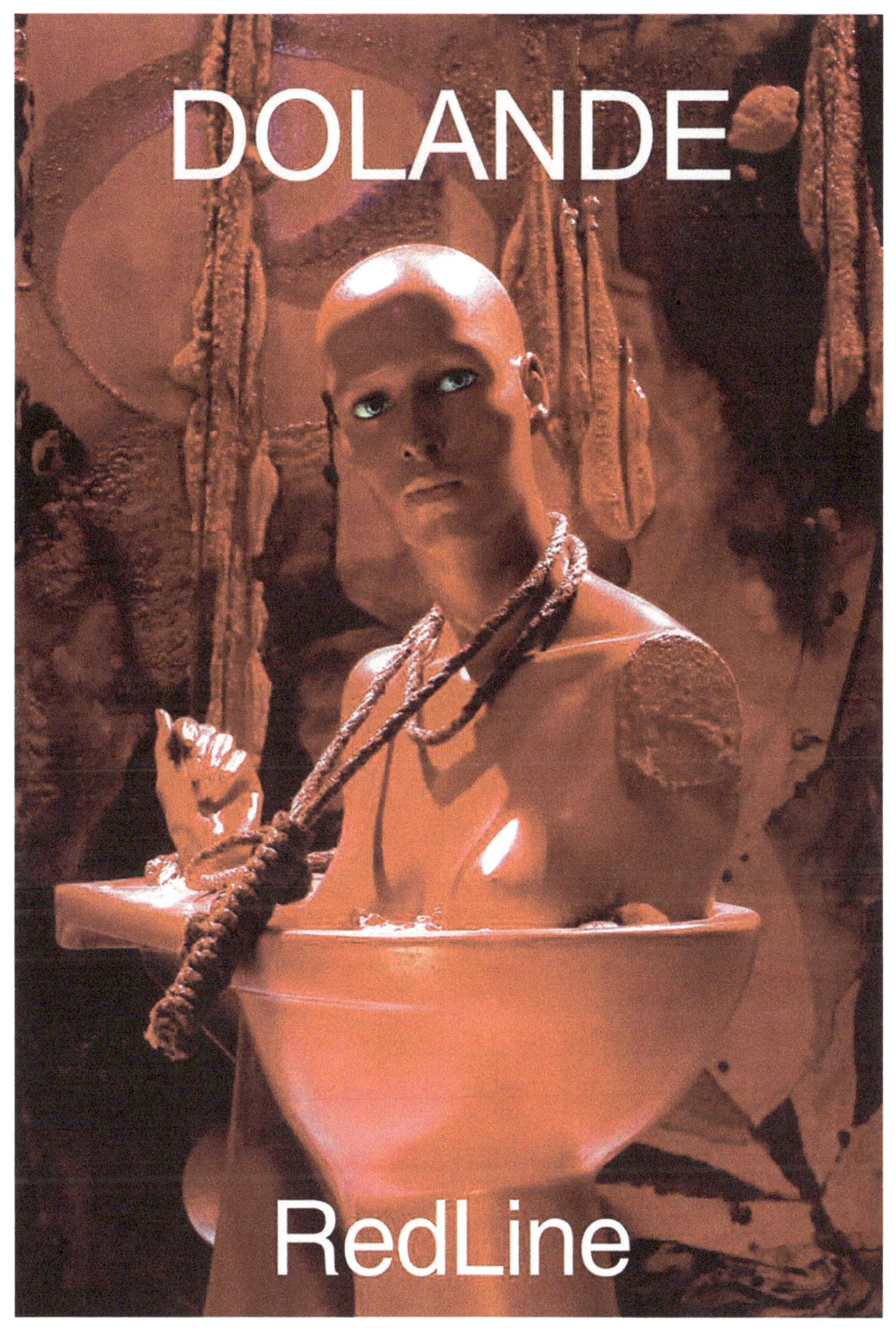
DOLANDE
RedLine

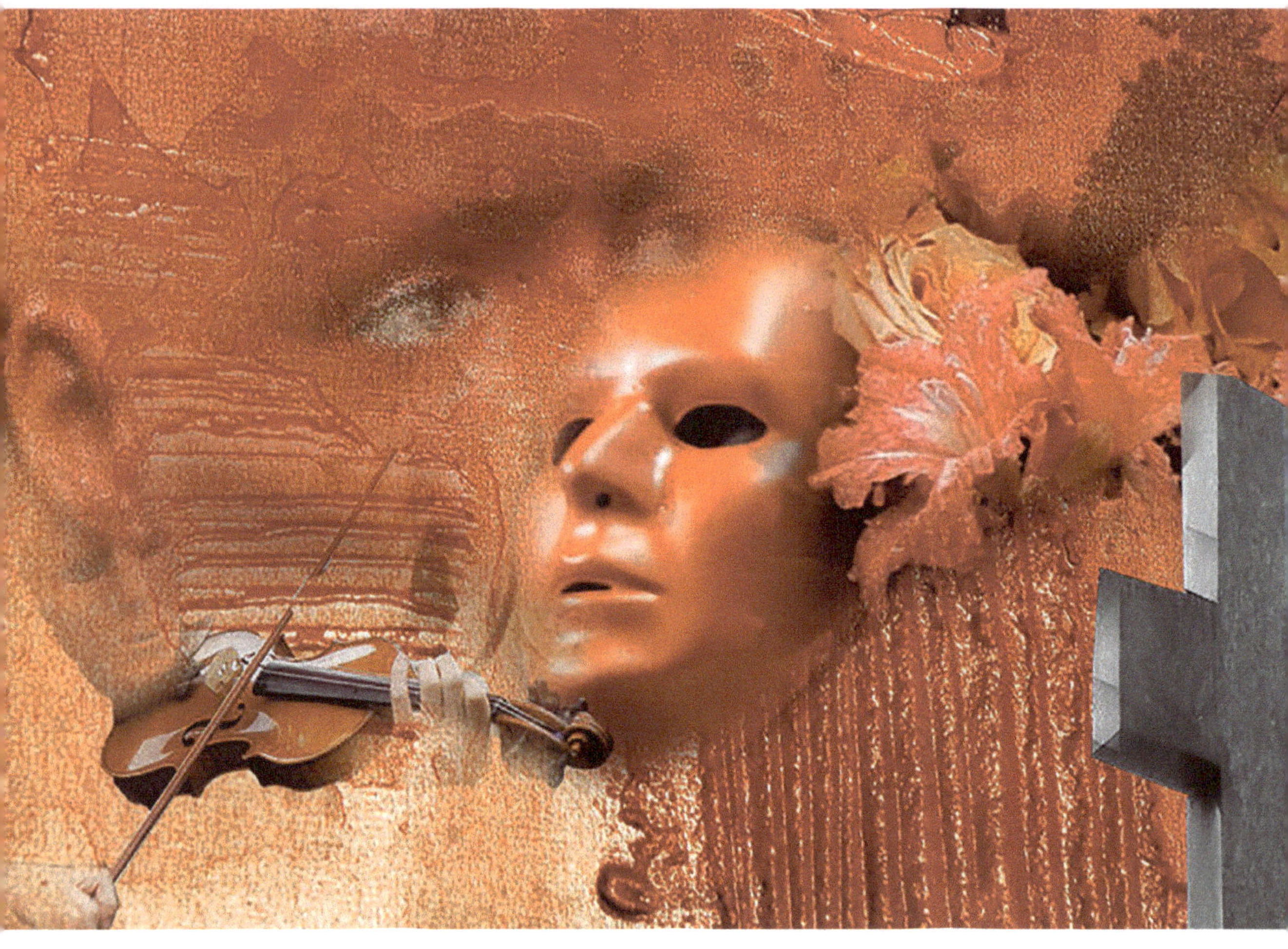

A gong sounds and the man in the mask appears, holding a mallet. It is, of course, the artist himself, and at each subsequent stroke of the gong he smashes a toilet and its contents, the room fills with the dust and din of shattered porcelain and plaster. It is a uniquely savage spectacle that yet contains within it an extraordinary beauty, "la poésie du mime" in Jean's own words, the poetry of mime, and in a few short minutes, eight months of work is strewn in pieces across the gallery floor. But the spectacle is not quite over. I neglected to mention that there is a thirteenth toilet, placed separately from the others, painted white and containing white-painted balls. There is something curiously redemptive about this one contrasting item when viewed before the beginning of the show, and how often have we seen in our newspapers or on our TV screens, when an apartment block has been blown up in some arbitrary and unnecessary war, among the twisted metal, smoldering rubble, ruined furniture, and blood-stained bodies, a single beacon of hope, a miraculously unharmed baby, perhaps, or a bouquet of flowers in an impossibly unbroken vase. So now, having symbolically destroyed a dozen of the world's greatest evils, the wielder of destruction comes to this, the thirteenth toilet. But these white-painted balls do not represent another evil; rather they represent life. When this installation is smashed, it is not with the intention to destroy but to liberate, to set free. The performance ends with a violent explosion of hope.

I once spent the day with Jean Dolande. This was back in October 2017. We met at the Nesles Gallery on the Left Bank where he was discussing with the owner an upcoming exhibition of his work. We strolled down the street to the Café Montparnasse for lunch. It was a beautiful autumn day, a Saturday, and we sat at a sidewalk table and talked in a strange medley of broken French and fractured English, about painting and poetry and the extraordinary artistic and literary legacy of the French capital, especially here, in an historic café where Picasso and Modigliani, Hemingway and Cocteau would once have drunk their glasses of red wine and eaten their *croque monsieurs* just as we did that day. There can be few finer experiences than sitting outside a classic Paris café in the October sunshine with one of the best contemporary painters in France. In person, Jean Dolande has the necessary charisma of an actor and performer,

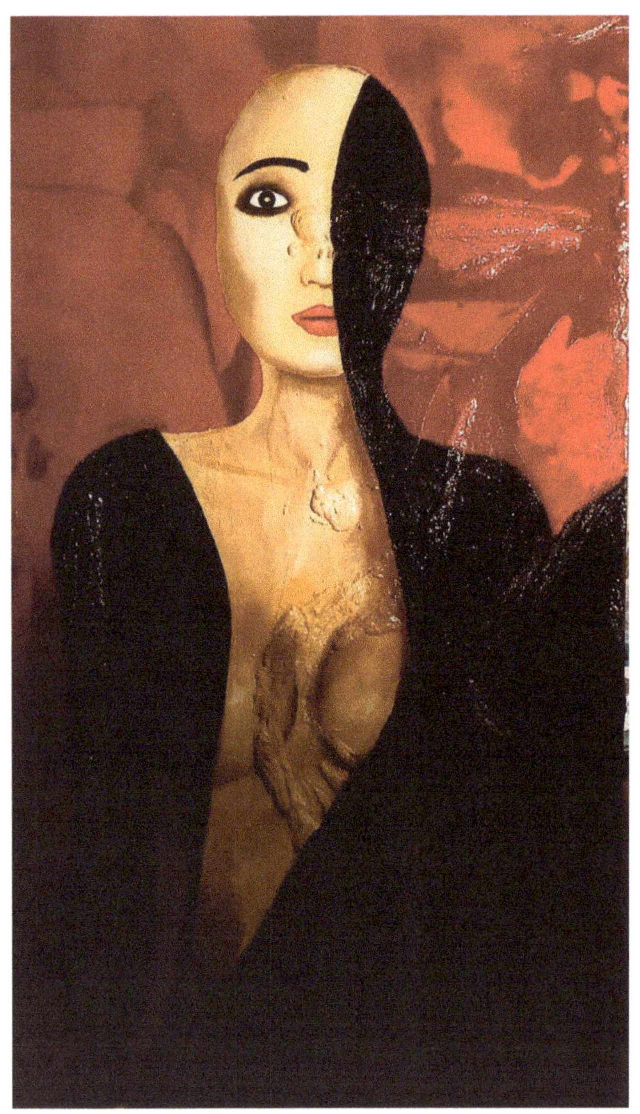

but with none of the posturing, none of the sense that he is playing a part. A modest man, quietly spoken, and with old-world courtesy, he likes to dress in pale blue, right down to his suede espadrilles, and is as keen to listen as he is to speak. His commitment to art is both aesthetic and intellectual; there is an exact balance between the two that gives all he does a combination of beauty and profundity, and this applies as much to his paintings as it does to the performances described above. After lunch we jumped in a taxi and went across the river to his studio on the Right Bank. As with all artists, the privilege of being invited to the studio and be in the presence of works in progress is to see the finished work in a whole new light. Jean uses oil and acrylic and uses them with strenuous disregard for the surfaces of his atelier: the walls, the floor, the easels, tables, shelves, the windowsills—not just spattered but literally textured with paint. The experience is to feel that one has been absorbed into a work of art, that one is simultaneously inside of and part of the painting itself. The actual paintings are large bold abstract works, as remarkable for the physical application of the paint as they are for their beautifully worked out combinations of color and shape. Jean even invites me to touch one of his paintings, a nearly finished canvas taller than myself, to better appreciate the sheer physicality, the essential feel of the paint.

"Yes," he says, in answer to my unspoken question, "texture is very important. It is how I transpose emotion to the canvas. An artist must completely trust his own emotions. Each color resonates a different energy and becomes like a volcano. And that is what makes the texture and emotion of the painting."

Two days later, on Monday, I paid a visit to Père Lachaise, the extraordinary cemetery in the 20th arrondissement, in fact not so much a cemetery as a beautifully constructed and serenely tranquil town of the dead, in which have been buried such icons of the art world as Frederic Chopin, Honoré de Balzac, Oscar Wilde, Marcel Proust, Sarah Bernhardt and Edith Piaf, plus a painting by Jean Dolande! But for the story of how that came about we must rewind the tape and begin in the Louvre Museum.

Journal Le Parisien • Le 4 novembre 2008 à 07h00

LE PEINTRE PROVOCATEUR a encore frappé. En juin, Jean Dolande avait accroché de force une de ses toiles au musée du Louvre. « Le Louvre, c'est le Père-Lachaise de l'art. On n'y expose que des morts! » avait-il clamé avant de se faire expulser au bout d'une minute. Dolande avait renouvelé l'opération un peu plus tard au musée d'Orsay. Samedi, à l'occasion du 1er novembre, le peintre abstrait a sorti l'une de ses oeuvres au Père-Lachaise avant de la recouvrir de terre. Il voulait à nouveau dénoncer le conservatisme qui règne, selon lui, dans les musées français. « Je suis le premier artiste enterré de mon vivant », a-t-il déclaré.

THE PROVOCATIVE PAINTER has struck again. In June, Jean Dolande forcibly hung one of his paintings at the Louvre Museum. "The Louvre is the Père-Lachaise of art. Only the dead are exhibited!" he had proclaimed before being expelled after only a minute. Dolande then repeated the operation a little later at the Musée d'Orsay. On Saturday, November 1st, the abstract painter took one of his works to Père-Lachaise before covering it with earth. He again wanted to denounce the conservatism that reigns, according to him, in French museums. "I am the first artist buried in my own lifetime," he declared.

We are once again fortunate that, as with ***L'Atelier*** and performances of *Red Line*, we have the scenario preserved on film, and there is a little more to it than got reported in ***Le Parisien***.

"Previously, I had hung a painting in the Louvre (there is a video of this), and I was basically saying that the Louvre is the Père Lachaise of art; that you had to be a dead artist to be hung in the Louvre. So, the next logical step was to do a mock funeral at Père

Lachaise. Having no official permission, I staged this event on the grave of a family friend."

"I have seen the video," I reply. "Several times, in fact. On the way to this grave, you stop at the grave of Gilbert Becaud and place a rose on the sarcophagus. Why?"

"Why Becaud? I met him several times, so why not! He is an immense French artist of the twentieth century."

"Also, you have an entourage of half a dozen or so people. Why do they wear red masks?"

"These red masks are part of the aesthetic of the staging. Also to preserve their anonymity. We had no official permission to be there."

His six or seven red-masked accomplices do not just walk alongside him. Two of them carry his ***Red Line*** torso in a toilet with a noose around its neck, while another plays a hauntingly beautiful accompaniment on the violin. It was the sound of that violin that I myself could hear as I stood at the monument to Albert Leveque (the family friend mentioned above) and saw in my mind's eye the painting (a small red abstract), then the black earth being thrown over it, and then the raindrops spattering the earth as Jean fielded questions from umbrella-sheltered journalists. It was a profound moment of spiritual connection with one of the most innovative and charismatic painters and performance artists of the modern era.

Merci beaucoup, Jean. Je t'embrasse, mon ami.

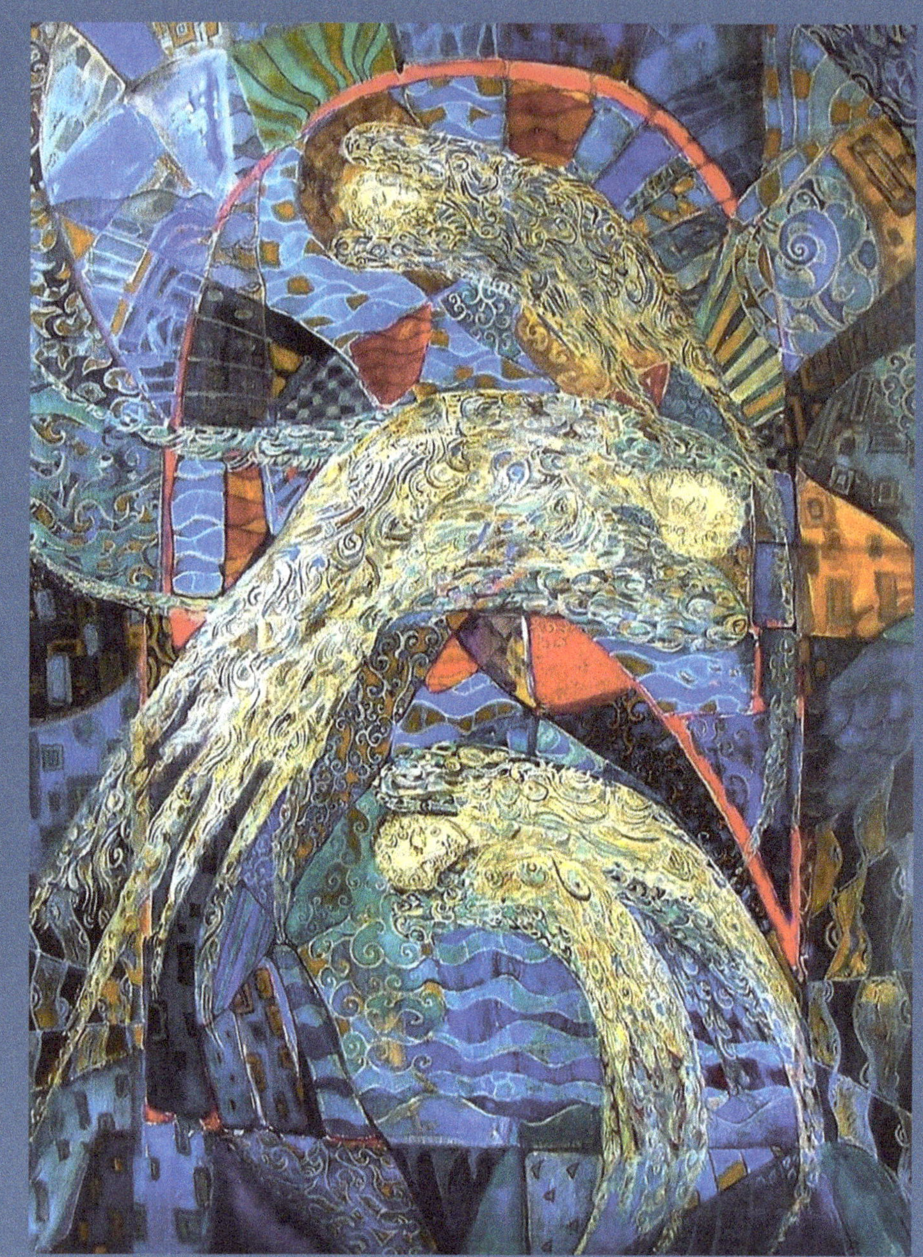

VICTORIA MERKI

"Enterprises endowed with virtue and talent, even if very often at the start they seem merely commonplace, always gradually climb higher; and they never pause or rest until they have reached the height of glory. This was clearly illustrated by the slight and common origins of the Bellini family and by the rank it then achieved by means of painting. Thus Jacopo Bellini, a painter of Venice and once a disciple of Gentile da Fabriano, worked in competition with the same Domenico who taught Andrea del Castagno how to color in oil. But although he labored hard to achieve excellence in that art, he did not acquire fame for it until Domenico had himself left Venice. But then, when he found himself without any rival to equal him in the city of Venice, adding all the time to his fame and reputation, Jacopo reached such a pitch of excellence that he became the greatest and most renowned man in his profession. And so that the name he had won for himself in painting should not only be preserved but grow greater still in his family and successors, he had two sons who were very much inclined to the art of painting and of shining intelligence: one was called Giovanni and the other Gentile, whose name he gave him as a loving father in fond memory of Gentile da Fabriano, his former master."

— Giorgio Vasari, *The Lives of the Artists* (1568)

Victoria Merki was born in Baku, the capital of Azerbaijan, in what was then the USSR, in 1972, but moved to St. Petersburg with her parents when she was eight years old. It is tempting to wonder whether, had she been born five hundred years earlier, she might have been the only Russian, to say nothing of the only female artist, to have been featured in Vasari's ***Lives***, and when I say that I am being only half-glib. For Victoria, in true Renaissance style, was born into a family of professional artists and had no other career in mind once she went to study art in Moscow at the age of twelve.

From the age of fifteen to twenty she studied in the studios of Vladimir Kiereev and Alexander Ponomarev, and also spent two years in the private sculpture school of Valery Sadomov, during which she started work as an illustrator at the

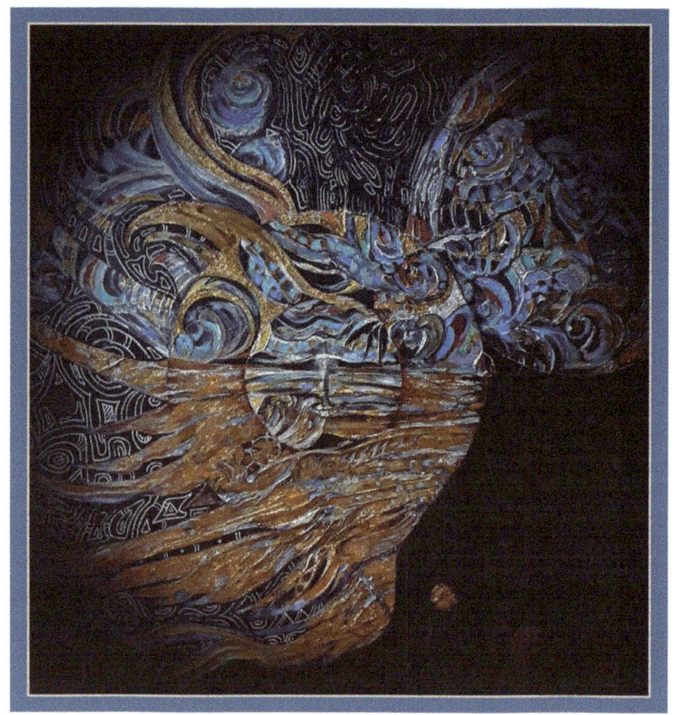

publishing house Sirius in Moscow. She gave her first international exhibition in Berlin in 1992; she was only twenty years old. Since then she has had exhibitions in Russia, USA (New York and Miami), Italy, Austria, Switzerland, and Dubai, and her paintings are in private collections in the UK, France, Germany, Italy, Switzerland, Austria, Canada, Sweden, and the USA. There is no doubt, in my mind at least, that she is the greatest Russian painter of her generation. But before we meet Victoria herself, I would like to stand back a little and place her within the context of Russian art as a whole.

When I was sixteen I saw a televised production of ***Petrushka***, with Rudolph Nureyev in the title role. It tells the story of three puppets: Petrushka himself, the Ballerina, and the Moor; all of whom are brought to life by the Charlatan, and from there the tragic consequences unfold. For those of you unfamiliar with the plot, Petrushka loves the Ballerina, the Ballerina loves the Moor, Petrushka challenges the Moor, the Moor kills Petrushka with a scimitar, Petrushka returns from death to curse the Charlatan, and Petrushka subsequently dies again of a broken heart. It was my first experience of Russian art, of Russian visual art, for I had already, however precocious it may sound, read most of Dostoyevsky, Turgenev, Pushkin, and Tolstoy. With music by Stravinsky and designs by Alexandre Benois, it remains one of the most beautiful productions of the Ballets Russes and as good a way as any to fall in love with the magic realism that has characterized Russian art since way before the term was invented to describe the fiction of Latin America.

But I have made my usual mistake of beginning in the middle (to say nothing of beginning with myself), and so let us rewind the spool to almost exactly five hundred years before Diaghilev died in 1929 and sit at the deathbed of Andrei Rublev, watched over by his Orthodox brothers at the Andronikov Monastery in Moscow, with—it is rather beautiful to imagine—one of his gorgeous icons, the icons for which he is immortal, nailed to the wall of his cell. If art historians cannot exactly agree on the date of Andrei Rublev's death, there is no disputing that he stands in relation to Russian art as Giotto does to the Renaissance. And if there was not exactly a renaissance in Russian art, then that only emphasizes Rublev's importance; there was no Russian Michelangelo to eclipse his achievement.

But, before we move forward, there is one of Andrei Rublev's icons I especially want you to take another look at. It is the *Holy Trinity*, the original of which is in the Tretyakov Gallery in Moscow. Take a look at those colors: a predominance of blue and gold, a connecting thread through nearly six hundred years of Russian art, bringing us right up to the most beautiful works of Victoria Merki. And in-between? Well, there were many fine Russian artists of the nineteenth century, not least, Aleksey Savrasov and his wonderful seascapes and the chilly, glittering beauty of Ivan Ayvazovsky's celebrated 1871 masterpiece ***The Rooks Have Come Home***. But I really want you to turn your attention to ***The Fallen Demon*** by Mikhail Vrubel. As with the works of Andrei Rublev, it is easy to find and therefore superfluous to describe. But it's those colors again, that gorgeous (and somehow very Russian) use of blue and gold, the same blue and gold of the Cathedral of the Assumption at the Monastery of the Trinity and St. Sergius at Zagorsk, and the whole texture of the piece, a sense of feathers in the brushwork, constitute a languid (but not insipid) sweep across the canvas, and all the time that beautiful combination of classicism and romanticism, of opulence and discipline, all of which could equally well describe Victoria's work.

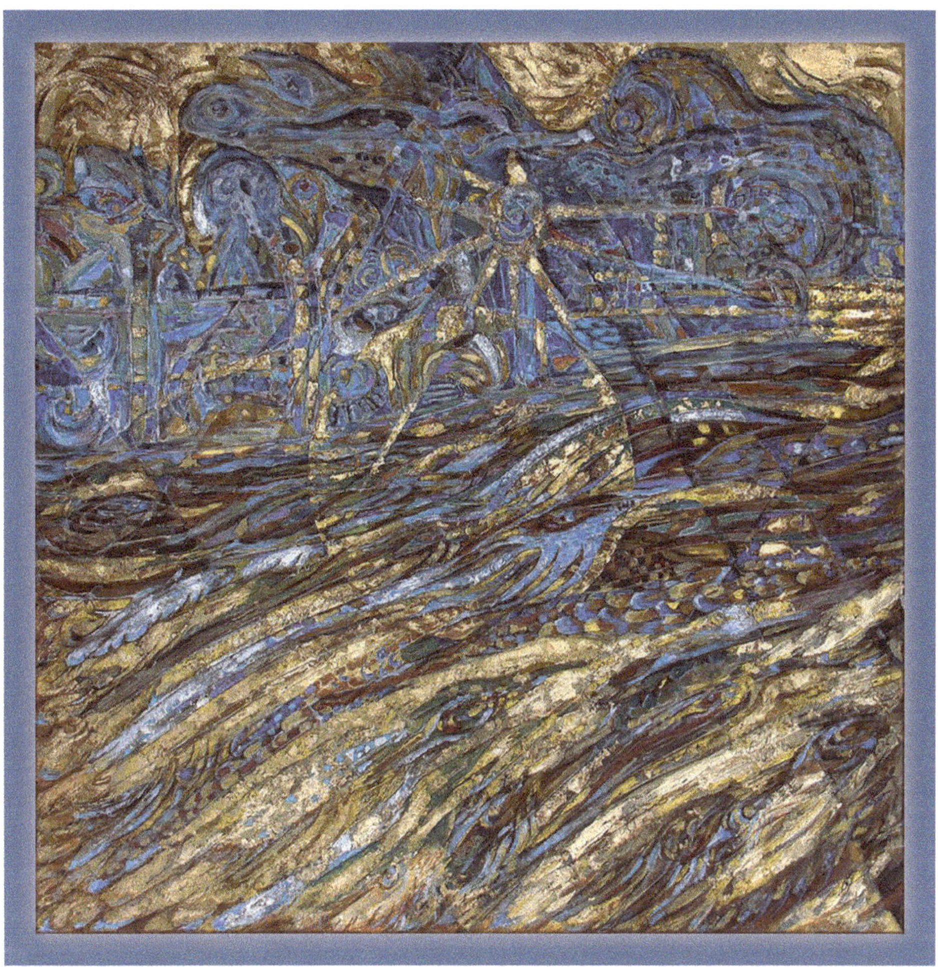

And then the twentieth century, of course. Vasily Kandinsky, Kasimir Malevich, Natalia Goncharova, and fifty or a hundred others, for the glamour of pre-war Paris and the often brutal modernism of post-war New York and London make us tend to forget how many fine Russian artists there have been in the last hundred or so years. But it is really Marc Chagall I am thinking about with specific reference to Victoria Merki. The gentle surrealism, almost a surrealism that develops from reality rather than rejecting reality altogether, the sense of freedom, of flight, and the solid grounding in Russia itself; all of these indicate to me that Chagall might have had some influence on Victoria's work.

It's a few days later and Victoria calls me from her apartment in Baden-Baden, the celebrated German spa town where Dostoyevsky once famously gambled away his wife's underwear. Her voice is simultaneously earthy and seductive, the words pouring out in her excellent (but heavily accented) English, a torrent of passion and enthusiasm laced with infectious humor that exactly expresses Victoria's personality and which is very difficult to reproduce on a cold white sheet of paper. One subject will blend into another, a word or a phrase jump-starting a recollection that bears only the most tenuous connection to the question originally asked. While I sip a glass of red wine and listen to Victoria's wonderful voice, I am glad this is not an attempt at a "real" interview, just a chat with a friend over the phone that might at the same time give me (and you) a few extra insights into her art.

"You mention Mikhail Vrubel. Oh, my god, you're right! I love him! Wow! My grandfather loved him too. There was a painting of Vrubel's in front of my bed when I was a baby. Other influences? El Greco for sure. Maybe Picasso, Dali. But you're wrong when you mention Chagall. He was never my inspiration, also my mother didn't like his work. But his life was an inspiration. The relationship he had with his wife. That is a special corner of the heart for me. And of course, in drawing it would be Albert Durer, Hieronymous Bosch . . . "

Of course! It is easy to forget, when looking at Victoria's large and gloriously colored canvases, her stunning use of not just blue

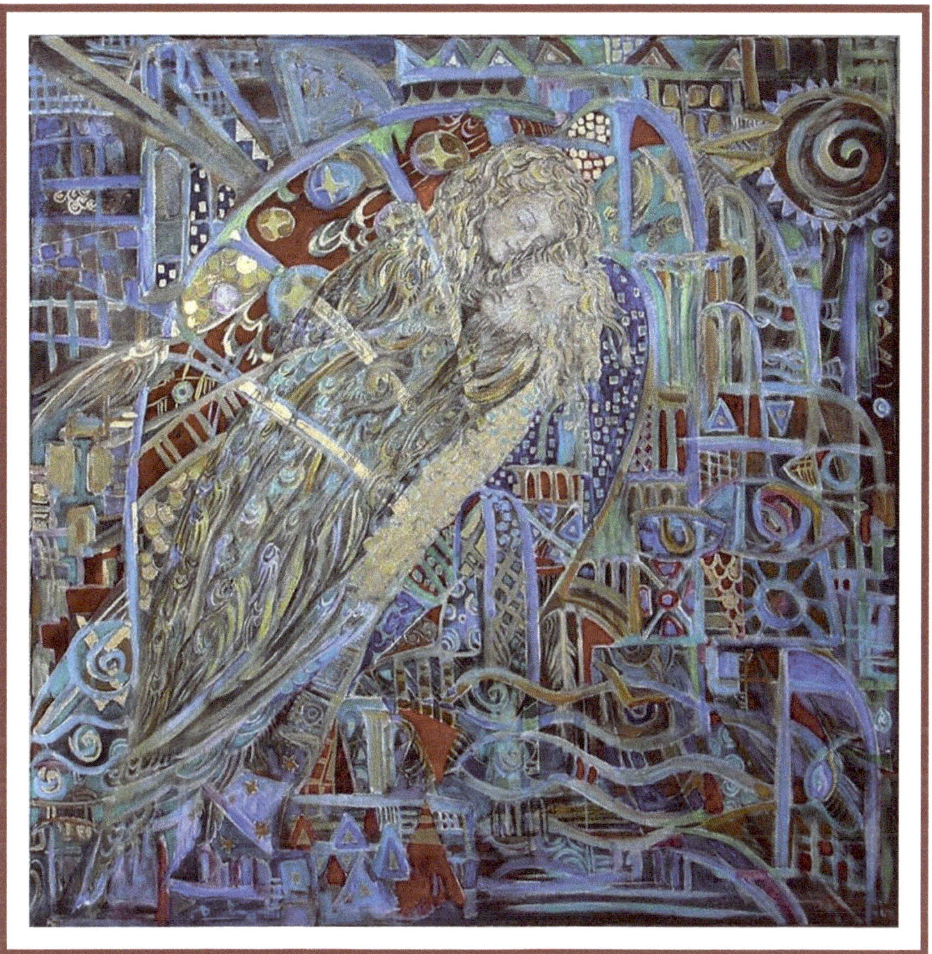

and gold but also red and green and silver, that she started out as a book illustrator.

"Yes, but you must know that my grandfather was the main artist of Azerbaijan, he was the main illustrator of Dostoyevsky. He was bringing me to his studio when I was two years old. So this is how I begin—when I was two! Then, when I was seventeen years old, we did the illustrations together for the transformation story by Kafka. You know this story?"

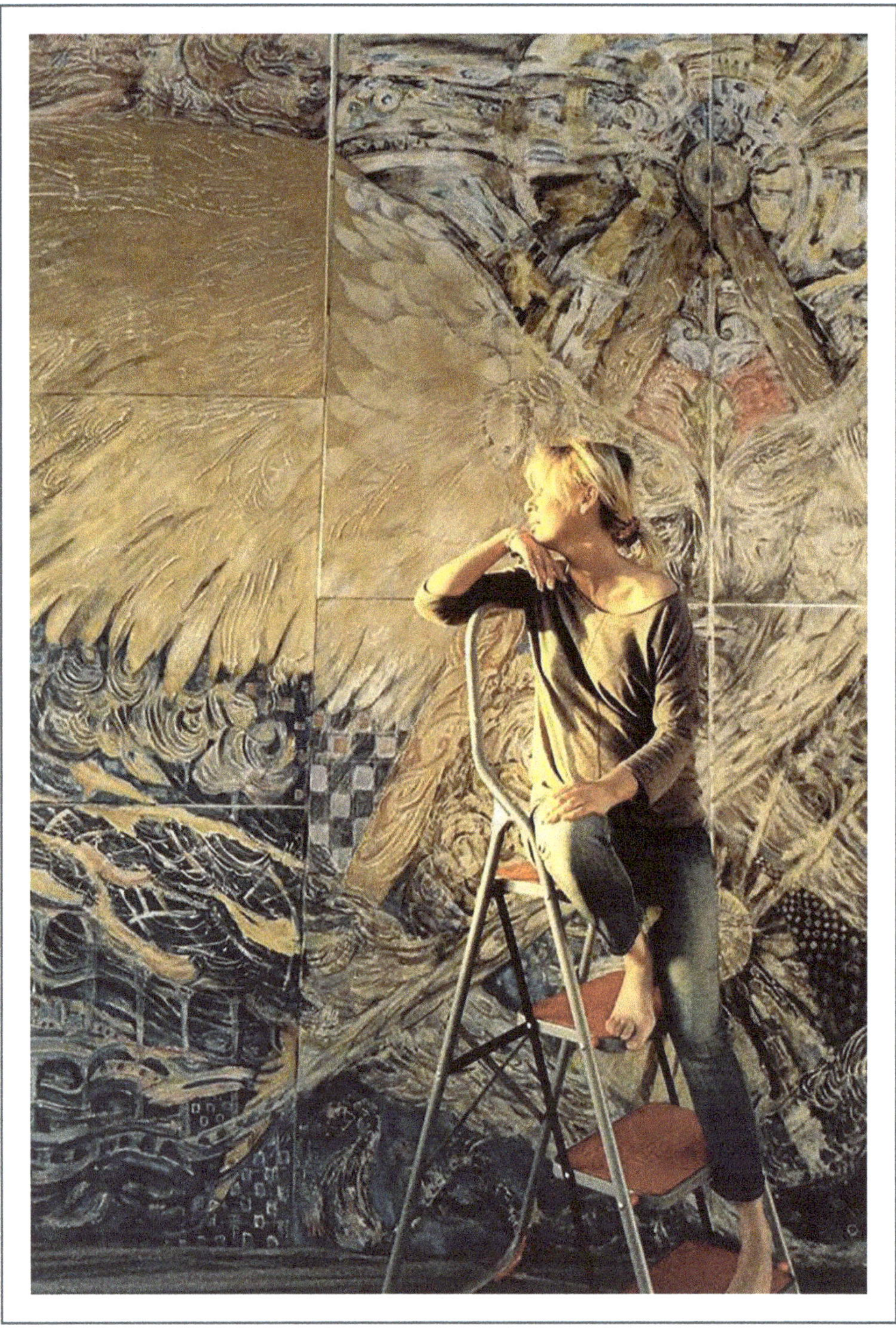

I respond: “Of course. ‘Metamorphosis.’ Where the guy wakes up turned into a giant beetle. It’s a wonderful piece.”

“Indeed. So next thing a publisher come to our house, he is from Sirius Publishers in Moscow, and he asks me, “Can you make illustrations for us?” So I say, “Yes,” and I started working for Sirius when I was eighteen years old and continued for twenty-five years.”

There is a pause, probably while she lights a cigarette.

“Then, when I was still only eighteen years old I was accepted as a professional artist by the Union of Artists in Moscow. They didn’t know I didn’t have a classical education!”

I am editing, of course. Our conversation takes in China—which Victoria has visited many times and where Susan and I lived for the first seven years of our marriage—her ex-husbands (there are three), her current boyfriend (a chef), and inevitably, the war in Ukraine:

“I believe in quantum physics, not nationalism. Nationalism is total shit! Or should I say crap?”

“Shit is better,” I say. “Crap is kind of wishy-washy.”

“Good! Then I say shit!”

But before we lose sight of the purpose of this call, I remind Victoria to tell me more about the enormous painting, the one where, in my favorite photograph of her, she is sitting on a stepladder, barefoot, beautifully lit, the truly amazing work as a backdrop.

"Oh my god, it was very hard. I destroyed myself completely with that work! Three meters times eight meters. It was commissioned by my husband at that time and sponsored by Sparkasse, a big bank in Germany. The studio they gave me, it was eight hundred square meters. You could land a helicopter in it! In structure, it is a giant mosaic. Twenty-two very big canvases. The title then was ***Mercurias***. The subject was a classic fairy tale of good and evil, but told in symbols. And when at last I fixed it on the wall, it was very beautiful. You know how it is made? You delete the first layer of color with a drill [I assume she means with an attachment for sanding, but I don't want to interrupt the flow to clarify], then the gold inside becomes very smooth. It took four months to complete, and I wanted $100,000 for it. Four months work is $25,000 a month. Not bad. Then my husband, he consults an art valuer, and she decides, based on previous sales of my work, that it is worth $350,000. And he finds a collector who says, "I will buy it for my castle in France." And I am more and more unhappy, I am so unhappy. So I destroy the whole work into small parts. And those small parts I turned into a new work which is called ***Spheres of Galileo***. This is my great connection to Vrubel because he also destroyed many of his paintings."

Creation—destruction. On that profound note we pause in our conversation, five hundred miles apart and connected by the invisible thread of technology, until I suddenly remember that I wanted to ask her about a series of pen and ink drawings titled ***Chronos***, which I particularly admire.

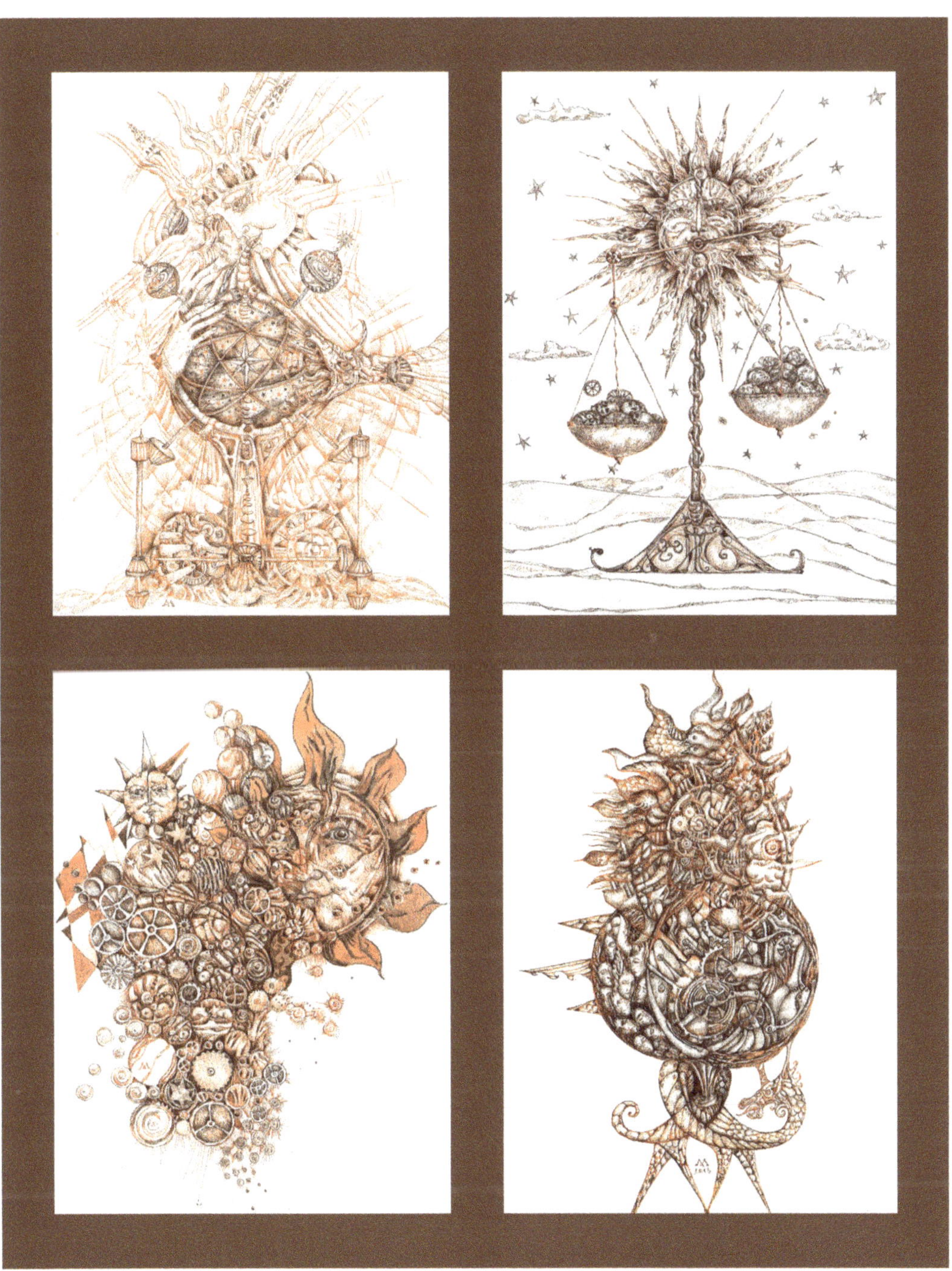

"Now this is a very interesting story because in the year 2000 I had a near-death experience. I actually died. And after that I saw a lot of funny things. For instance, I could see energies, and I began some very complicated drawings. You know alchemy? Of course. So I became very interested in how things are transforming one to another. Anyway, my husband at that time, this is my third husband, he was a professional watchmaker, one of the best, you can still see his work in many international catalogues, and he asked me if I could make something about Time. So I said, "Alright, I will do this," and I was then reading books about quantum physics, especially Einstein and Stephen Hawking. Also my favorite author is Borges, you know? Jorge Luis Borges."

"I have a copy of ***Labyrinths***. He's a great writer."

"He is! When I go on trips, I do not take the Bible, I take Borges! So I was inspired too by that. In total there are twelve drawings. Ten of them I have at home, two have been sold."

I think about the ***Chronos*** sequence, those extraordinary and exquisite drawings inspired not just by classical sources and techniques but also referencing old maps, Greek myths, alchemical textbooks, and the insides of watches themselves, which, of course, is where it all began. At that moment I was thinking of Greek myths, and Victoria reads my mind. She picks up the conversation by talking about another, more recent set of drawings based on the story of Theseus and the Minotaur and Ariadne's Thread.

"In the labyrinth we meet our fears. At this time I am reading Carl Gustav Jung. She, Ariadne, gave him intuition with this thread, so he could see the light outside. It is a beautiful true story, but I have turned it into symbols. My own interpretation. I show it is really a fight within oneself."

"And the labyrinth—that must surely be another reference to Borges."

"No, there is no connection to Borges. Anyway, not that I was aware of."

"Maybe subconsciously. Surely. It's too good not to be."

"Well, maybe you are right. I had not thought of it like that before!"

"In that case I am a real art critic. I have found an interpretation you didn't even know yourself!"

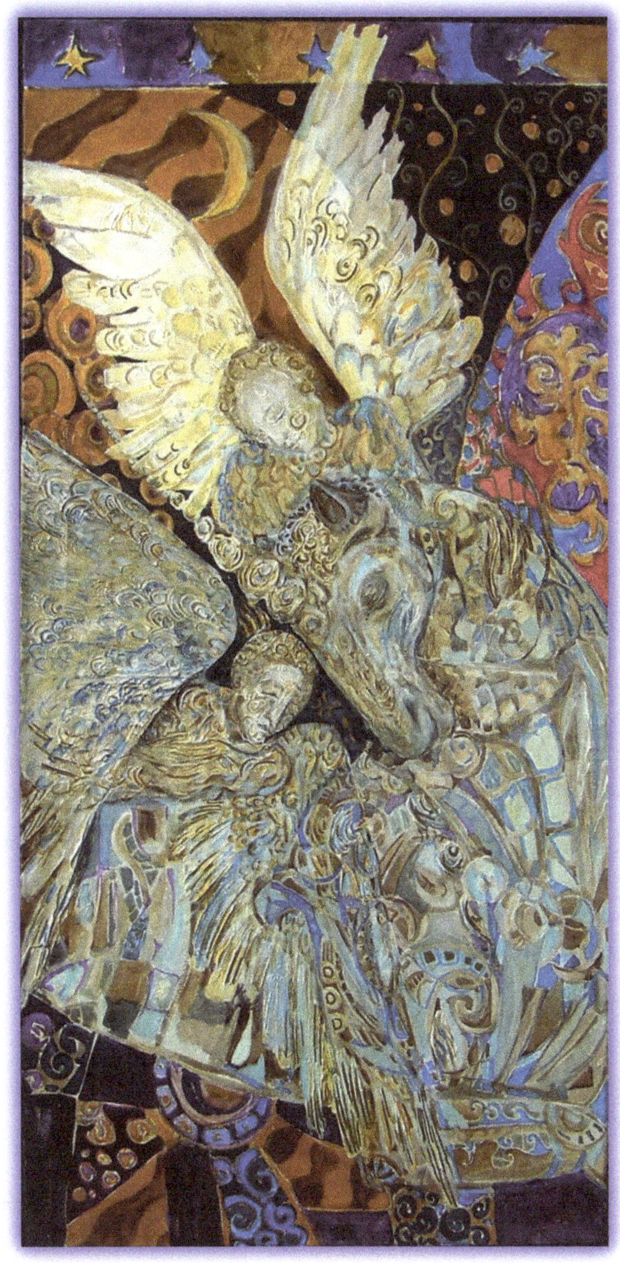

We both laugh, but it is time to think about saying goodbye. Victoria's voice is beginning to sound a little tired, and I realize we have been talking nearly non-stop for well over an hour. We conclude with the usual promise to speak again soon "and love and big hug to Susan!" and hang up our respective phones. But a little while later, still hearing her wonderfully warm and expressive accent in my mind's ear, I see, on one of the half-dozen sheets of paper I have been scribbling on during our conversation, the following:

"I don't want to justify my life. You must finally come back to yourself. With a little bit of wisdom. Hopefully."

❧

I end more or less where I began, for however early I may have read Dostoyevsky and Tolstoy, the ballet ***Petrushka*** remains for me the touchstone, the secret door that allows me to enter the fantastical garden of Russian art. The stage is quiet; Petrushka has been slain. The puppets' booth is empty, and the haunting woodwinds of Stravinsky's beautiful score have been reduced to a few mournful notes. But—how wonderful!—the dead puppet has come back to life! But here, if you will forgive me, is where my version of ***Petrushka*** differs from Diaghilev's original 1911 production choreographed by Michel Fokine. In my version, the Moor and the Ballerina are forgotten. Instead, Petrushka climbs a stepladder against the backdrop of Victoria Merki's 8 x 3 meter ***Mercurias***. He looks at the painting, transfixed by its sheer size

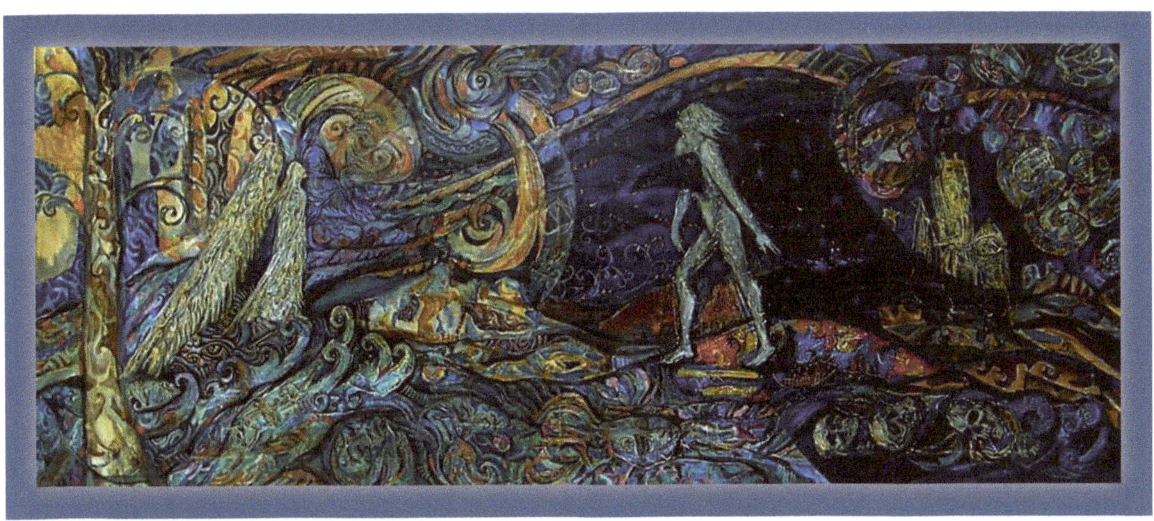

and beauty, then slowly turns to face the audience. He smiles and then bows with elaborate grace to acknowledge their applause. A bouquet of flowers is thrown onto the stage, followed by another, and then a third. He is joined from the wings by Sergei Diaghilev and Igor Stravinsky and Alexandre Benois and Michel Fokine and Victoria Merki. Together in a line, with Petrushka still poised on his ladder, they step forward, exchange smiles, and then bow to the audience. A bouquet of roses lands at Victoria's feet. She picks it up and, with a graceful gesture, acknowledges the gentleman in the box who has thrown it (myself, impeccable in evening dress, of course!) and then steps forward again to receive a round of rapturous individual applause.

Her masterpiece has been resurrected. The curtain comes down.

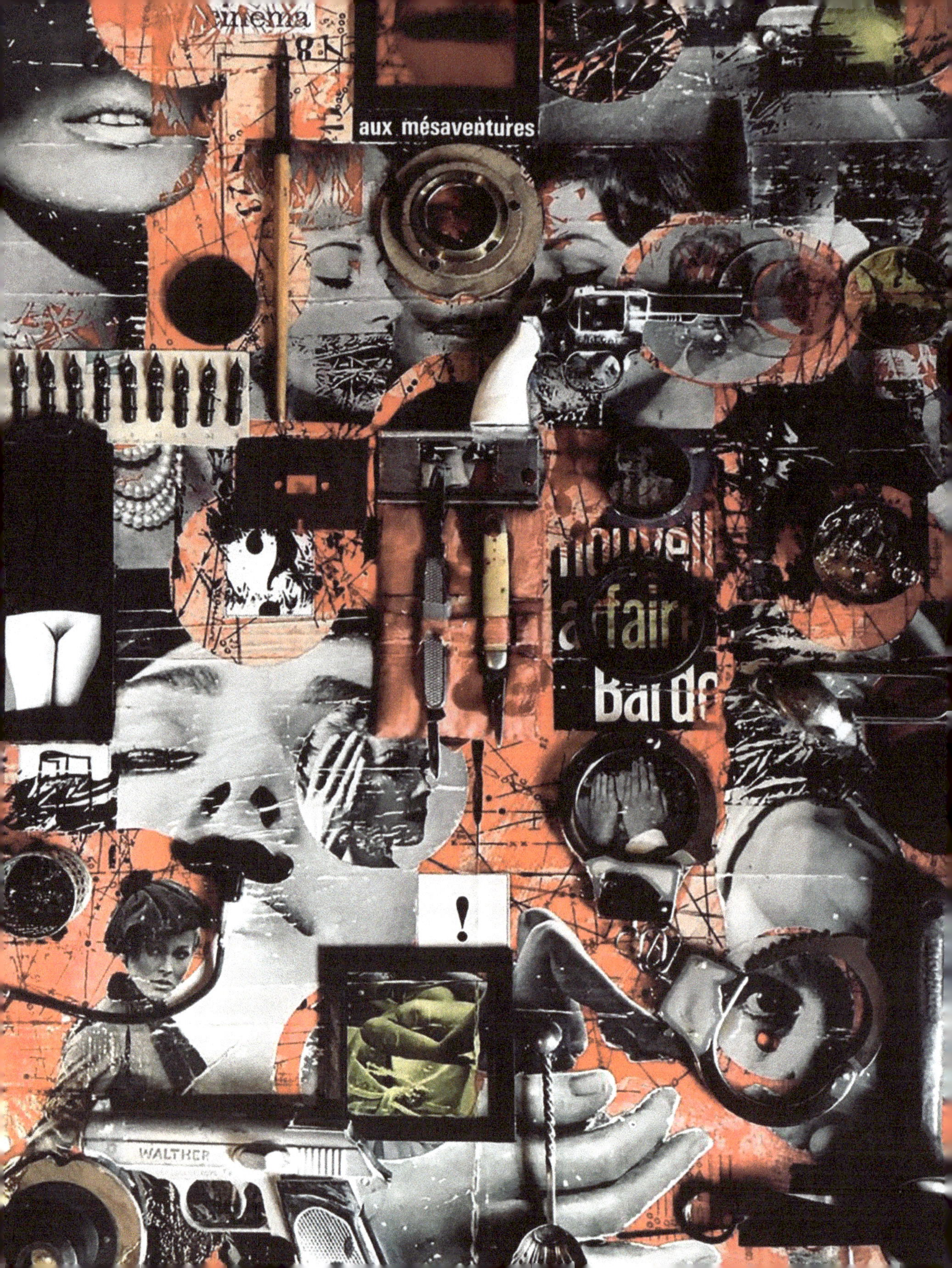
aux mésaventures
WALTHER

9 STUDIES FOR A PORTRAIT OF MICHAEL WOODS

1

"I was eight years old. I didn't want a camera for Christmas, I wanted a bike. I went out on Christmas Day and photographed the other kids on their bikes. The next thing was, they didn't want their bikes anymore—they wanted a camera. After that I took pictures of everything. Absolutely everything. It was a way of exploring my world through the camera lens."

Born in London in 1952, Michael Woods, the photographer, surrealist painter, collagist, and maker of assemblages, is quite simply one of the most significant British artists alive today. I cannot hope to properly illustrate the range of his talents and achievements, to say nothing of his legendary friendships, in an essay of reasonable length—one day there will be a full-scale biography to accomplish that feat—but what I can do is attempt to put together a portrait, making use of the fragments of material I possess first-hand. For it is my privilege to know Michael, to have drunk coffee and smoked cigarettes with him in his favorite hangout—the Golborne Café in London's Notting Hill—and to have had the rare honor of being invited to his home, itself an extraordinary combination of Aladdin's cave, bric-a-brac museum, and Joseph Cornell box.

As for Michael himself, well, hopefully you will have a fairly decent idea in fifteen or so pages time, but let us begin with a physical description: he is of medium height but, like most slender, well-dressed men, appears taller. And by well-dressed, I mean very well. I have never seen him except in a waistcoat, jacket, and tie. The jackets themselves are those of a true *boulevardier*, with panels on the back or fancy needlework around the collars. There are cufflinks on his shirt cuffs, and he always carries a cane. A fedora completes the effect. One of his closest friends, George Melly, in the pages of their joint book ***Paris and the Surrealists***, described him thus: "Tall and thin, with a deceptively reticent air, Michael has the head of a carved medieval saint framing the eyes of a slow loris. His principal interest is photography." I am not sure about the loris bit, maybe because I've never met a loris, but for me they are the eyes of a man who never ceases to observe, but never stands in judgment of what he sees. They are the eyes of a man both compassionate and wise. They are the eyes of a man who, with an almost zenlike tranquility, knows what you know before you yourself are aware of knowing you know it. They are, of course, a photographer's eyes. A painter's eyes. A surrealist's eyes . . .

But before we begin, I need to tell you: this is not an essay about Michael Woods. It is an assemblage.

2

In the National Portrait Gallery in London's Trafalgar Square there are eleven photo-portraits by Michael Woods:

Christopher Battye,
Harry Diamond,
Ivor Abrahams,
James Birch,

Frank Avray Wilson,
Bruce Lacey,
Conroy Maddox,
Eva Urvasi Neurath (née Itzag),
John Mortimer, Matthew Parris, George Melly,
Michael Peppiatt,
plus a portrait of himself with the great Soho photographer Harry Diamond.

MPH: So how did you meet Harry Diamond?

MW: I met Harry Diamond in the French House on Dean Street in Soho. He'd recently been painted by Lucien Freud. He talked like a gangster in a forties movie. There was a bloke sitting down at the bar and Harry got the idea he was looking at me strangely. He said, "You want me to do 'im? You want me to sort 'im out?" And every time he said it, he clicked his fingers for emphasis. He really was a very simple soul. He could be quite childlike. I used to do all his printing and his framing. Why? Because he never had any money! We gave an exhibition together at St Leonards in Sussex. Two hours before the opening—no Harry. I eventual-

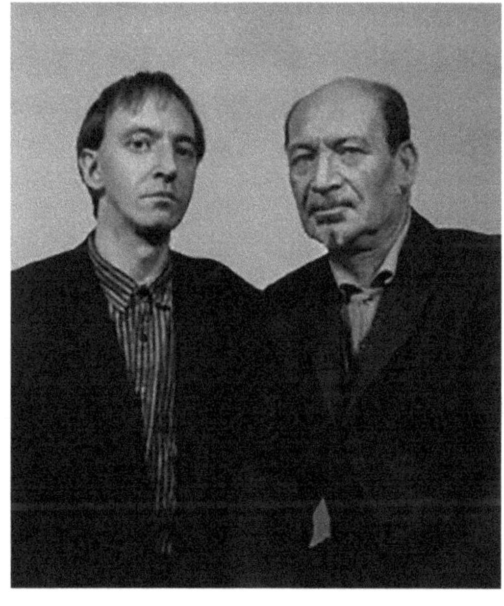

Michael Woods and Harry Diamond

ly found him sitting on the beach, looking out at the sea, in a state of obvious distress. "What's the problem, Harry?" I asked. He replied, "This stuff called Blu Tack. I don't understand it. How does it work?" I said, "Is that the problem?" He nodded. I had some Blu Tack in my pocket, and I showed him how it worked. It completely transformed his mood. He smiled happily and said, "This Blu Tack—it's fuckin' magic, innit?"

3

"I first met George Melly in 1984. He actually lived quite close to me in Notting Hill. He'd been commissioned by the ***Daily Telegraph*** to write an article about my work. 'A New Eye on London' was going to be the title of the piece. I went round to his flat with my photo portfolio, and we ended up just drinking and eventually getting dead drunk together. The second time was the same. The third time, as soon as I arrived, I said, 'Look, we really must do some work.' So George gave me a book to read while he sat down to write the article. Handwritten. The whole thing. And the book was ***Paris Peasant*** by Louis Aragon, and I absolutely loved it. And not much later, George said, 'Why don't we do a book on Paris together?' Which, of course, eventually became ***Paris and the Surrealists***.

"But first I had to go to Paris to do research, and I got so fascinated with the city that photographs weren't enough. So that's how I became a collagist and assemblage maker."

Michael's first important exhibition was ***Six Surrealist Artists*** at the Crawshaw Gallery in London in 1987, followed by the collaborations with Harry Diamond mentioned previously. In 1989 he was in Milan for ***I Surrealisti*** and then back in London for ***Living British Surrealists*** at Murray Feely Fine Arts, in which he appeared alongside Desmond Morris, Eileen Agar, Leonora Carrington, and Conroy Maddox. Solo exhibitions of his assemblages were held, again in London, in each of the next three years.

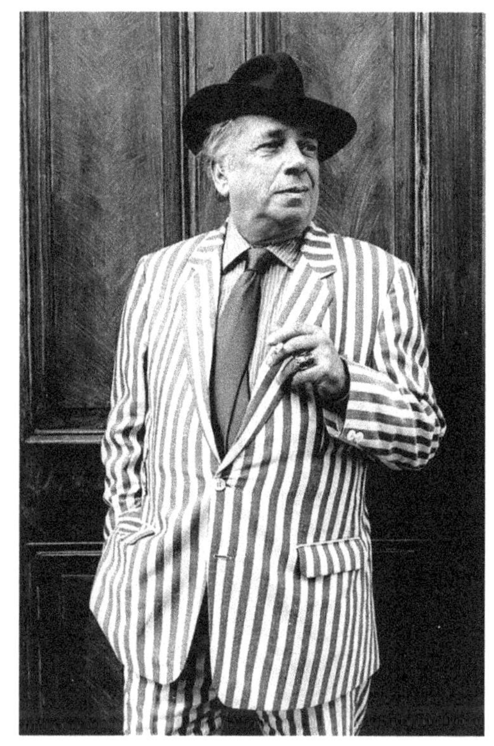

George Melly

"Yes, Joseph Cornell and Marcel Duchamp were influences on my collages and assemblages, but also Eileen Agar and Anthony Earnshaw. I exhibited with Eileen Agar as part of the ***Living British Surrealists*** in 1989, and we became friends. I used to take coffee and apple flan around to her flat."

Eileen Agar b. Buenos Aires, 1899. Friend of Ezra Pound. Lover of Paul Eluard. Photographed by Lee Miller. d. 1991. Buried in Pere Lachaise, Paris (re. Jean Dolande).

Anthony Earnshaw b. West Yorkshire, England, 1924, and was, according to his obituary in the Times on August 25, 2001, "a painter and graphic artist, a surrealist and anarchist, a composer of aphorisms and insults."

Conroy Maddox b. Herefordshire, England, 1912. Surrealist painter whose ready-made *Onanistic Typewriter I*, with spikes protruding from the keys, is a direct reference to Man Ray's *Cadeau*. When Maddox died, in 2005, George Melly turned to Michael Woods at the funeral and said, "You're the last of the surrealists now!"

4

Paris and the Surrealists, published by Thames & Hudson in 1991, is a modern classic, a beautifully produced homage to the artistic inventors and innovators and the city in which they lived and loved, worked and drank, formed lasting friendships and bitter enmities, and in the process created a mythology that pervades the streets and cafés of Montparnasse to this day. George Melly's text manages to be simultaneously elegant and erudite, informative and entertaining; his prose style never descends to mere journalism and, more importantly, never becomes precious or self-conscious. It is a saxophone solo that never thinks itself more important than the band. But the photographs, well, they are something else again. The first thing you note (after how exceptionally well-chosen they are) is that they perfectly illustrate a book on surrealism without falling into the obvious trap of trying to be works of surrealism themselves. The second, and really most extraordinary thing, is that after reading Melly's text you are immediately drawn to reading (or probably rereading) ***Paris Peasant***. And I think the beauty, in fact sheer genius of Michael Woods's photos is that they illustrate Aragon's masterpiece just as well as they do the book they are actually in.

Paris Peasant
(Louis Aragon, 1926)

A shop selling canes and walking sticks separates the Café de Petit Grillon from the lodging house entrance. A perfectly honorable salesman offers to a questionable clientele a wide choice of luxurious examples of these canes, displayed so as to show stems and handles to their best advantage. A whole art of spatial panoply is at play here: the canes lower down form fans, while those higher up are crossed like Xs and, as a result of a strange tropism, inclines toward the beholder their bouquets of pommels: ivory roses, dogs' heads with jeweled eyes, damascened semi-darkness from Toledo, niello inlays from delicate sentimental foliage, cats, women, hooked beaks, countless materials ranging from twisted rattan to rhinoceros horn and the blond charm of cornelians.

I remember a shivering waxwork figure at a hairdresser's, her arms crossed in front of her chest, her unpinned permanent tresses soaking their permanent wave in the water of a crystal bowl. I remember a fur shop. I remember the strange dumb show put on by the electroscope's strips of gold leaf. O top hats! During a whole week you presented, for me, the black appearance of a question mark. On the threshold of palpable emotion, a mere nothing could induce me to think that there must be more certainty in my restrictive and particular concept of each thing than in the absolute intuition I had of it. That state of affairs did not last long. Then, without feeling reluctant any

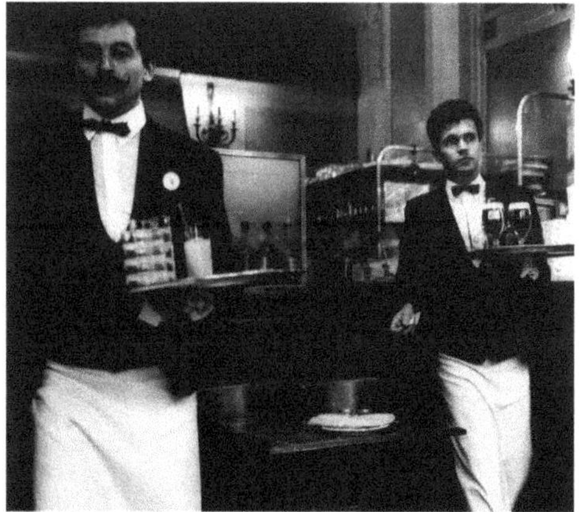

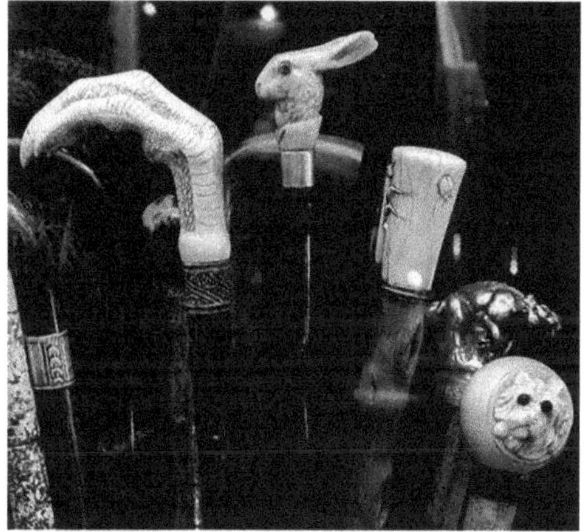

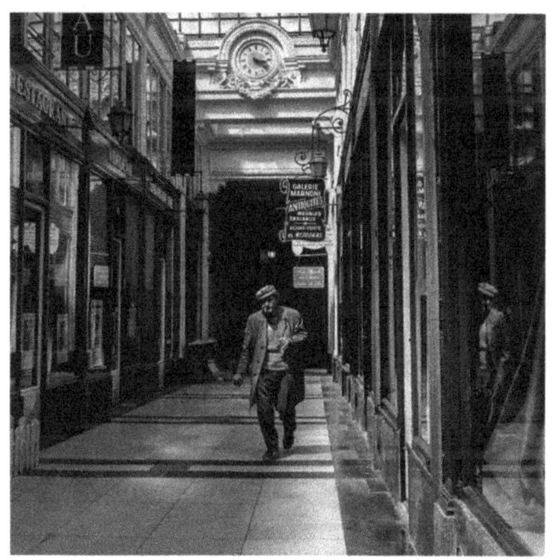

from *Paris and the Surrealists*

longer, I set about discovering the face of the infinite, beneath the concrete forms which were escorting me, walking the length of the earth's avenues.

5

In Response to a Query about a Sequence of Forty Paintings entitled *La Belle Captive* and Based on the Work of Alain Robbe-Grillet

"You ask if my series was based on Robbe-Grillet's novel or film *La Belle Captive*? Neither! I can't visualize my paintings, I can only feel them. I buy boxes of junk for not much money, often on the Portobello Road. Then, a few years later, I turn them into something. It's all in the unconscious. When everything is in front of me, I play around with it and see what works. But what you have to understand is that I have no visual memory. Small vessel disease has severed the pons link between my body and my brain, so I can't see things and store them to memory. I am, if you like, a man without a pictorial history, and part of my compulsion to create art is to both lose myself and find myself, always trying to create a visual memory outside myself. For that, I have had to learn to see in a different way. The irony is that previously I was trying to be a surrealist, but now I can't contrive anymore. I am a true surrealist because I don't have conscious control. Aristotle said that the inner self is 'something other.' So you could say I'm trying to capture an image of the inner self."

6

5 – 4 – 3 – 2 – 1 flickers suddenly on the screen. The spool unspools, *flapper-flapper-flapper-flapper-flap*; a small white face looks down from the projection booth at an empty theatre, the worn

scarlet plush of the chairs revealing their metal frameworks; ice-cream wrappers and hot-dog napkins scattered in the aisles; the screen, unlit, merely a dirty sheet, creased and time-stained, like the back of an old photograph . . .

Nicolas Roeg, director of
Don't Look Now and *Walkabout*,
dies, age 90.

Influential British director
behind run of acclaimed movies
in 1970s and early 80s dies

The Guardian, Saturday, 24 November 2018

"I know you've told me before, but please remind me. How did you and Nicolas Roeg meet?"

"I met him in 1992. He'd just got back from New York, where he'd bought three copies of ***Paris and the Surrealists*** and went into a shop on the Portobello Road to get a picture framed. And in the shop they had a copy of the book, and he said, 'Oh, I've just bought three copies of that.' And the proprietor said, 'Well, would you like to meet him?' So he gave Nicolas Roeg my phone number, and he called me and that was how we met. He wanted me to sign the three copies he'd bought. And, of course, I did, and we became friends. With Theresa Russell, too, who was his wife at the time. I used to look after his dog while he was away filming. Anyway, in 1995 he was making a film called ***Two Deaths*** with Michael Gambon, and he asked me to work on that. So I turned up on set and said, 'What do you want me to do?' But Nic didn't work like that. He just said, 'Whatever you like.' And that became me doing the title and credit montages, and we worked together on all his films after that.

ʊʊ

Those collaborations continued all the way up to Nicolas Roeg's last film, ***Puffball*** (2007), featuring, among others, the star of ***Don't Look Now***, Donald Sutherland. Michael Woods was second unit cameraman and in charge of special effects. But by far the most interesting of their collaborations, for myself anyway, is perhaps the least known—a fifteen-minute piece for the BBC called ***The Sound of Claudia Schiffer***, first shown in 2001 and entered in the Venice Film Festival. A surreal montage that begins before the celebrated fashion model (or perhaps even our solar system?) is born, it incorporates many of the effects that have since become familiar in video installations, and utilizes a number of voices, not just Claudia's own, as well as archive footage from (I assume) 1920s Berlin. A glorious mix of profundity and experiment, symbolism and playfulness ("I was given free rein to do whatever I wanted!"), it is really impossible to describe it in any meaningful way. It is available to watch on

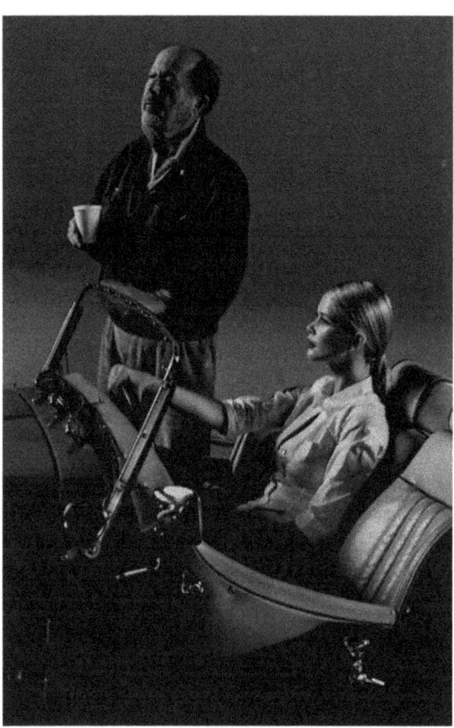

Nicolas Roeg & Claudia Schiffer

YouTube, and I sincerely suggest that you do, treating it as an extension of the pictures that illustrate this essay. When you reach the end, you will see that the credits say, **Artwork and Photography MICHAEL WOODS**, but there is more to it than that. Anybody who knows Michael's work well can see him and his style thoroughly incorporated into the fabric of the film; indeed, it is the most profound form of collaboration because it is really impossible to tell where Nicolas Roeg ends and Michael Woods begins.

7

"When I was thirteen I saw Francis Bacon's ***Three Studies for Figures at the Base of a Crucifixion*** at the Tate. It blew me away. Such fascinating strength and beauty. Years later I was introduced to him at the Colony Club in Soho. Ian Board, who had taken the place over from Muriel Belcher, said, Whatever you do, don't ask to photograph him.

"Oh, I wouldn't dare.

"Anyway, a few minutes later Francis Bacon comes in and Ian Board introduces us, and the first thing I say is, Oh, Francis, could I photograph you? And he lets out a squeal of anguish and runs out the door. When he comes back, I say the same thing again, and again the same thing happens. After the third time he sits down and looks at me and says, If you photograph me, what can you add that hasn't been done before?

"Nothing, I replied.

"Well, have some champagne then.

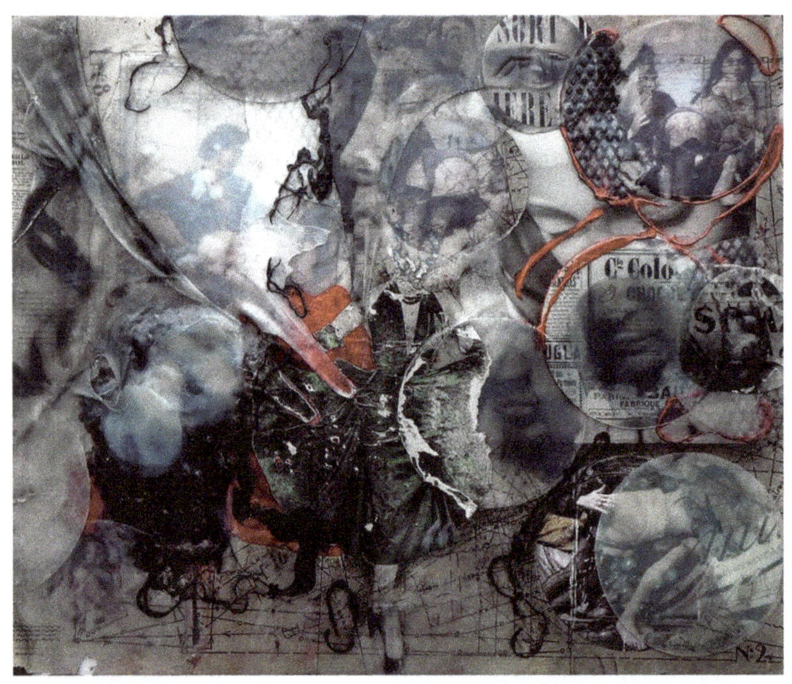

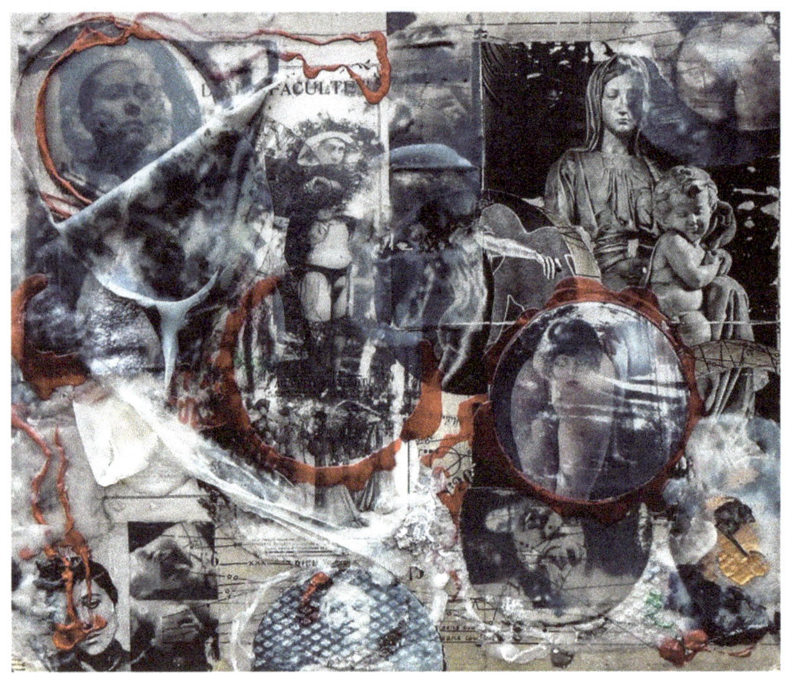

from *La Belle Captive*

"Anyway, two weeks later I was passing Dean Street and happened to have my camera around my neck when I went up to the Colony, and Francis Bacon and Ian Board were sitting at the bar and Francis said, Why don't you take a photo of the two of us?

"And I said, What's the point, it's all been done before . . .

"Francis smiled. Then he said, Do you masturbate?

"I was taken aback. I said, Well, um, sometimes.

"I masturbate before I do a painting. When do you masturbate?

"Oh, I don't know. When I'm tense maybe.

"And Francis had his hand on my knee, and he started squeezing so hard that it was painful and he grinned. He said, Are you tense now?

"And we became great friends after that. But I never did photograph him."

8

When I spoke to Michael on the telephone a few days before starting this essay, he told me: "When you are writing your piece, please remember that the emphasis for me is the work I've done exploring the consciousness, or more specifically, the connection between the heart and the brain. Of course, you can't paint consciousness, but I am attempting to capture consciousness."

In 2012 a specially commissioned assemblage ***Arena of Hearts—Cardiology in Medicine, Art and Consciousness*** was unveiled in London's Royal Brompton Hospital. It is majestically large, measuring eight feet by five, and represents an ongoing collaboration between Michael Woods and the eminent physicist and neuroscientist Professor John Taylor. It is, according to Michael, "a distilled metaphor for the heart as featured in art, literature, poetry, etcetera," and represents an ongoing engagement with extending the reach of surrealism to incorporate not just the philosophy of Hegel and Sartre but also the most up-to-date medical and psychiatric research into what constitutes the inner self. Subsequently, he began a sequence of internal self-portrait paintings called ***Wounds***, difficult to describe but which remind me of a darker, more visceral version of that 1966 sci-fi movie ***Fantastic Voyage***, and which he now tells me he has abandoned after fifty canvases "because my wounds became too painful. I didn't like what I saw, what was going wrong inside my body." Nevertheless, it has been superceded by an even more expansive project, a work-in-progress entitled ***Self in Non-Thetic Consciousness***—"It's the most powerful work I've ever done. The most unified, the most expressive"—which currently numbers approximately four hundred canvases . . .

"How many exactly?"

"I'm an artist. I don't count my work!"

. . . one hundred of which are already on display alongside ***Arena of Hearts*** at the Royal Brompton Hospital. When the inevitable biography, as mentioned earlier, is written, its author will have sufficient pages to adequately explore and explain the intensely complicated relationship between medicine, psychiatry, neuroscience, and philosophy in Michael Woods's most recent

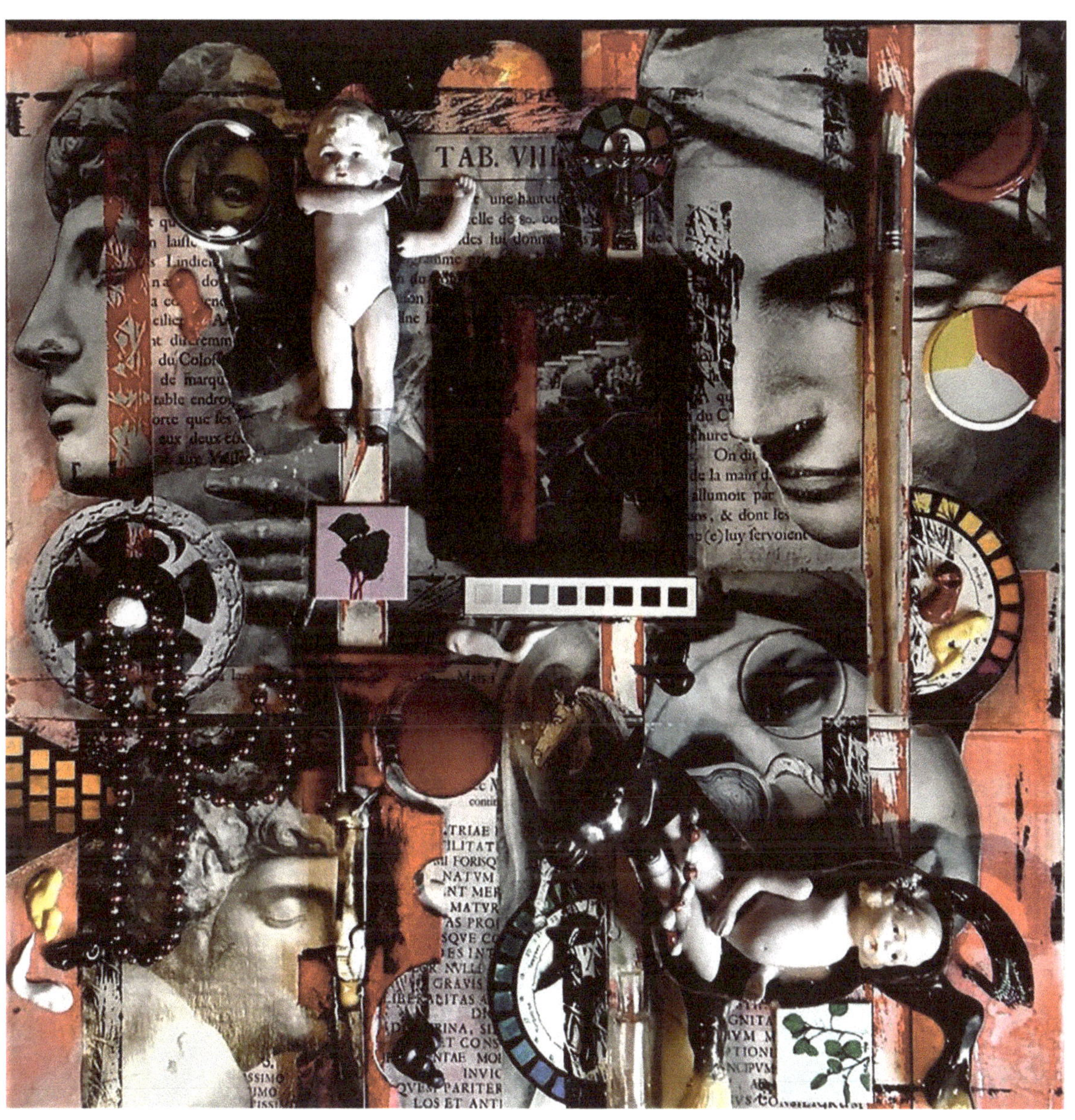

work. In the meantime, we have a neat summary from Nicolas Roeg: "You," he once told Michael, "are an artist chasing your scientist's tail!"

9

I am sitting with Michael at a pavement table outside the Golborne Café on Golborne Road in London's Notting Hill. It is a beautiful mid-September morning, so warm, in fact, that I have ordered a Coca-Cola, although Michael is drinking his usual coffee, and we are both smoking cigarettes. He is, of course, impeccably dressed, and there is the habitual pound coin on the edge of the glass-topped table, ready for the waiter who served him before we arrived. Our talk takes in what he's been doing recently and his upcoming projects, most notably a collaboration with the Scottish film director Lynne Ramsay on an adaptation of a Margaret Atwood story set on a cruise ship in the Arctic, starring Julianne Moore with location shooting in Greenland and Iceland, plus, when he has the time, a continuation of a long-planned autobiography, provisionally titled ***A Memory of Eye***. Somehow we get on to Jacques Prevert, perhaps because I once published a chapbook based on the great French surrealist poet, and I now remember that Michael has a copy of my ***Six Variations on a Theme of Jacques Prevert*** and gave me a sincere thrill by expressing admiration for it a couple of years ago. And so an hour drifts pleasantly by before Michael's car, a Jaguar, pulls up on the other side of a Sunday-quiet road, his driver sitting patiently behind the wheel. A hug and a kiss for Susan and then the same for me because Michael is one of those rare and lovely men who instinctively inspire affection and entirely reciprocate it, whether you are male or female, just so long as you are *sympathique*—and then the familiar stiff-legged, beautifully suited, cane-steadied walk to his car and a brief wave through the open window as it pulls away from the kerb.

Whenever I say goodbye to Michael, whether in person or on the phone, but more so in person, I am aware of a certain unknowability about him; however close we might seem to be, there is a vacant lot between our two houses that can never quite belong to either one of us. But then I remember something he once said to me:

"Francis Bacon told me, 'I don't call myself an artist, I call myself a painter. And once I've been understood, I've failed.'"

In that case, Michael, and with all respect to my readers, I prefer not to, at least completely, understand you, or, indeed, open the window on your art so wide that you can be completely understood. So for now, let us leave it there, with Susan and I finishing our drinks at a pavement table outside the Golborne Café and an idea for a literary portrait already forming in my mind. Afterward we may take a walk along the Portobello Road. It is, after all, a beautiful day and I have been told that one can find some excellent assemblage material there . . .

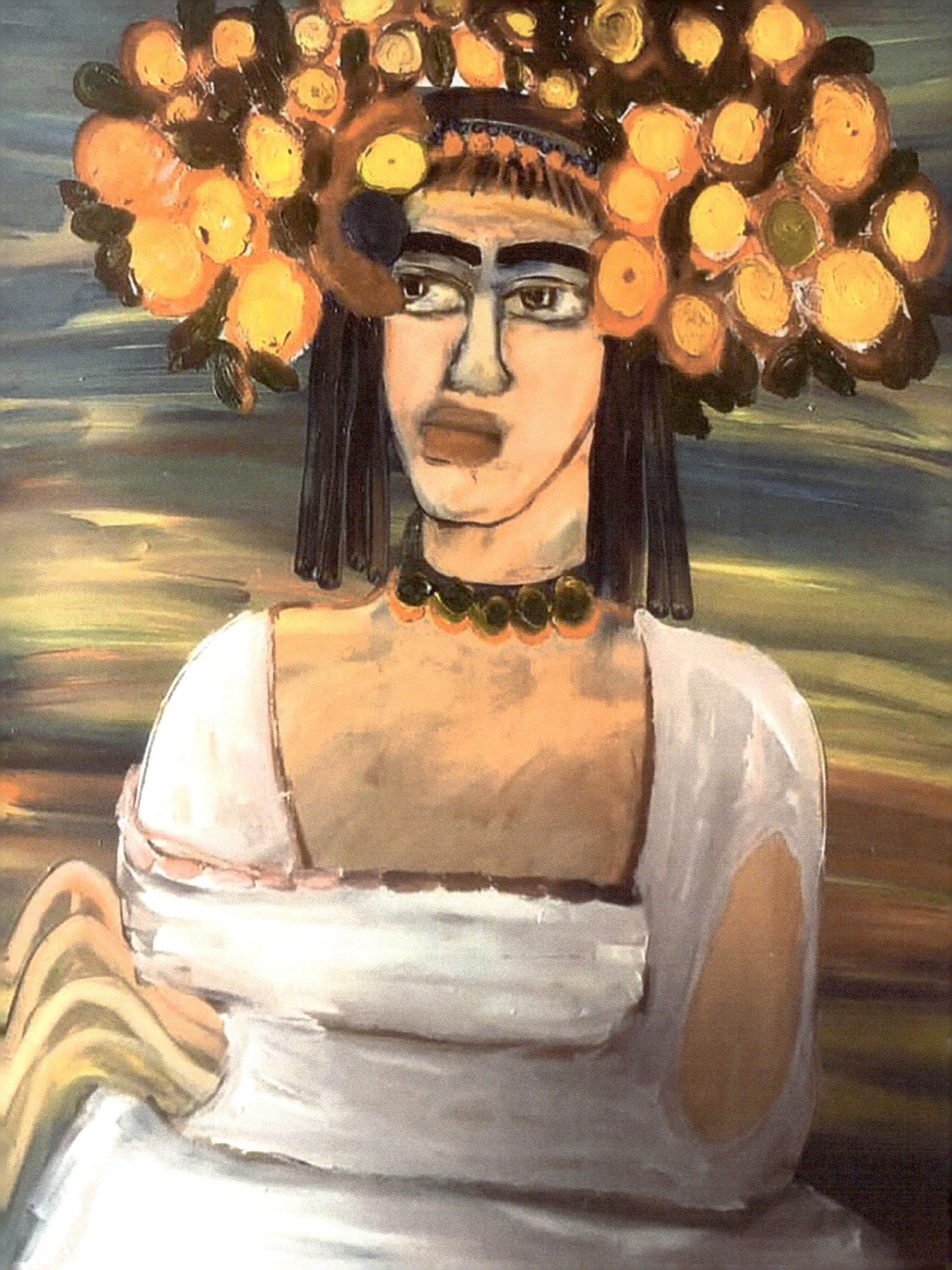

MYSELF, MY WIFE, KONG NING AND THE LITTLE BLUE MAN

In the late afternoon of May 17, 2018, my wife and I were standing in the arrivals hall of Bristol Airport waiting to meet the celebrated Chinese artist and environmental activist Kong Ning as she flew in from Paris on her first visit to the United Kingdom. It was one of those beautiful spring days when the light appears diffused through a yellow filter, all sounds seem to come from slightly further away, and an almost tangible aura of cider orchards combined with the ethereal atmosphere of Victorian railway stations. She emerged from Customs as an already extravagant figure, pulling an enormous wheeled suitcase with one hand and in the other holding a large square bubble-wrapped parcel that turned out to be her larger-than-life-size portrait of Susan. For the next two nights Kong Ning stayed with us in our flat on the southwest coast, my writing room converted into a makeshift bedroom, before we all took the train to London where she had rented a town house on Beauchamp Place, just a short walk from Harrods and almost opposite the atelier of fashion designer Bruce Oldfield.

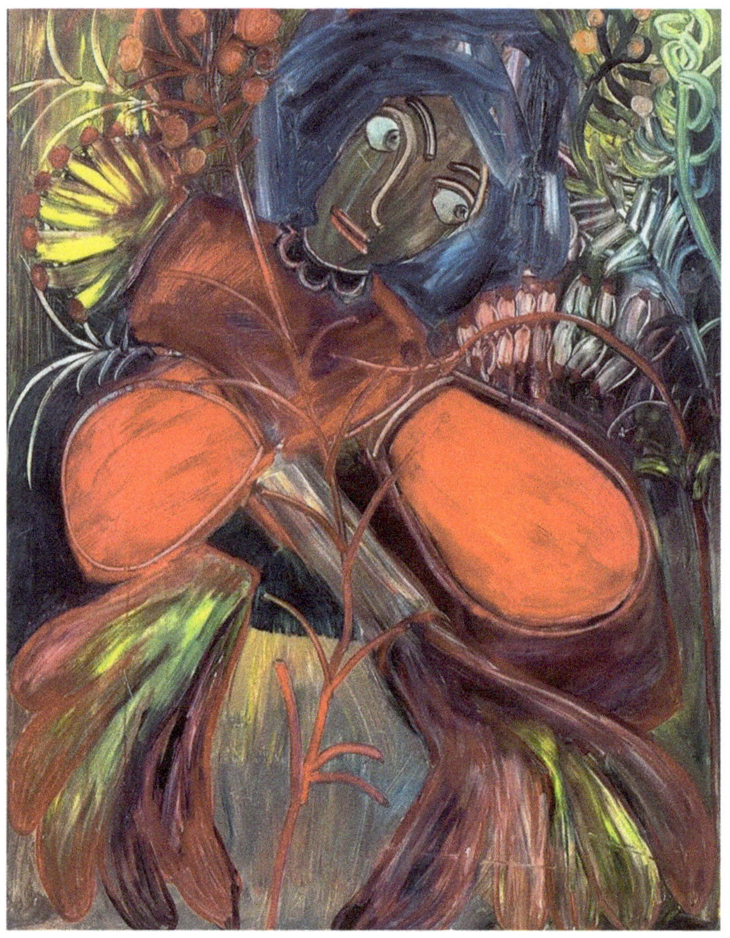

The Buddha

I remember the next few days as a sequence of striking and contrasting events emerging from the overall unreality of living far beyond a literary writer's modest means. On Sunday Susan took Kong Ning to Soho and Chinatown and then introduced her to fish and chips in a restaurant off Leicester Square. Meanwhile, I stayed behind at Beauchamp Place, drinking Gordon's gin with Marks & Spencer's tonic, near-enough chain-smoking Gauloises cigarettes, and coming up with performable versions of Susan's translations from the original Chinese of two of Kong Ning's poems.

On Monday we invited the photographer Paul Polydorou to lunch at San Lorenzo, once Princess Diana's favorite restaurant, where he took several pictures of Kong Ning against the backdrop of its conservatory, crossing the street afterwards to take several more portraits in our rented living room. The next evening, Tuesday, May 22, Kong Ning and I performed her poems on the stage of the Poetry Café in Covent Garden, myself reading passages in English while Kong Ning, like a sort of Greek chorus, spoke a counterpoint of the original Chinese lines:

Father,
You sleep so deeply
You sleep so soundly
You are within an endless dream.

Father, I know
You worry I feel cold.
Is this why you have planted a field of sunflowers on my black skirt?
And sewn a thousand flowers of cotton on my green blouse?

You worry, too, that I'm afraid of the dark.
But oh, my dear Father—look!
You have asked the stars to decorate my bedroom window.
You're standing on the rooftops and holding the moon like a lamp,
Directing its beam on me.

You know I love sunflowers
So you've planted ten thousand of them in my eyes.
You know I love roses
So you've told the roses to bloom in my studio every day.

Father, you're perfect!

Look, I have painted a beautiful red horse for you.
Go, go, Red Horse, gallop across the grasslands upon
which my father loved to ride,
Go as fast as possible on this most special day
And carry all his favorite presents to where he sleeps
and waits for you.

Father,
Have you received them?

Father,
Don't be sorrowful if I speak the truth—
It is not as though I blame you for dying.
But since you began your endless sleep
I haven't celebrated Chinese New Year.
The thought of a Spring Festival without you
Turns my eyes into fountains of tears.

But the tears water the sunflowers
You planted in my eyes. They spill over and water the roses
In my studio. They are beautiful tears!

I was so pleased for Kong Ning because in a demanding venue we received a standing ovation.

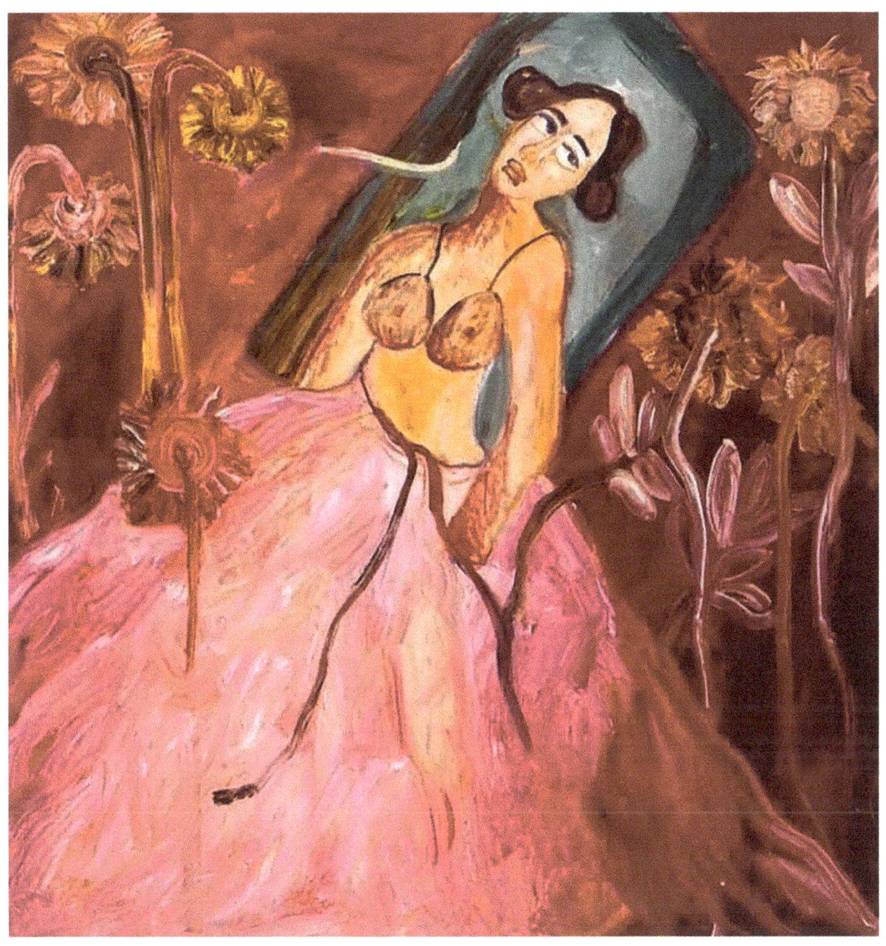

The Lines of the Universe

The following day at about ten o'clock we all clambered—with some difficulty, for Kong Ning had changed into one of her most extravagant public outfits—into a black cab and told the driver to take us to Waterloo Bridge. But while you have the image of us driving through the streets of London on this particularly warm and sunny May morning, Kong Ning's blue extravaganza virtually filling the passengers' space behind the driver, shall we take a look at who exactly Kong Ning is and why the significance of her visit in the first place?

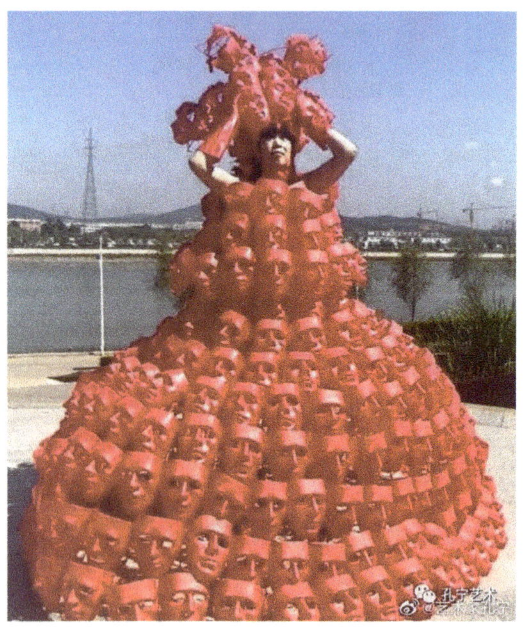

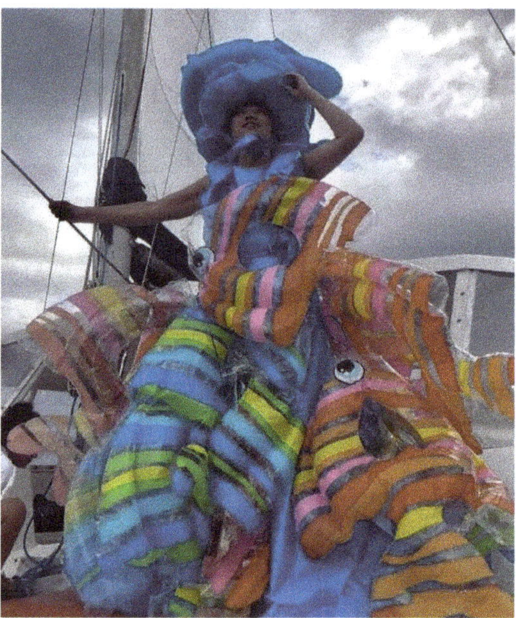

Kong Ning was born in Manzhouli, Inner Mongolia, on August 29, 1958. With her extraordinary costumes and flamboyant personality, she has become one of the most celebrated and recognizable performance artists of the twenty-first century. As a self-styled Bride of the Planet clutching her trademark Little Blue Man, she has been a gift for newspaper photographers and TV reporters in over forty countries since she first burst onto the scene of environmental activism street performance in 2007. But there is a darker side to this than meets the eye, and for the origins of her art, we must go back to when, having taken a law degree, she worked in the Chinese judicial courts.

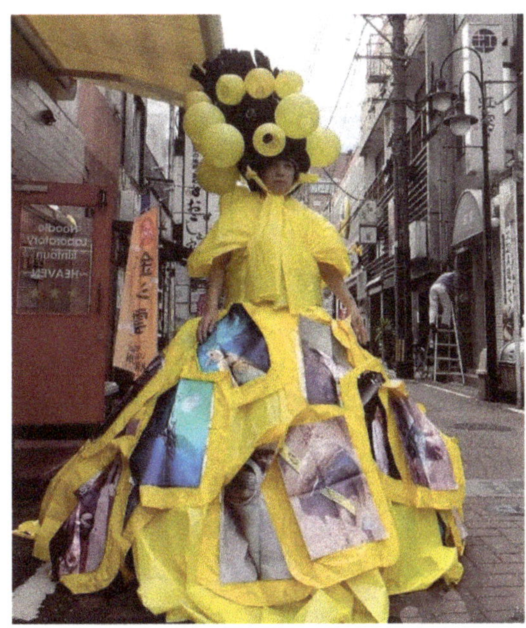

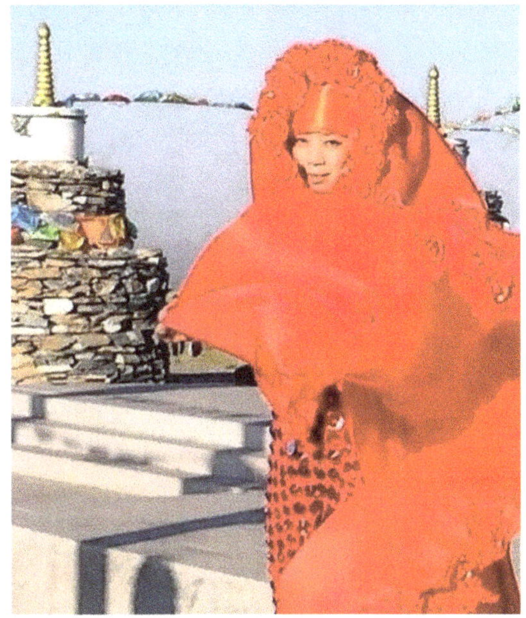

"I often had to deal with prisoners who had been condemned to death. On one occasion I was an administrator during a multiple execution. When it began, I fainted. But I wasn't just revived, I was literally kicked awake. What I saw then was that one prisoner was still twitching. Just as I realized he was still alive, a guard with a small pistol came forward and shot him in the head. He died instantly. From then on I had a horror and hatred of the death penalty and gradually this expanded to a wish to protect all life on this planet. But my experiences in the law courts were where it all began."

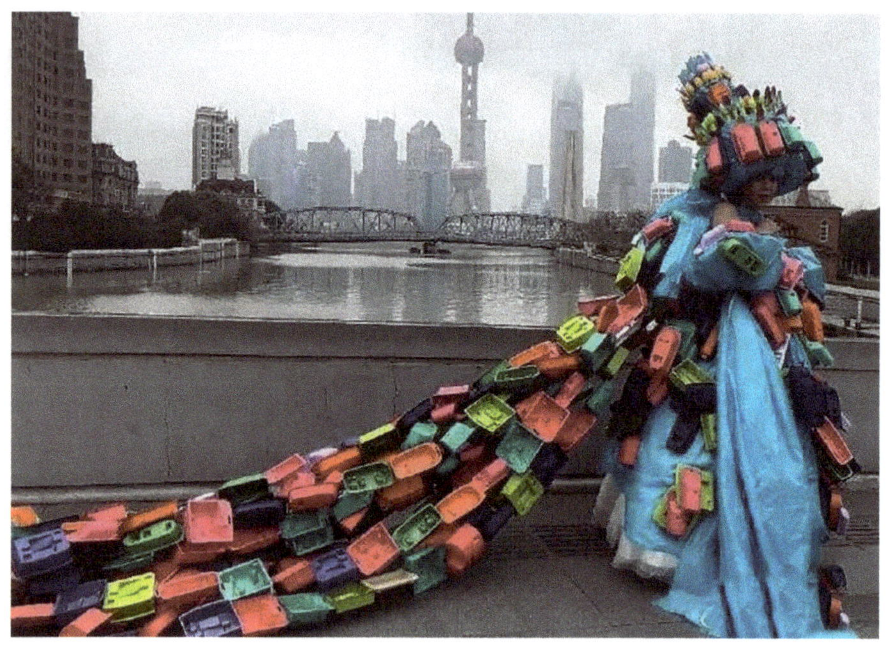

She then decided that, in a world full of sound and fury, with everybody competing for media attention on an overcrowded world stage, with state-sanctioned blood being shed in the name of justice and law, only a magnificent gesture would be sufficient—and a magnificent gesture is exactly what she has made.

"I worked as a lawyer. But I got so depressed, I quit. I felt that I had to express myself in order to survive the memories of what I'd seen. Being a witness to that execution mentally scarred me. I only hoped that my art could be of some comfort to me; that through it I could help restore the planet to somewhere we all can live."

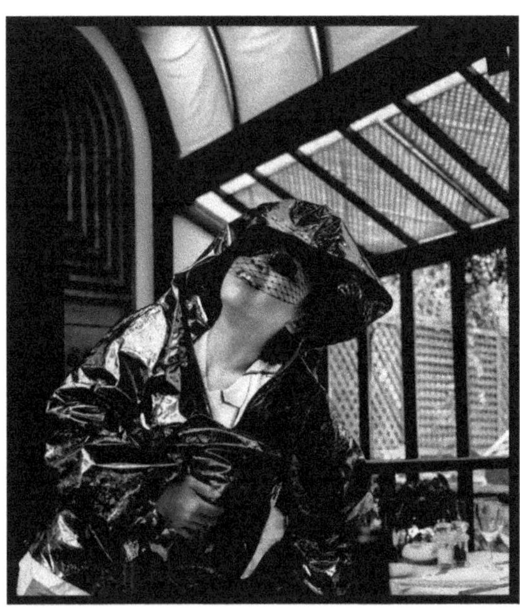

Portrait by Paul Polydorou, London, 2018

But behind all the multinational performances, the photographs in leading newspapers, the ever-growing legion of fans, there are, as in any performance, whether one's stage is a theatre or a boulevard, hours of unseen technical detail. She designs her own costumes, and they can take as little as two days or as many as ten to create. At the time of this writing, she has worn over a hundred costumes, but this does not mean quite literally a hundred different dresses. Where possible she recycles one to make another; the material can be dyed blue or red, and different ornaments or decorations can be added to produce a different effect. Fish, leaves, balloons, surgical masks, children's rubber-studded sensory balls (which, painted black, bear a striking resemblance to spherical viruses, symbolizing how pollution diseases the planet) are just a few examples. On April 22, 2016, the highly respected UK newspaper ***The Daily Telegraph*** published a picture of her wearing a faux wedding dress studded with a thousand biodegradable eggs. I remember saying to her once, "These dresses, they're so extraordinary—they should be exhibited somewhere, like in a fashion museum. Have they been?" To which she replied that, no, they hadn't. Although she subsequently admitted that some are in private collections in Germany, France, and Greece.

And then, of course, there is her *poupée* (as the French call it), her famous mannequin, a sort of mute ventriloquist's puppet, the oft-mentioned Little Blue Man, symbolizing, according to its creatrix, "water and sky." Here we have a description from a 2018 French brochure:

Un Projet par Kong Ning

A chaque rencontre avec un representant etatique, Kong Ning offrira une poupée eco-concue a partir de paille, de ble et de mais. Comme la robe Little Blue Man, ces poupées sont biodegradables et contiennent chacune une graine. Lorsque la poupée sera use, elle pourra etre plantee en terre et fera eclore une fleur. Cette poupée incarne le lien eternal entre Terre et la consummation energetique. Elle es tune offrande a la terre, symbolique et materielle.

L'idee de la poupée est une action pedagogique destinee aux enfants et transmet un message: l'harmonie entre l'homme et la nature est fondamentale.

Les poupées Epouse de la terre transmettent des valeurs universelles et une vision sans frontier. C'est une demarche oppose au concept de classe, au culte de l'argent et la discrimination.

A Project by Kong Ning

At each meeting with a state representative, Kong Ning will offer an eco-designed *poupée* made from straw, wheat, and maize. Like the Little Blue Man dress, these *poupées* are biodegradable and each contain a seed. When the *poupée* has been used, it can be planted in the ground and will make a flower shine. This *poupée* embodies the eternal link between the Earth and energy consumption. It is an offering to the earth, symbolic and material.

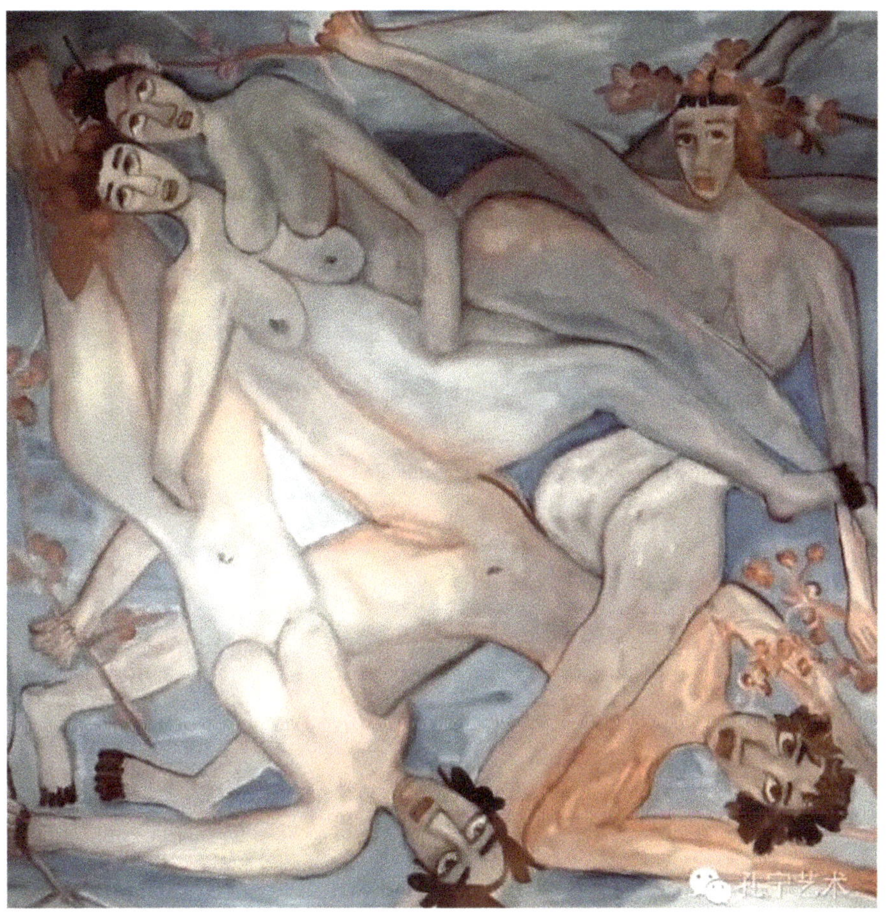

The Season of the Horse

The idea of the *poupée* is an action pedagogique intended for children and conveys a message: harmony between man and nature is fundamental.

The Bride of the Earth dolls transmit universal values and a vision without borders. It is a step against the concept of class, the cult of money and discrimination.

It may come as a surprise to Kong Ning's many fans, or should I say, the fans of her charmingly realized Little Blue Man, that since his relatively recent inception in 2017, he has had over two hundred incarnations, although not all of them have been planted in the earth. There are a few more permanent examples. The three-foot-tall mannequin she brandished above her head during her walk along the Embankment from Waterloo Bridge in 2018 is made of foam-filled blue plastic, handstitched at the seams, and now sits propped-up in our bedroom next to my wife's dressing table. It is, whichever way you look at it, an interesting souvenir.

ꕥ

May 23, 2018
Xinhua News Agency
Waterloo Bridge

Chinese artist Kong Ning, famous for her art works calling for environmental protection, showcased her performance art *Little Blue Man* here on Wednesday.

Wearing dozens of "Little Blue Men" made of degradable corn materials, Kong Ning made her debut walk along the Thames River, starting from Waterloo Bridge and proceeding to Westminster Abbey.

Before coming to Great Britain, Kong Ning gave art displays in France, Monaco, Italy, Greece, and Morocco. She plans a global walking tour with her Little Blue Man, hoping her voice can be heard all around the world.

"I want to convey the idea of environmental protection. Life is just like a drop of water, gently coming and going without adding any weight to the earth.

"By performing as a blue man, I try to convey the concept of environmental protection as well as a peaceful world.

"I hope the skin of our planet could all change to blue color."

ꙮ

However much Kong Ning has been feted in London and despite the many countries in which she has been enthusiastically received, Paris remains the city in which she feels most appreciated. There, in 2017, she was the top reported artist in ***Le Figaro*** and twice had television documentaries made about her. It says something that in every country she visits, she writes a letter to the head of state stating her artistic and environmental objectives. Emmanuel Macron, the French president, is one of the few to have personally replied, expressing his support.

If Kong Ning the performance artist has a starring role on the world's stage, her work as a painter is no less important, although perhaps inevitably attracting less media coverage and, therefore, less public attention. Kong Ning began painting seriously in 2005, but has tended to be dismissed by the critics both for being self-taught and for failing to fit into any recognized trend in modern art. In fact, she has no interest in classical Chinese painting or calligraphy and denies any influence from her contemporaries, although she will admit to having, when she was a young girl, admired some of the western old masters who worked in oils.

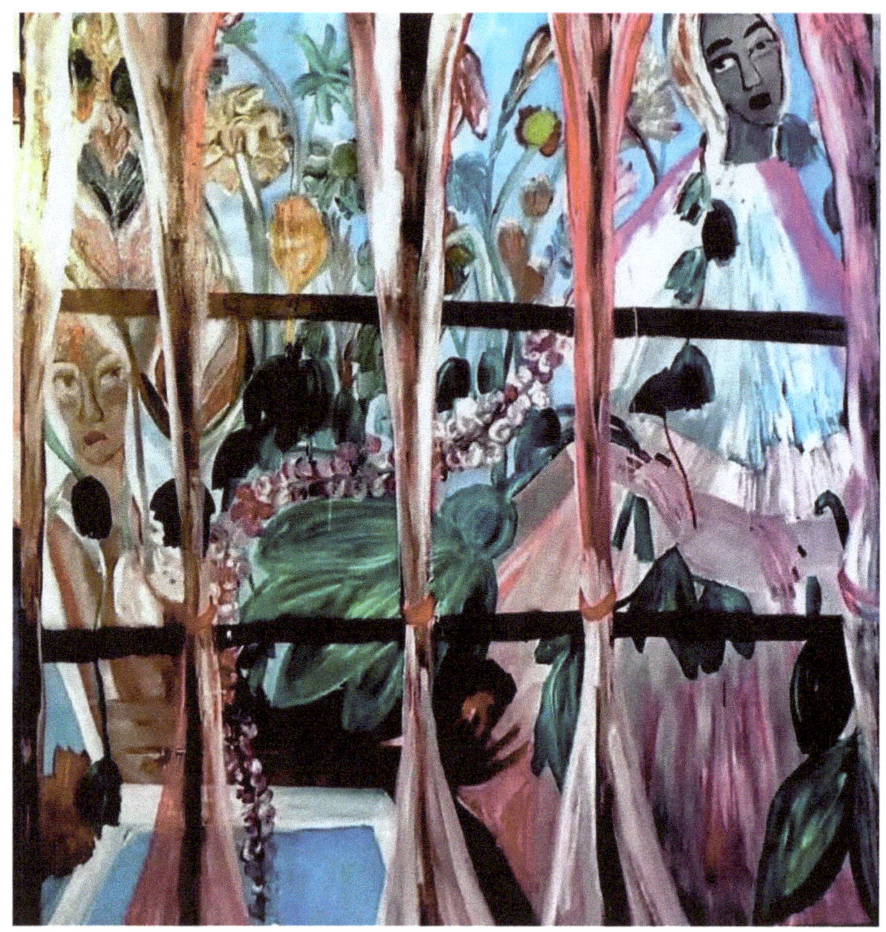

Living All the Way

Be that as it may, wherever it developed from, her style is immediately recognizable. Strangely elongated figures with almost luminous eyes emerge from the canvas like previously unknown sea creatures coming into focus through the portholes of a diving bell. Fascinating and surreal, they entice the viewer into another world—exotic, for sure, but also filled with a certain tension. A Kong Ning face is immediately recognizable: usually female, sometimes androgynous, larger-than-life eyes, a flatly delineated nose, and a pointed chin make these faces as distinctive as any in contemporary art. The hairstyle is such that it usually reveals the ears, but apart from this detail, the face is not Kong Ning's own. These are not an endless series of self-portraits, at least not in any literal sense. They are a portrait of the age in which we live, an Age of Anxiety, if one might lift a line from Auden, for there is certainly anxiety in the expressions of many of them, and often you feel that they would prefer to fade back into the lush, almost tropical backgrounds that the artist has set them against; for to be thrust into this world in all their nakedness and fear is to be exposed both literally and figuratively; and to experience it briefly with wide-open eyes is as much as the human soul can sometimes stand.

There have been exhibitions of her work in France, Germany, and the USA as well as her native China, and paintings have been bought by private collectors in France, the UK, the USA, Taiwan, China, and Korea. In fact, one American collector, who prefers to remain anonymous, has bought sixty of her canvases over the past few years, and each sells for up to fifty thousand dollars. This helps to explain why Kong Ning, when not traveling around the world performing her art on the streets, resides in a beautiful Beijing mansion called the Rose Palace where many of her artworks, be they canvases on the walls or street performance costumes on shop-window mannequins, are on permanent display.

Kong Ning is one of the most remarkable artists of our time. To walk with her along the banks of the Thames, to see her stand magnificently on Waterloo Bridge like some modern incarnation of a Wagnerian myth is to knowingly be in the presence of greatness. But what is she like as a person? One can almost open a box of adjectives and sprinkle them on the canvas of the page like the rose petals she loves so much. Easy-going, demanding, generous, warm-hearted, big-hearted, infuriating, captivating, emotional, impulsive, traditional, curious for new experiences—be they in life or love—broad-minded and single-minded, completely unselfconscious and absolutely committed to being the twenty-four-hour-a-day incarnation of her own conception of herself, she is completely impossible and totally irresistible. She is the guest for whom I once cooked a traditional English breakfast of sausage, bacon, and fried eggs, untraditionally washed down with a bottle of Italian sparkling wine, and who decided, after several anxious moments in our apartment's galley kitchen, that it was "*mei we de!*" ("delicious!"). But before I congratulate myself too much on my skills as a chef, I might also add that after her London performance, which finished at Buckingham Palace, not Westminster Abbey as Xinhua stated in their press release, we had supper at Paul Polydorou's Notting Hill flat where she even better appreciated his and his wife Masami's excellent homemade fish pie.

In conclusion, she may or may not be the savior of our planet, but ultimately, she is a significant performance artist who has brought renewed attention to the conservationist cause and a painter who has found a way to symbolize the anxieties of the modern age. And let us not forget that she is also a poet, the poet who wrote, and with whom I once performed, at London's Poetry Café, these lines:

I chose to catch the wind and die last night.
It was the time of my choosing.
Death! But something was wrong and I opened my eyes.
I came back from the edge of eternity,
Back to the unhappiness of this world.

O, Mother, forgive me . . .

I have metamorphosized without your permission.

My ribs have become a cage of bamboo,
My legs are divided between land and sea. Behold!
One leg is a poplar, planted deep in the earth,
The other an ocean-dwelling mermaid's tail.
One eye is a fireball launched from the sun,
The other a bowl of purest water lit by the moon.
One arm is the wing of an aluminum swan,
The other the stubby feather of a chick learning to fly.
One foot is a burning roller-skate,
The other a blade of sharpened ice.

O, Mother, how can I not remember
Any night as a child I slept with you?
How did you not know my fears and solitude?
The two-year-old girl afraid of caterpillars,
The three-year-old in love with a beautiful blue skirt?

I chose to catch the wind and die last night,
And returned because it was the wrong time to go.
Sometimes you only recognize true love
When your life is nearly ended . . .

Mother, yours was the truest true love I nearly died to recognize.
You neglected me to make me strong.
You empowered my whole body to marry the universe.

You committed your own child to the planet,
To be lost like air . . .

Tell me, Mother, have I fulfilled your dream?

Nice, South of France | 25 April 2018

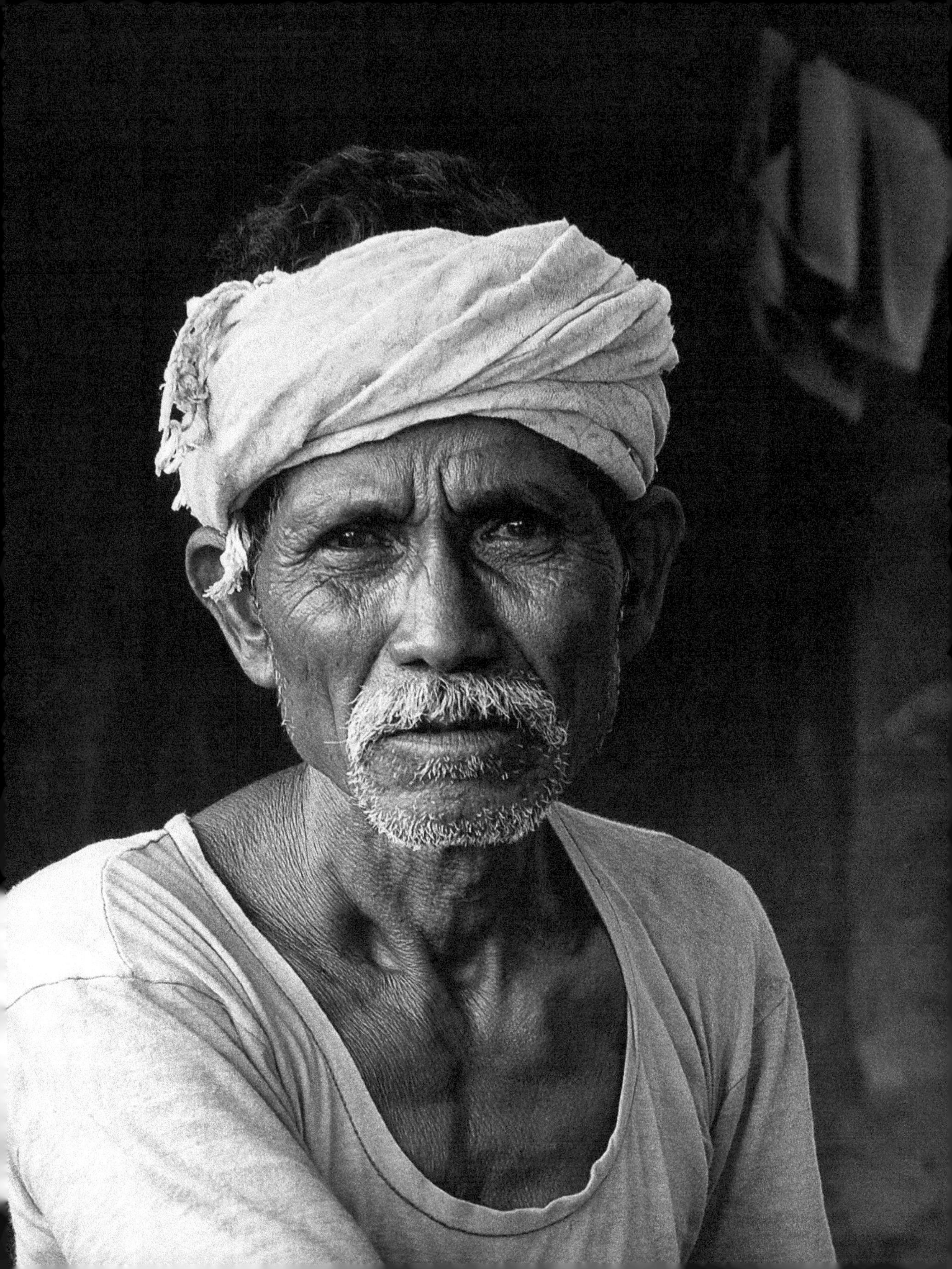

FROM A DISTANCE

THE PHOTOGRAPHY OF PAUL POLYDOROU

"I normally photograph from a ways back so there's room to make shapes and tones balance. But whether they're taken in Japan or Ladakh, or in the Lake District or the Hebrides in Britain, the pictures I feel work best and want to exhibit have nearly all been taken while away from home. It would seem that it's only when in an unfamiliar environment that I'm able to really see and make something work . . . "

Paul Polydorou was born in 1958 in a town called Asha, now part of Turkish-occupied northern Cyprus. He has few memories of it, however, for when he was just three years old his family made the life-changing decision to emigrate to England.

"In 1960 Cyprus became a republic after many years of British colonial rule. Following this it was possible for people to emigrate to Britain, and so my parents came here for economic reasons. Of course, people gravitate to places where their own communities already exist, the better to find assistance and employment. For us it was South London."

Along with speaking Greek at home with his parents, Paul grew up and assimilated into the English environment and progressed through its educational system. A significant event, though hardly one to be aware of at the time, was being given a camera when he was sixteen.

"It was an Ilford Sportsman, a very basic, totally manual film camera. You adjusted the aperture and limited shutter speeds based on whether it was sunny or cloudy! My first roll of film was black-and-white, and my first photographs were mostly taken in the woods behind where we lived."

Paul began taking photographs increasingly seriously during his student days, having enrolled in a humanities course at what is now Greenwich University in the southeast of London, even setting up a darkroom in the kitchen under the basement stairs of the house where he lived in Blackheath.

"The kit I ended up with was a Nikkormat (35mm SLR) and a Mamiya C220 (120 roll film). Most pictures I took were of friends and . . . nothing much . . . just out and about. However, I did go on my first journey at this time where taking photos was important. The year was 1979. I went on a cycling holiday across Ireland to the west coast. And it was during this trip that I took a photo of The Gates in Kilkenny, which I've since reprinted many times in various formats. You could say this was the beginning of my photographic journey. It gave me the confidence and feeling that I could maybe do something with photography."

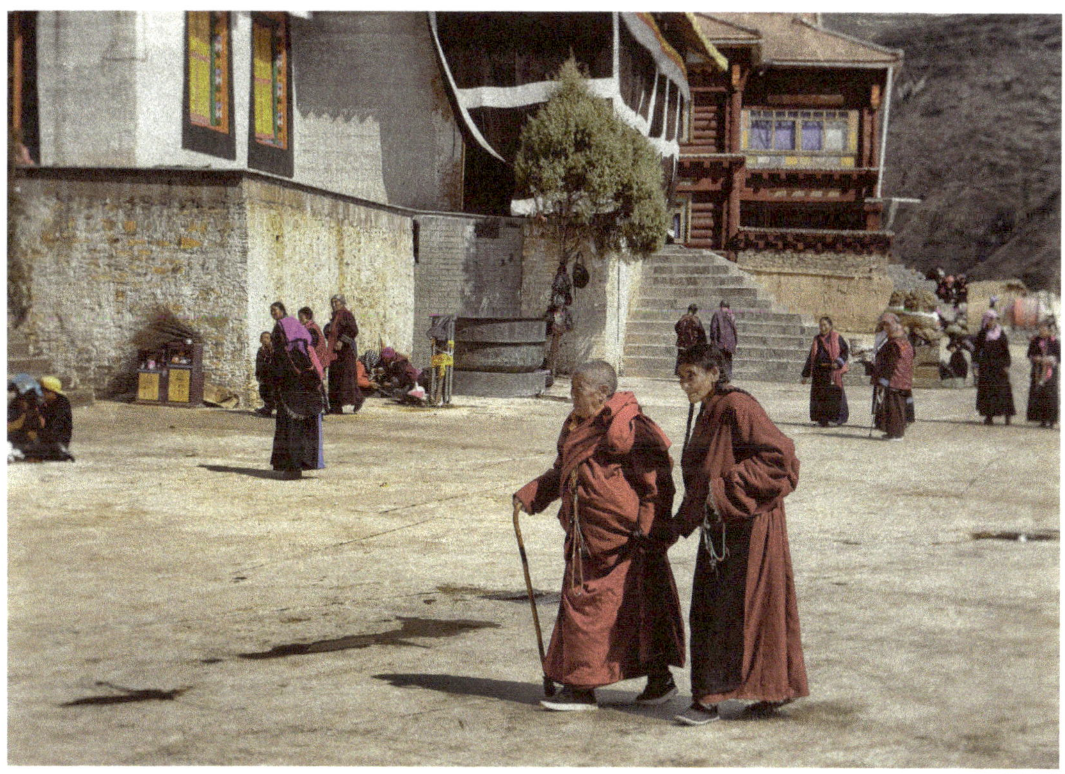

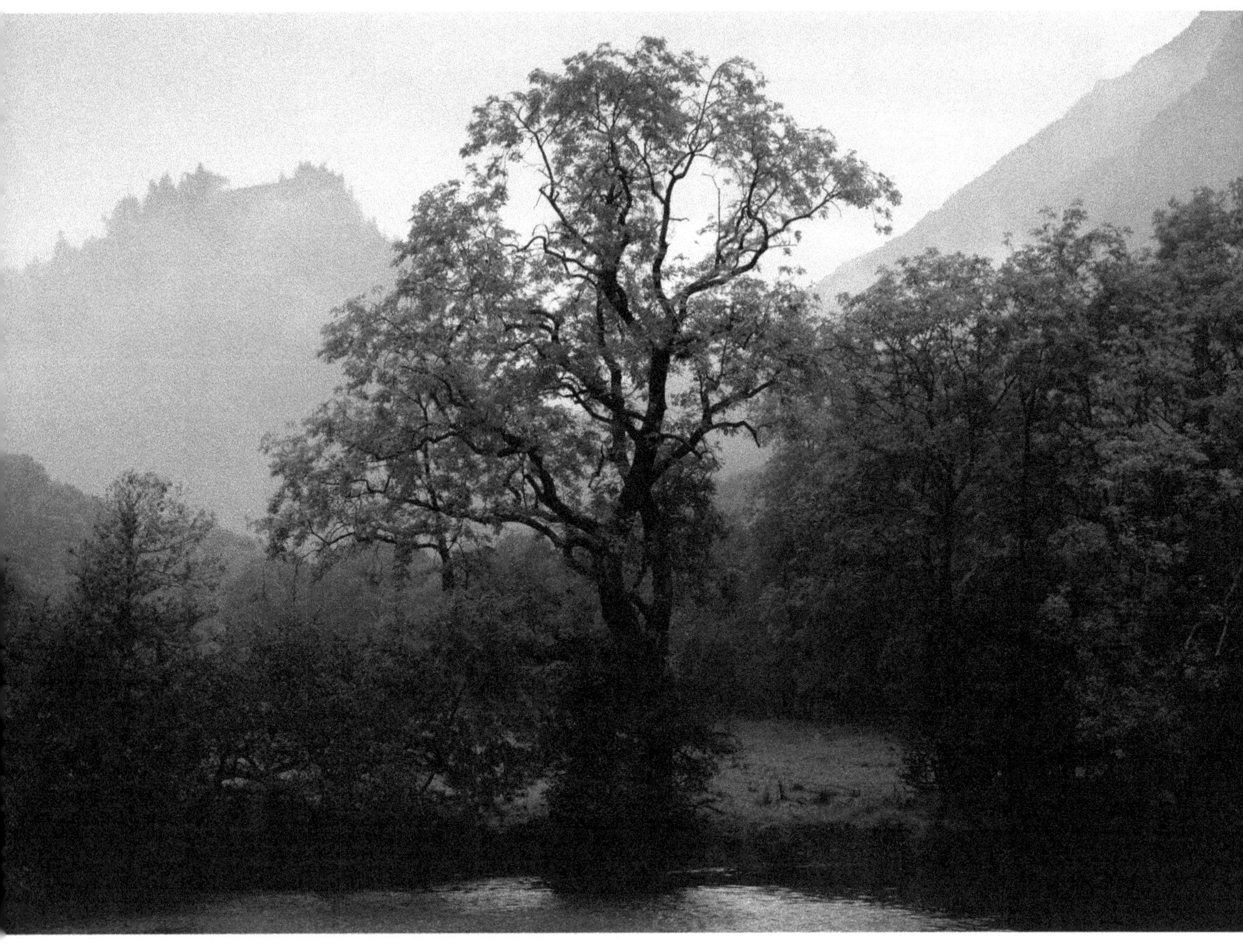

That love and engagement with photography was maintained through several years working with disadvantaged children, followed by a long stint working in information technology. A passion for exotic lands and their photographic possibilities, however, was never far away, and in 1993 Paul quit his job to enroll as a student in London's world-famous School of Oriental and African Studies, majoring in Indian, South East Asian, and Islamic Art. "It provided me with the inspiration and grounding for later travel and photography in Asia," is how he explains it. But the best explanation is surely in the results. Over the next twenty-five years Paul Polydorou traveled extensively and used his camera to capture what he saw, quietly establishing a portfolio and a reputation.

It is surprising, however, how long it's taken for his work to be exhibited and is only in recent years beginning to be properly seen and appreciated. Finally, in 2015 he had a solo exhibition in Holland Park, London, titled ***Travels East***, showing work spanning from Eastern Turkey, Syria, Uzbekistan, and through Ladakh, Burma, and Cambodia. This was followed two years later by ***Floating Light*** at the same venue that included some of his very early black-and-white pictures along with other travel work from Japan and Europe.

What follows is an interview conducted in Paul Polydorou's London apartment, ironically situated on the top floor of what used to be the home of W. H. Hudson, ornithologist, explorer, author of ***Green Mansions*** and ***The Purple Land***—a suitable residence for someone whose art has frequently traveled far from home.

MPH: Your subject matter is extremely varied and I'd like to begin by asking whether there is an underlying theme to your work, something that connects a North of England landscape, for example, with an Indian street scene?

PP: In terms of actual subject matter then, yes, they are fairly disparate, but stylistically I would hope they are all well-composed and have my own imprint. There are few that are really close-up, I normally photograph from a way back so there's room to make shapes and tones balance. But what I'd say is common to them, though, is that whether they're taken in Japan or Ladakh, or the Lake District or Hebrides in Britain, the pictures I feel work best and want to exhibit have nearly all been taken whilst away from home. It would seem that it's only when in an unfamiliar environment that I'm able to really see and make something work.

MPH: How do you decide whether a photograph, be it of a landscape, a man-made monument, or a portrait should be recorded in color or black and white? And do you have an inherent preference in respect of color vs black and white for any particular subject or composition?

PP: In the past I used black-and-white film almost exclusively, mainly because I could then process and print it myself. Now with digital you can decide to convert it into a color or black-and-white image file. My natural leaning is towards black and white—it's what I first learned to "see" in—and, to quote a phrase, "the colors are better in black and white." However, the richness of some of the tribal women I photographed in Central India, for example, would have been lost if not produced in color, whereas I find that most of my landscapes tend to work better in black and white.

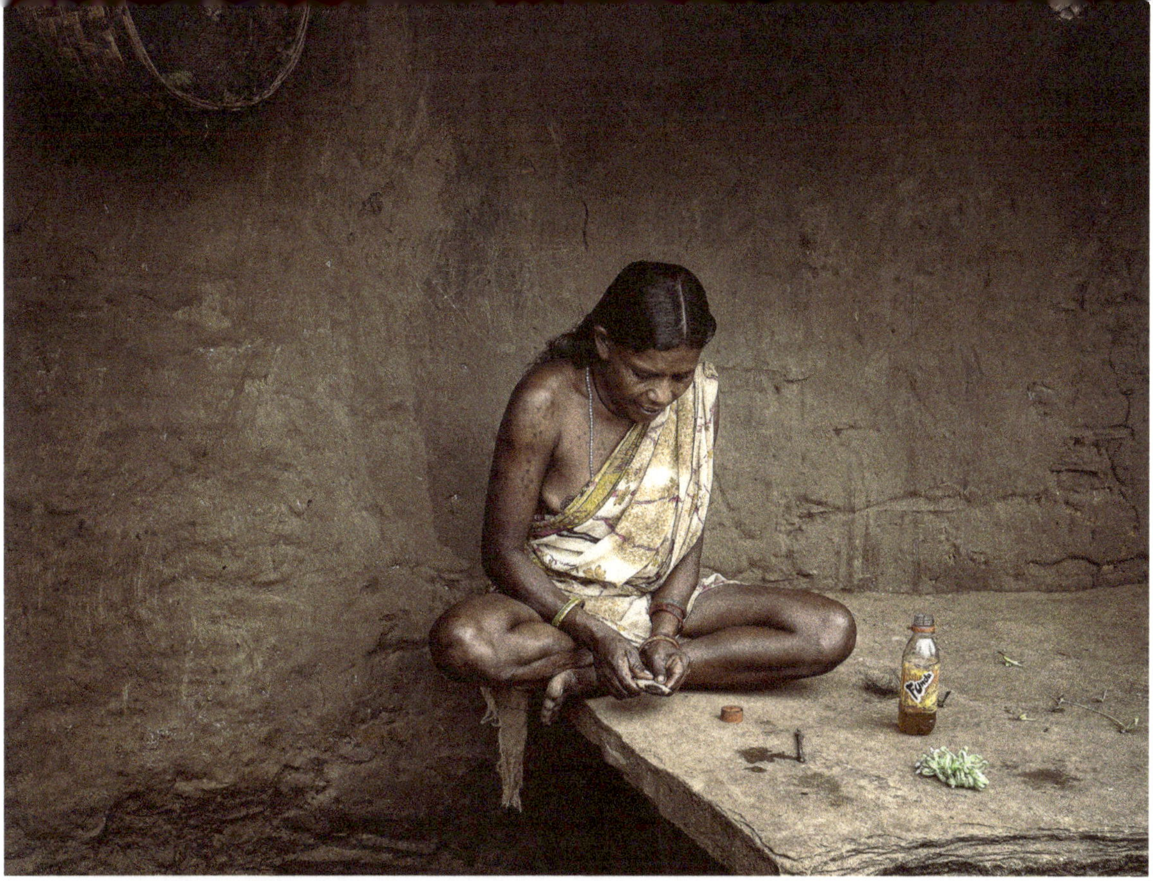

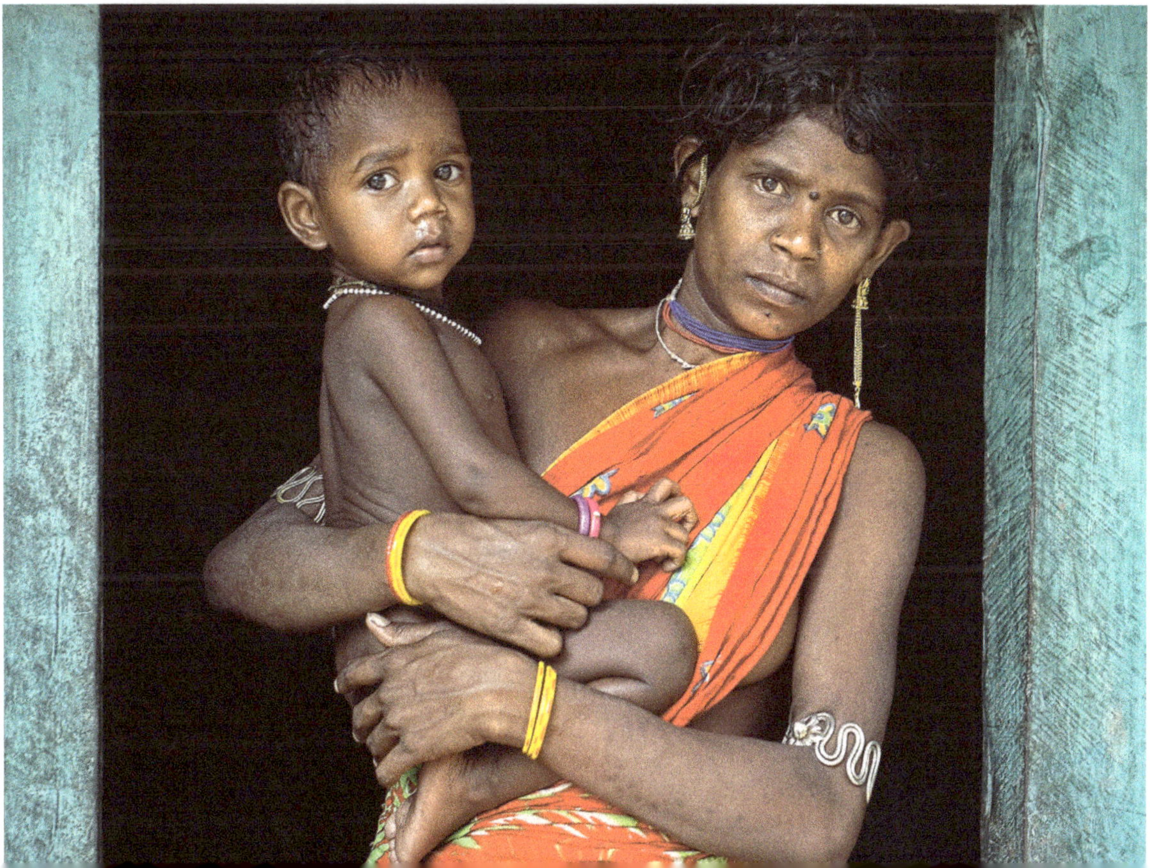

MPH: Of all the great photographers, past and present, are there any in particular you would acknowledge as influences? Are there any specific photographs in the public domain of which you might say: God, I wish I'd taken that?

PP: I remember very early on getting excited by the still lifes of Edward Weston and his portraits of his muse Tina Modotti. Later, while I was writing my final year dissertation for my humanities degree on Walker Evans and American documentary photography of the 1930s, I spent a lot of time looking at Evans's work, and this was just about the time I began to produce serious photographs myself. His clean, direct, understated, almost "pure" documentary approach was a very strong influence. Subsequently? Well, the recently discovered Vivian Maier I think is wonderful, along with the Hong Kong photographer Fan Ho. In more recent times, there's a Finnish photographer called Pentti Sammallahti whose actual prints (darkroom) are probably the finest I've seen. In answer to the second part of your question, no, I'm not envious of anyone else's particular images. You have to explore your own vision, and also you don't know what they, these great photographers, might have endured to get that particular picture one admires.

MPH: The greatest revolution in photography in my lifetime (and we are of a similar age) would seem to me to be the almost universal transition from film photography to digital. Do you agree? And has the transition to digital affected your style in any way? Furthermore, do you think there might still be a place for traditional film photography in the modern digital age?

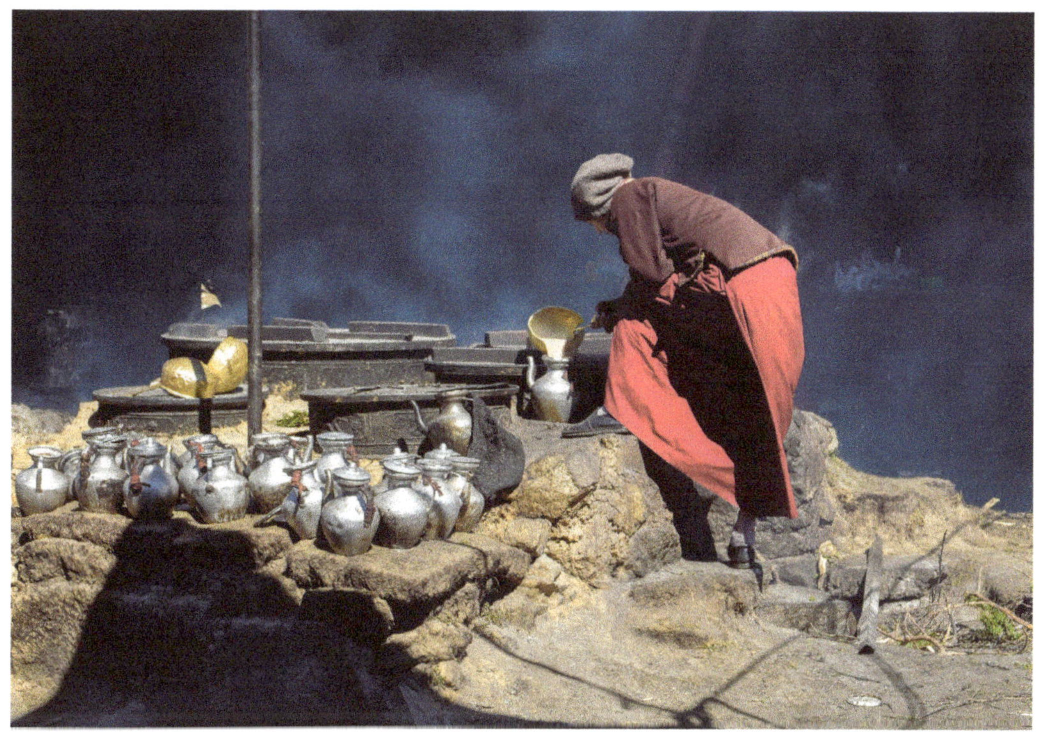

PP: In 1900 Eastman Kodak introduced a camera called the Brownie at a price of just one dollar. This was probably the first real revolution in photography since its inception. It democratized the medium so that ordinary families could photograph themselves and their activities, such as being on holiday, without needing to visit a studio. A few years later it allowed both military photographers and ordinary soldiers to take candid snapshots of the front line during the Great War. As for digital—well, it has certainly facilitated the ease of taking and processing photographs quite significantly. I now use digital equipment primarily, but I try and take the same considered approach as I would if using film. What that essentially means is that I don't take hundreds of pictures in a day.

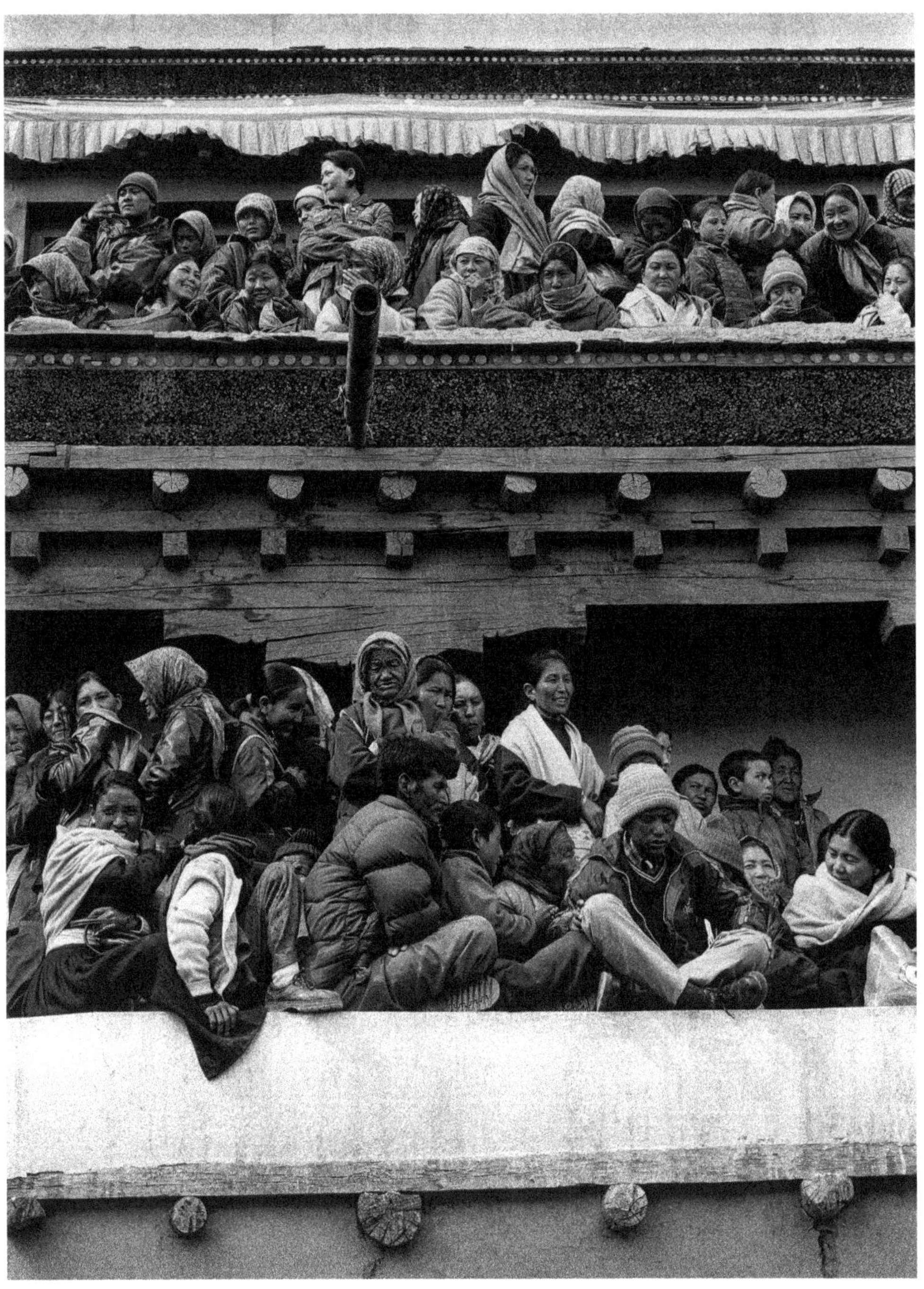

However, I believe film's particular aesthetic means it will remain in use for some time. In fact, there is growing interest in using earlier nineteenth-century alternative photographic processes such as wet collodian plate photography. When people compare digital and film, they tend to focus on the image quality, which is understandable as each medium has some advantages over the other, but what is rarely considered is the longevity and preservation of the captured image, and of course that was the real invention of photography—the fixing of an image onto a flat surface of paper or glass, not simply an image being reflected through a lens as that had been used by artists long before. I'm constantly unearthing negatives from thirty-odd years ago and am able to view and make prints from them, either digitally through scanning or chemically in a darkroom. At least a negative bears some material correspondence to the image it holds. My concern with digital photography is the unknown longevity of the binary components that are arrayed to form pixels that only become an image when interpreted by a software application and displayed on a device. Will these digital files retain their formatted structure and still be readable in fifty years' time? Also, will there be those moments of serendipity in the future when people stumble upon old family albums held on some hard drive as there are with printed photographs? My advice for preserving family snaps or other photographic work is not to make yet another digital backup to be stored somewhere but to produce good quality prints; properly cared for they should still be around in a hundred years.

MPH: There is an almost haunting quality to many of your photographs, not just in the portraits taken in the streets of India or the Middle East, but even the monuments and landscapes that provide a setting for the human element of your work. To what extent do you empathize with the subject matter of your photographs, and do you think it is ever possible to take great photographs dispassionately, as in the sense of being a consummate technician rather than an artist?

PP: Why one is drawn to photographing certain things and in a certain way, which is the backbone of the creative process, is inexplicable. In discussing his work with students at Yale, Walker Evans said, "almost all good artists are being worked through with forces that they're not quite aware of. They are transmitters of sensitivities that they're not aware of having, of forces that are in the air at the time." I look a great deal at other good photographers' work and am sure that their way of seeing seeps into my own way of seeing. One is obviously drawn to a subject or scene for various reasons, but I'm not sure how much empathy is going on at the time, at least not consciously. You're more focused on how things are fitting within the viewfinder. There's an inherent voyeurism in taking photographs, and using a camera legitimizes the act of looking but at the same time separates you from the subject. You're engaging with your subject—the person or landscape—but it's through the window of the viewfinder, so you're one step removed, you're looking from a distance. But, yes, I'd say I'm drawn to scenes that show human constructs in a natural environment, such as a Roman pillar on a tumulus mound, or a stupa on a mountainside in Ladakh, or simply a park bench beneath a tree. And then after taking the picture, you can treat it in so many different ways and impose a certain

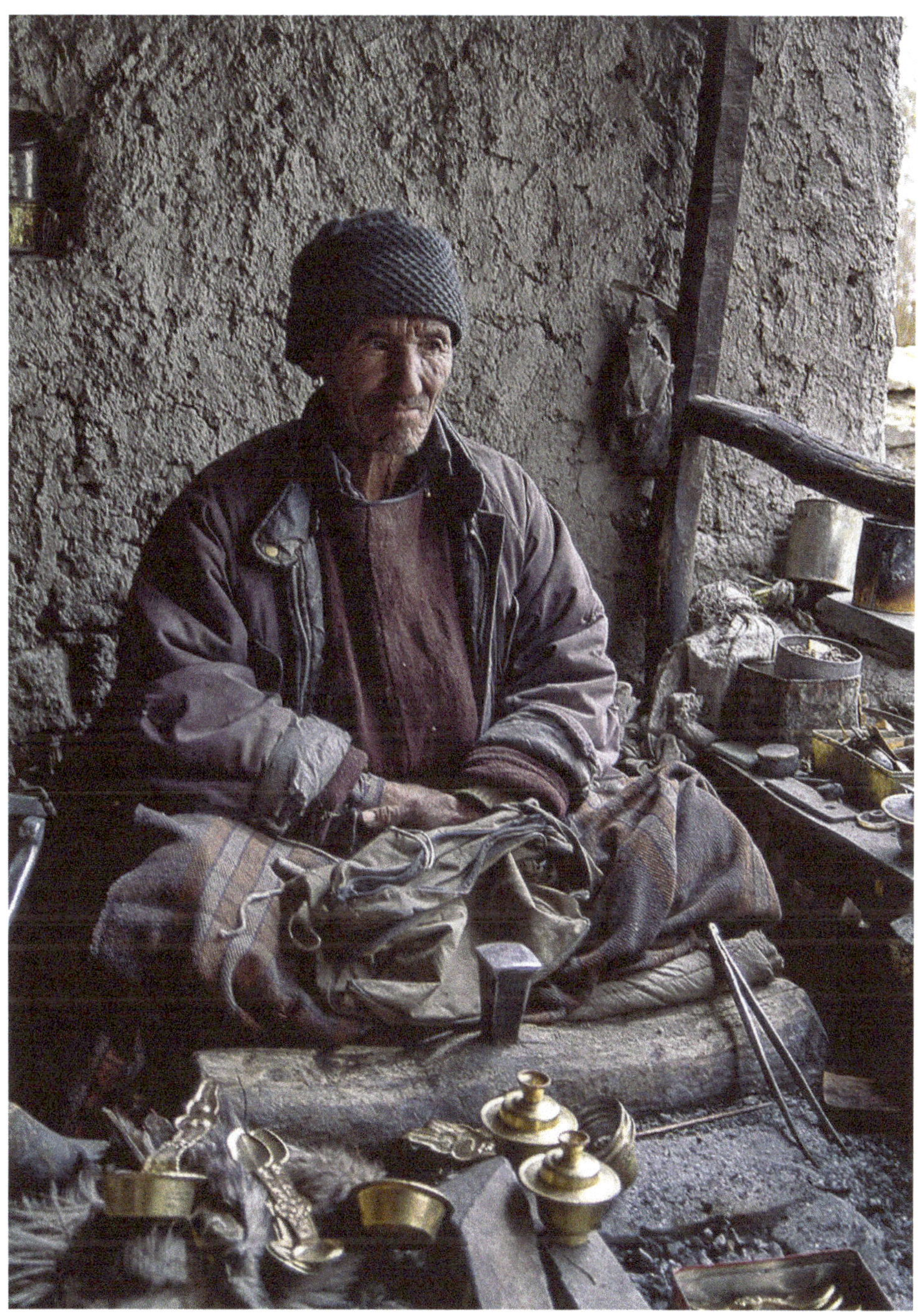

look or mood to it, even though that wasn't how that scene necessarily looked when originally taken. But then isn't that what art is primarily about?

MPH: Looking at your books, and especially ***Indian Portraits***, although also those recording your trips to Myanmar and Sichuan, I am struck by how much your subjects reveal themselves to the camera, how they seem perfectly willing to have you, a foreign photographer, a stranger, look beyond their eyes and into their soul, or else catch them at moments of spiritual tranquility when I myself would be shy to disturb them. What is your technique in this respect, or does it merely depend on the willingness of the subject?

PP: The photographs of the people presented in ***Indian Portraits*** were made under unusual circumstances insofar as access to the "tribal" areas of the Indian states of Odisha and Chhattisgarh is tightly controlled, with a permit and guide required to travel there and photography prohibited in many of the public markets. And so with a guide, I visited small villages where he was known. He would engage with the people and say whether it was okay for me to take pictures. Mostly it worked out okay, but sometimes, even when he gave me the nod, I knew from their expressions and body language when I raised my camera that they weren't comfortable with it, so I wouldn't proceed. There'd be no point as I wouldn't produce anything good and just create a difficult, intrusive interaction.

As to technique, I think it's maybe more about intention and having or not having preconceived pictures of what you want to produce. I learned a lot from looking at the work of the documentary photographers of the 1930s in

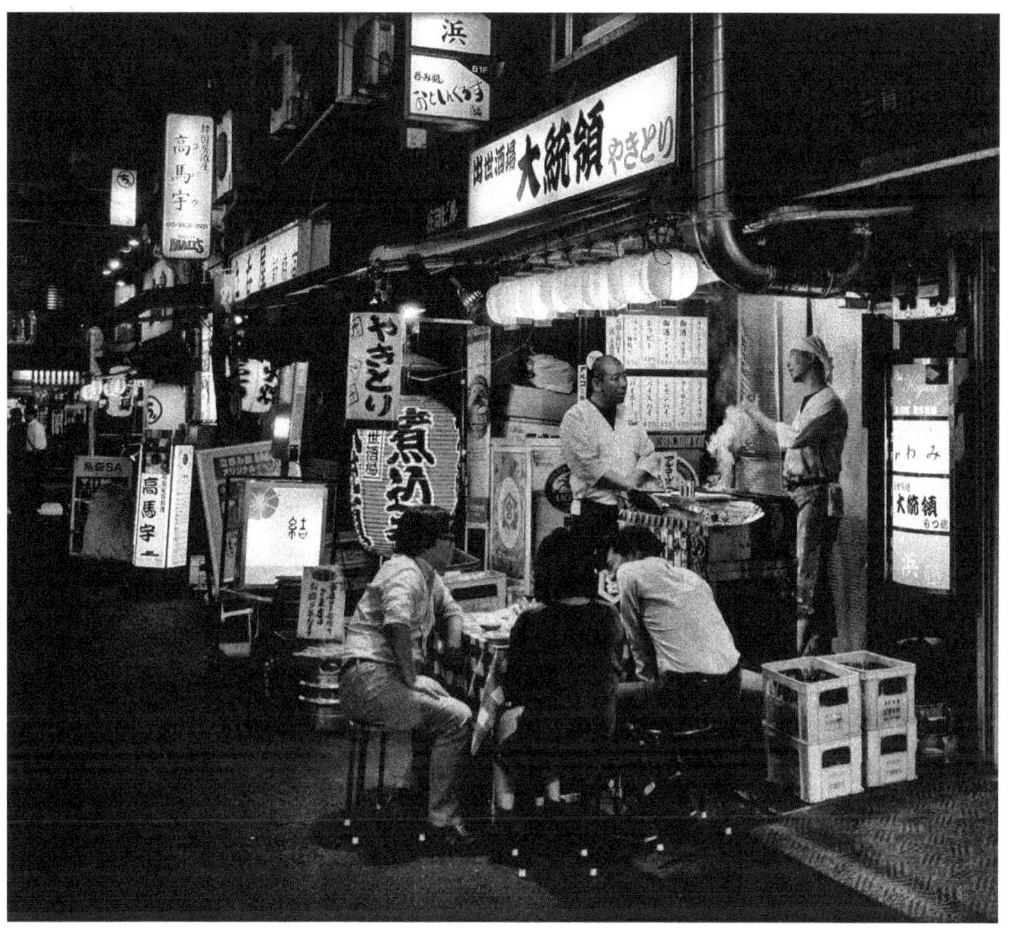

that many had an agenda to fulfill and the result was a depiction of anguish and poverty rather than portraits of unique individuals who happened to be experiencing difficult circumstances. This is evident in the often oblique angle of the shot or "ironic" context created. Going back to Walker Evans, his approach was different, straighter, more understated perhaps, but he gave his subjects the space to present themselves as they wished. I try to direct as little as possible, maybe shift position so the light falls more favorably or the background offers a better composition, but to ask a stranger to change their expression? There's a fine line between creating a documentary record of people and their culture and trophy hunting the exotic; between producing a genuine portrait and constructing a glorified fashion shoot. I'm not sure I've always got it right.

MPH: I would like to conclude by asking about the future direction of your work. Are there countries or peoples you particularly want to photograph but have not yet done so? Or is there perhaps that "one elusive perfect shot" that is waiting around the corner, over the next hill, in the yet-to-be-discovered Asian bazaar?

PP: When we last spoke about my work a few years back, I might have mentioned an interest in visiting some Buddhist communities on the Tibetan plateau before their culture becomes even more eroded and diluted. This, I'm pleased to say, I managed to do in visiting the Kham region in Sichuan Province, where the monasteries seem to be thriving even though they exist under the tight controls of Chinese authority. However, where they're deemed as becoming a threat, the sites are closed down or destroyed, such as at the remote Buddhist monastery / city of Larung Gar, where somewhere between ten and forty thousand monks and nuns lived.

Since that trip some rather significant world events have taken place that have curtailed the ability to travel and also forced people to question and reassess how they work and what they engage in. The restrictions of the COVID pandemic have begun to ease, but issues around reducing our personal carbon footprint are not going to subside, so I'm questioning the appropriateness and need to be traveling to far-flung places so much. I don't want to sound downbeat about it though. Last year, a little closer to home, I visited the islands of Mull and Staffa in the Hebrides, which offered some wonderful photographic opportunities. What is depressing is the increasing homogeneity of the world and, at least from a photographic viewpoint, the ubiquity of electronic devices. In one of the Indian tribal villages I was taken to, a man proudly showed me a lethal arrowhead he used to hunt wild pigs in the forest. I wouldn't be surprised if I returned there now, eight years later, to find him still using his bow and arrow, but his two young daughters whom I photographed now texting or chatting with their friends in the next village.

MPH: Thank you, Paul. It's been a sincere pleasure, and thank you for sharing your thoughts on photography and, indeed, your photographs.

PP: You're welcome!

CLAUDIA MASCIAVE

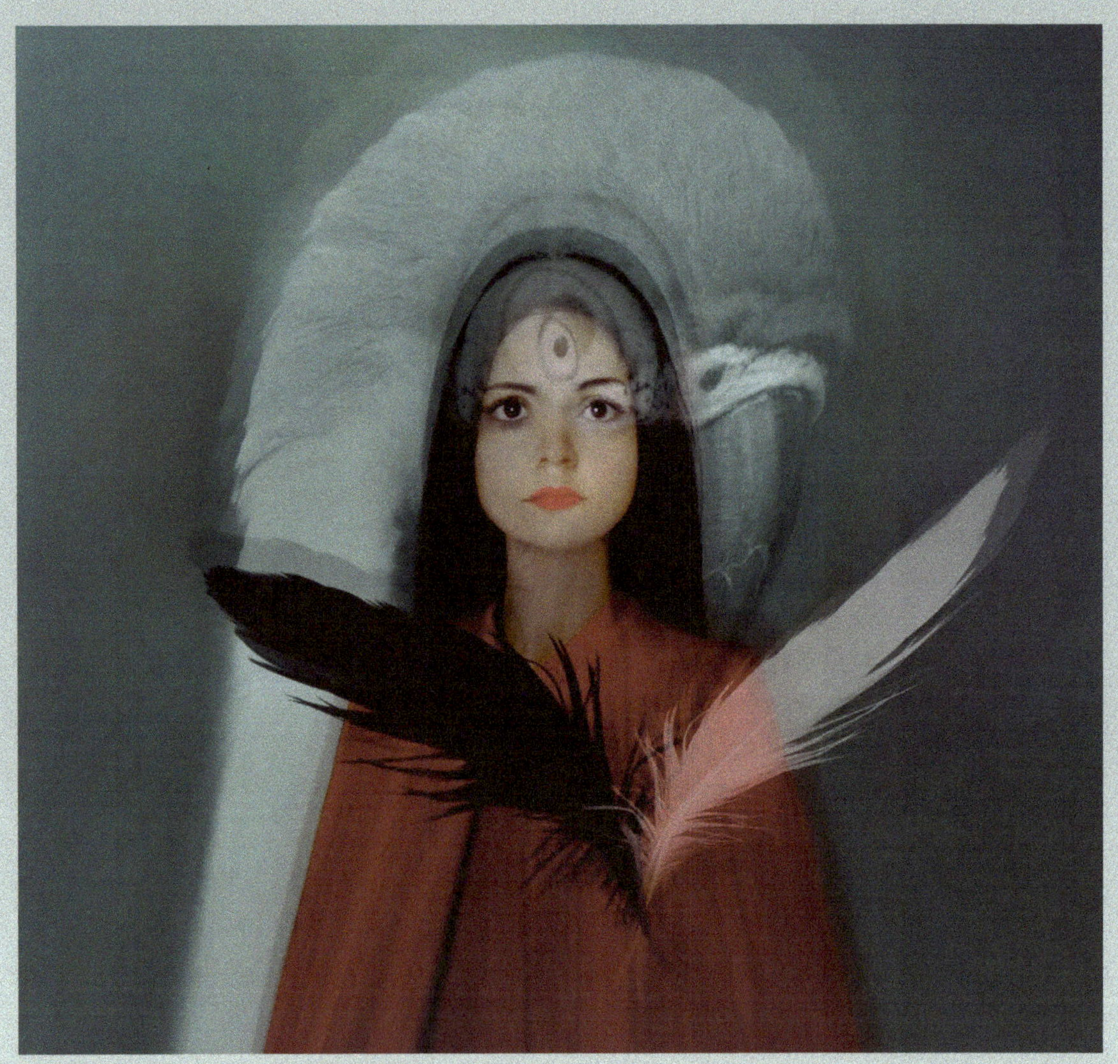

THE MULTIPLE SELF

"The Other precisely reveals himself in his alterity, not in some shocking negation of the I, but as the primordial phenomenon of gentleness."

—Emmanuel Levinas

"The clues of the lost object are to be found in my images that express the relationship with oneself, the Other, and the visible and invisible world that surrounds us and influences or conditions the course of our existence. All my self-portraits are for me a way to try to understand the functioning of the world, the consequences it implies on human relations as on my own history. Thus, the image of the mobile phone on my face clearly addresses the subject of our addictions to technologies that, at the beginning, seemed to constitute so many possibilities of freedom of speech as human contacts."

—Claudia Masciave

The Salimoes and Negro rivers meet just east of Manaus and form the Amazon River, which itself gives its name to the state of Amazonas, of which Manaus is the capital and largest city. Situated in the center of Brazil's largest rainforest, it was the production and export of rubber that made it the richest city in South America during the late nineteenth century, earning it the title "Paris of the Tropics" among those attracted from abroad by its wealth, its electrification, its extravagant new opera house, and its imported champagne. But just as the bubbles in champagne are doomed to burst, so did the bubble of extravagance that inflated Manaus, and the end of the rubber boom after only twenty-odd years returned the city to subtropical violence and desperate exoticism, to the jungle that surrounded it, to the snakes and the alligators and the many-colored birds that illuminated the foliage, to Yellow Jack and the watery music of broken glass . . .

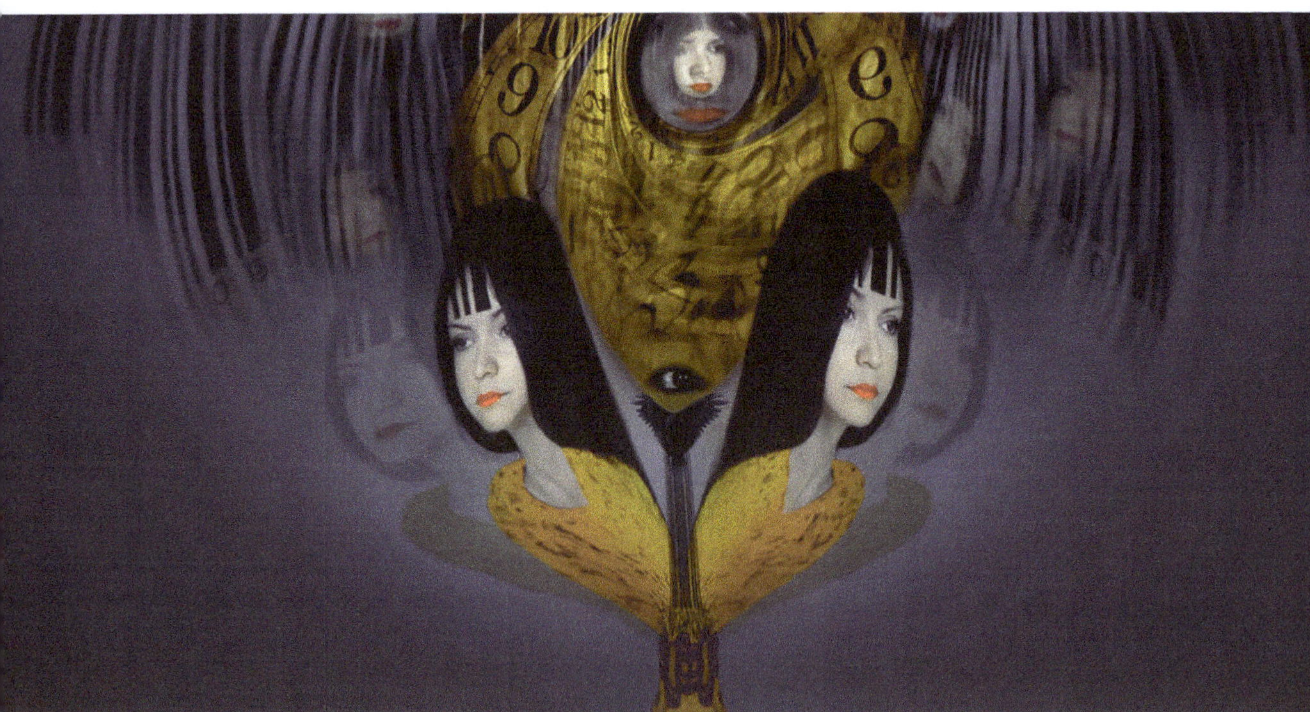

Claudia was born in Manaus, the city of Brazil's past, in the year of George Orwell's future, 1984.

✠

"The eighteenth edition of the ***Rencontres la photo***, which has just ended in Chabeuil, is a disappointment . . . There were some fragile nuggets, however, which made it possible to save the whole . . .

"Another beauty was visible at the Gaillard greenhouses: Claudia Masciave and her ***Textes sur la série***. This young photographer offers a kind of self-portrait with objects, unique and very colorful, which each present in their own inventive way the existential problems that challenge the lives of each and all of us. Drowning, choking, anguish, or suicide are treated cheerfully, with a simultaneously spiritual and joyful, ironic and combative recollection. The whole thing is very thoughtful, even cerebral, but at the same time playful, cheerful, irresistible.

"In summary, when the established male artists aspire to these precious spaces where they subsequently fail, the young women, extroverted or thoughtful—or both—blow the lid, in Chabeuil as elsewhere, off the old world of photography. Forza, girlzzz! When they compete directly, as here, it is the ladies who must now be expected to take the highest honors.

"[All this has escaped no one, of course, since Claudia Masciave has been awarded the ***Grand Prix des Rencontres*** and ***Grand Prix du Public***.]"

—Claude Meunier, 2018

ꝏ

I am sitting in my writing room looking out of the window and hoping that a cold northeasterly wind will drop sufficiently for me to be able to take a walk along the beach before lunch. It is the highlight of my day, a brisk march to the solitude of the estuary, my only companions the ducks and gulls and wading birds that populate these southwest England shores, the perfect antidote to the preceding three or four hours of writing and reading and self-editing a book on contemporary art. But if the wind is too strong and too cold, blowing in off the sea and using the waves to whet its edges, a walk ceases to become a pleasure and is merely an eye-watering, breath-taking endurance test, not even worth the glass of whiskey and Gauloises cigarette I will reward myself with when I get back to the apartment.

But in the meantime, when I am not gauging the weather, I am once again studying the sequence of photographs by Claudia Masciave entitled ***A la recherche de l'objet perdu.*** I have been expecting to hear from Claudia for the last few days. Ironically, it was only last week that she invited us to stay with her and her husband in their home in Grenoble, a trip we look forward to making when my book is finished, because I really want to get her personal take on the series. But for now I must fall back on my own judgment, my own interpretation of what is perhaps her most well-known series of photographic art.

Like all of Claudia's works, whether photographs or short films (known as phone-films), the subject is ostensibly herself, but the truth is that she is merely her own canvas—the screen upon which she projects her artistic vision—and why not? If an actress can, in concurrent repertory productions, play, for example, Medea, Lady Macbeth, and Hedda Gabler, and simultaneously be the same actress as well as the widely differing characters she portrays, then why cannot Claudia be simultaneously herself and others? The ***A la recherche*** photographs (the title is, of course, deliberately Proustian) are seemingly straightforward self-portraits, usually face-on and from the waist up, 36 x 36 inches (90 x 90 cm), which makes them about life-size, each displaying a different facet of the human condition—although with a definite feminist slant. As for the set-up:

"It's simple, I just put myself in front of the camera, with my tripod, then work in the colors of the photograph like a painting with the help of software. It's pictorial art photography."

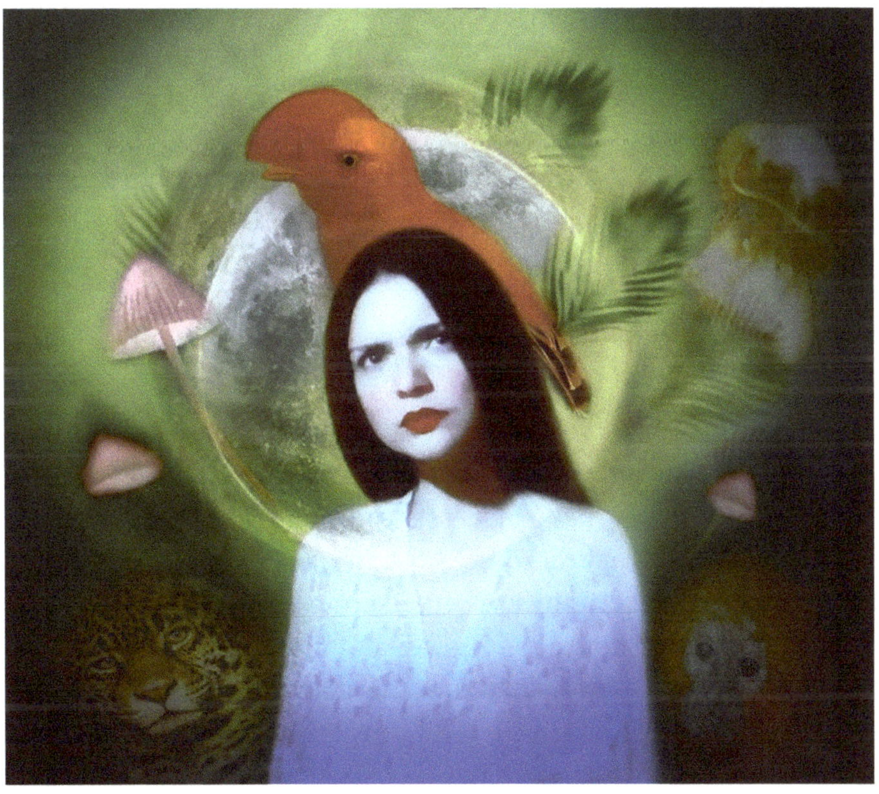

Making it sound simple is typically modest, but necessarily disingenuous. The genius of any great photographer is in the vision behind the eye behind the lens. It is thinking to shoot what others have not thought to shoot before. Mastering the technical process kind of goes without saying.

The vision behind Claudia's eye is not just aesthetic but deeply philosophical. However, before we examine the meaning of her work, the most striking, the most immediate thing about these photo-portraits is what I think must be the most glorious use of color in contemporary art. There is no modern painter, certainly no other photographer, who can rival her sheer clarity and boldness of palette, who can create an almost mystical third dimension by the instinctive knowledge of how to contrast and separate the colors used to make an image, and who can invest them with profundity as well as clarity. It is a clarity that one associates with pop art, but also with op-art; it has a wonderfully cleansing effect on one's vision; it liberates itself from the page or the gallery wall and makes an instantaneous but lasting connection with the viewer.

Each self-portrait is stripped down to a beautiful simplicity, emphasized by the primary colors used, but this simplicity is aesthetic rather than intellectual, and the contrast between the simplicity of the image and the profundity of its meaning creates the kind of tension that is necessary for great art. The fact that a number of these apparently straightforward photographs can be interpreted in different ways underscores the depth of Claudia's artistic mission. Some I confess I do not understand—I will need to ask Claudia exactly what it is she means when we talk over the next few days—but others offer ways of interpretation that strike me as valid, although necessarily somewhat subjective.

The genius of any great photographer is in the vision behind the eye behind the lens. It is thinking to shoot what others have not thought to shoot before. Mastering the technical process kind of goes without saying.

In one, for example, she wears a blue dress, down the front of which she spews a river of what we assume to be yellow vomit. Sick of being treated as a woman, as a second-class citizen in a male-dominated society? Sick of being patronized by (often male) critics who seem as enamored of her own beauty as the beauty of her art? But maybe this is too obvious an interpretation, a shallow response to a rather obvious problem. But, wait—let me look back at my own first sentence: I said a "river of vomit" and the fact that that image should spring automatically to mind makes me think that perhaps we should go further back, pick up on the river motif, and let it lead us to Claudia's birthplace, Manaus, and the mighty Amazon River that almost defines the character and topography of Brazil. Does Claudia see the artist as an aboriginal bringing forth the whole world, the ultimate creator? Is she creating (or re-creating) the Amazon River with its inevitable pun on the semimythical race of Amazon women, written of by Herodotus and Plutarch, but in fact living, if they lived at all, in modern-day Turkey? Or is she rejecting the land of her birth— for her childhood was difficult, although we do not talk of that— vomiting out the poisonous yellow fever-ridden waters in search of a new freedom in a foreign land?

In another she holds a basket filled with over-the-counter medicines—Humex, a well-known cold relief, is prominent. Her smile is bright, but strangely neutral. One suddenly thinks: is she customer or salesgirl? Is she smiling a fake smile because she has made a sale, or is she smiling blandly because her personality has been deadened by years of petty addiction to unnecessary pharmaceutical products? I must remember to ask Claudia whether she has ever seen and therefore perhaps been influenced by Jean-Luc Godard's 1967 classic ***Deux ou trois choses que je sais d'elle (Two or three things I know about her)***. There is a connection here, whether deliberate or accidental, that I find interesting, especially as I once wrote an essay on Godard that focused on this particular film.

As I look from photograph to photograph, from one carefully crafted image to the next, I become more convinced that ***A la recherche de l'objet perdu (In search of the lost object)*** is not just a single work but also a complete work, by which I mean it contains everything within itself to create an aesthetic unity and is most definitely greater than the sum of its parts. The way that certain portraits either compliment or form a contrast with one another (and not necessarily displayed adjacently) is another way in which Claudia's work expands out of its own proportions. For example, in one picture she contemplates a noose hanging from an out-of-shot ceiling; in another she hangs from a hook on the wall by virtue of a coat hanger within the back of her dress. I love the mordant wit of that. In another (potential) pairing she is shown wearing a neck brace and sporting a badly bruised eye and is, unusually for the series, looking to one side of the camera in a downcast, perhaps slightly ashamed manner; meanwhile, the subsequent

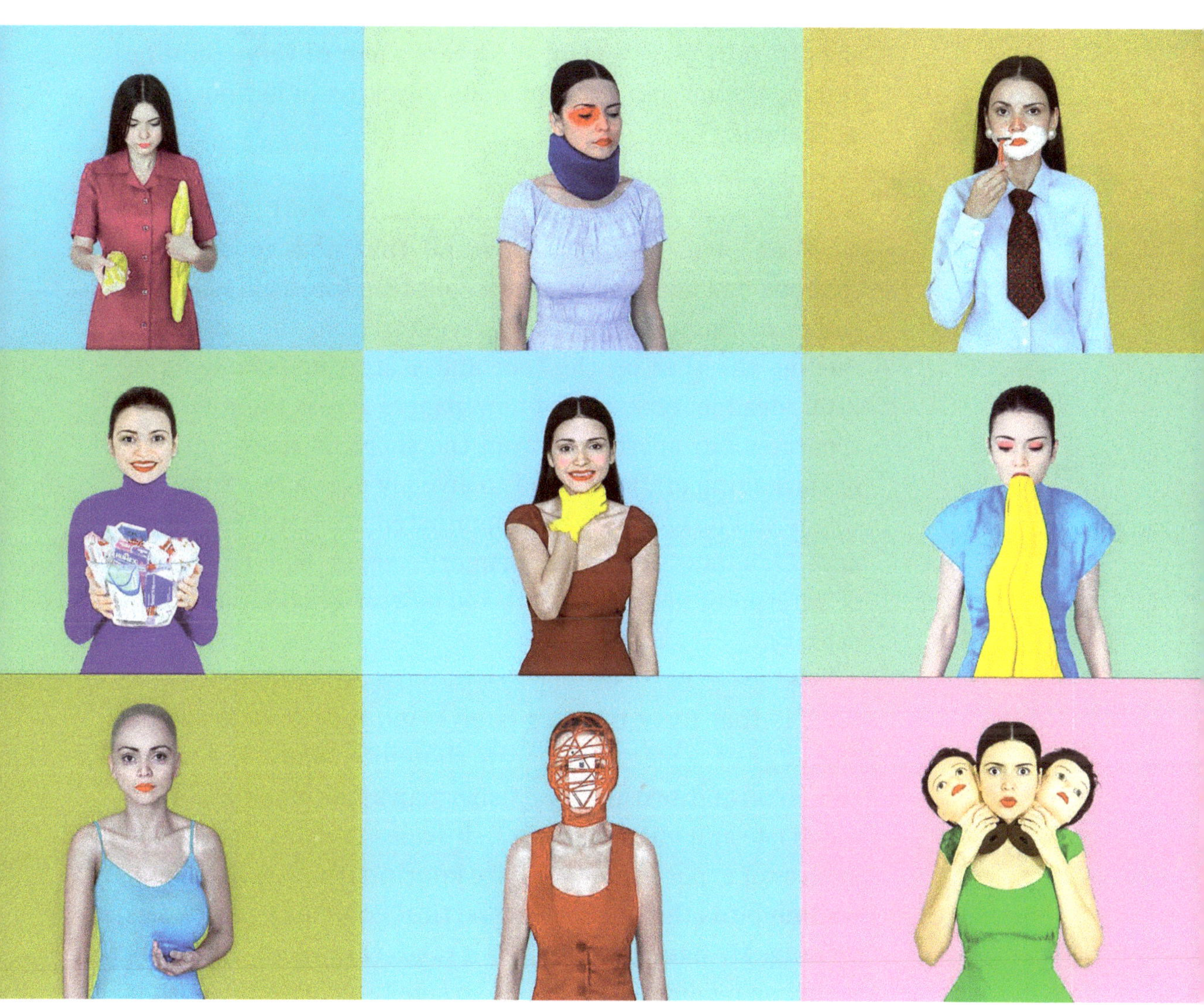

frame shows her wearing a shirt and tie, her face lathered with foam, drawing a red plastic razor down her right cheek, staring boldly straight ahead as one would into a mirror. The beautiful irony here is that in a photo where she playfully plays a man, she wears a pair of very feminine earrings, something conspicuously lacking in her portraits as "herself."

It is very easy to lose oneself in Claudia's work, to expand on one's own interpretations and find new connections that one had not noticed before, but I am interrupted by the sound of the wind, that bitter visitor from the northeast, rattling the tiles on the roof and scattering fragments of litter, dead leaves, and old newspapers across the road that separates our apartment from the shore. It shows no sign of slackening off, but I need to give my eyes a rest from the words and images that have dominated the last three hours, and Claudia's wonderful primary colors will find their counterpoint in the mudflats and pewter-gray waters of the estuary.

So it is that forty minutes later I find myself standing on the edge of a piece of narrow shoreline, where the sea is the color and texture of a fisherman's knife chipped with much use and blistered with fish scales, and the undulating shelves of exposed mudbank are imprinted with the tracks of wading birds that make neat, vertical columns like Chinese writing. My hands are chilled; it takes three goes to flip the wheel on my lighter to be able to smoke a cigarette. But it is refreshing to be out in the cold after the artificial warmth of our apartment. The world always changes a little when you brave the wind and the rain and mesh yourself up in the fabric of it. It certainly sharpens the mind.

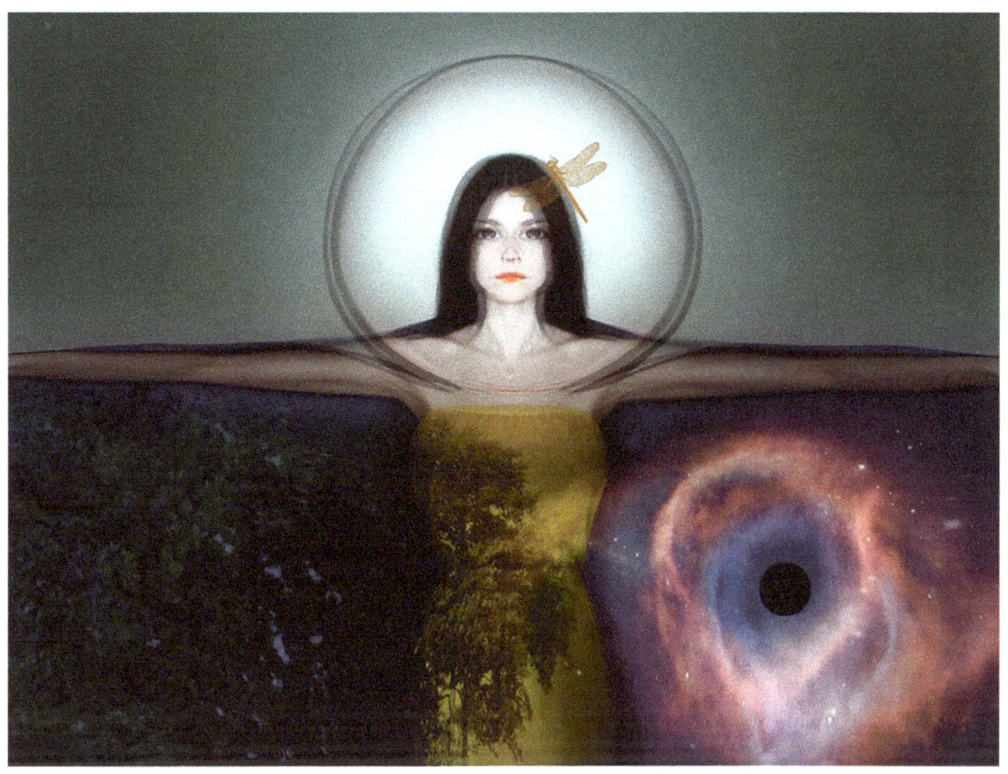

When I return home there is a message from Claudia waiting for me. I fix myself a large scotch with a splash of water and carry it through to my writing room. I'd almost forgotten that a couple of days ago I asked for some basic background information, influences and such, and here, exactly on cue, is her reply. In response to my query as to which photographers have most influenced her, she suggests Cindy Sherman and Francesca Woodman. Sherman's work I am familiar with, although I have always thought of her famous self-portraits as being somewhat random, with not enough sense of a clear aesthetic connecting the work as a whole. This is not to say I do not like them, but I feel that the best her work could have been for Claudia is a departure point. The second influence is more intriguing, for although the

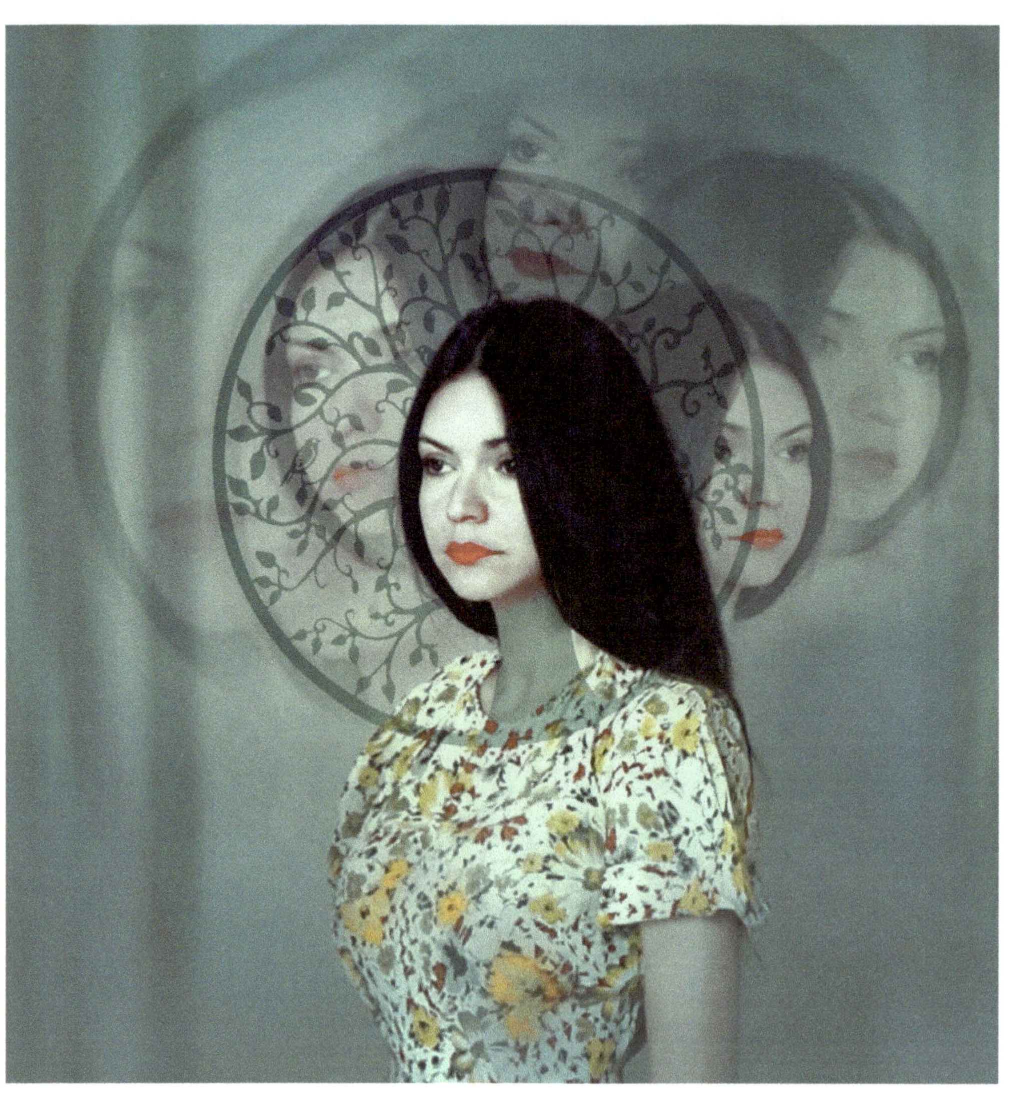

name Francesca Woodman rings a bell, I can't immediately bring her work to mind. I look her up and realize I am familiar with the work; indeed, there is that wonderful one taken on the beach where she stands over her own corpse, holding a mirror to reflect the dead woman's (upside-down) face exactly where her own face should be (but, of course, that is her own face)—but had forgotten the details of her short tragic life. Born in Colorado in 1958, she fell into a deep depression compounded by a failed love affair and lack of appreciation for her work and jumped to her death from a window in New York when she was just twenty-two years old. Leafing through images of her photographs I can see how the influence could be there: the use of herself to project moral, philosophical, and psychological attitudes; the technical confidence; the sheer intelligence on display. But wait—here is something I am finding out for the first time. Francesca Woodman did not just take the photo self-portraits she is famous for, but also made short videos with a running time of about twenty seconds to more than three minutes. Although Claudia's and Francesca's styles are very different (that the latter worked almost exclusively in black and white is an obvious and important difference) I find the fact that Claudia's own short video pieces, her ***Phone-films***, have a precedent enormously interesting. And I have to say, the more I reacquaint myself with Woodman's work the more impressed I am with it, and, furthermore, the more impressed with how Claudia has built on and expanded Woodman's original vision, creating something entirely fresh and original, respecting the past without imitating it, using the art of a previous generation (as, indeed, all artists do) to create the art that will be appreciated by the next.

Of course, Claudia's other, non-photographic influences are interesting too, perhaps more so because here we find ourselves behind (or should that be beyond?) the lens. In response to my question about which writers she most admires, she tells me Tolstoy, Dostoyevsky, and Dante. Philosophers? Emmanuel Levinas and Hegel. I'm not sure about Hegel, but Levinas makes sense because of his concept of the "Other"; it is something that Claudia has referenced in previous interviews when asked to explain the ***A la recherche de l'objet perdu*** photographs. And then finally she answered a question I had not asked, telling me that the women who have most inspired her are Mother Teresa and Marie Madeleine, the latter better known to English speakers as Mary Magdalene. I find it particularly interesting that, instead of the obvious candidates, the candidates I most certainly would have guessed, such as Isadora Duncan, Anaïs Nin, Katherine Mansfield, Frida Kahlo, Maya Deren, or Simone de Beauvoir, she chooses a Catholic nun who devoted her life to the poor in Calcutta and a woman who witnessed the crucifixion, burial, and resurrection of Jesus Christ. Does this mean we should attach a spiritual as well as a philosophical meaning to her work? Whatever, there is a great deal more to Claudia Masciave than, quite literally, meets the eye.

Claudia's work has been written about and exhibited extensively in her adopted country, France, and as director of ***Phone-Films*** she has been recognized at the recent Monaco Charity Film Festival. Of all the people featured in this book, Claudia holds a special place in my regard, for not only is she a great artist but she has the unswerving courage and enviable self-belief to look her potential audience straight-on and reveal herself with neither arrogance nor self-aggrandizement, but instead with a sheer commitment to art; to be an artist prepared to metaphorically strip herself naked in order to psychologically and aesthetically reveal herself as, indeed, an actress, as referenced earlier, might do in order to play Medea or Lady Macbeth; and furthermore to do all this with a wonderful spirit of adventure and delightful sense of humor. A new series, titled ***Humaine***, still a work in progress at time of writing, develops her photographic self-portraits in a particularly exciting and no less original way, utilizing multiple exposure and photo-collage and often directly referencing her Brazilian roots. Technically and aesthetically, they represent a significant new phase in her art. As I write she is preparing two new exhibitions; one, a new showing of ***A la recherche de l'objet perdu*** in Drome, itself in the southeast of France and close to Chabeuil, where she gave a prize-winning exhibition in 2018; the other a separate screening of the ***Phone-Films*** in Paris. In the meantime, it is only a matter of time until her reputation expands well beyond the French (and European) border and she gains the international recognition she unquestionably deserves.

The Color of Our Dreams

Combining Text and Images in Contemporary Art

ceci est la couleur
de mes rêves
—Joan Miro

It wasn't Picasso who started it, nor was it Braque. Neither was it Toulouse-Lautrec and the great poster artists of the *fin de siècle.* The simultaneous use of words and images is as old as art itself. In China they have been inseparable since the invention of paper more than two thousand years ago; while in the West, one only has to consider the medieval genius for illuminated manuscripts and the inclusion of the names of saints on pre-Renaissance frescoes. As Volker Klein puts it: "For me, writing has always been part of the grammar of visual art in equal measure as color, stroke, composition, surface, etc. And not just for me. Just think of the most ancient Christian paintings, of Arab art in which, for religious reasons, it is forbidden to represent man, as well as in the art of Orthodox Judaism. In modern art it was mainly reintroduced by the Cubists a hundred years ago. Then nothing new."

Nothing new, indeed.

For this section, I have selected five contemporary artists who, in their very differing ways, are redefining the parameters of modern art by incorporating the written word into their visual work in new and exciting ways. They are:

Toti O'Brien,

Volker Klein,

Alexander Christoph Sterzel,

Ruben Dominguez Leon, and

Erika Capobianco.

My choice, although necessarily personal, has been dictated by quality, originality, and the fact that they have all been extremely willing to discuss their aesthetic process with me for the purpose of this article. So willing, in fact, that I intend to mostly stand back as a writer and let them create this essay in their own words. If this gives the piece a somewhat random, patchwork feel, then all to the good; it is entirely appropriate to the subject matter. I would much prefer you—the reader—listen to what they say, look at the illustrations accompanying this article, and then form your own opinion rather than have me analyze these artworks for you. I would also like to thank these artists for giving so generously of their time. It is sincerely appreciated.

TOTI O'BRIEN

Born in Rome, but now living in Los Angeles, Toti O'Brien is a painter, collagist, poet, essayist, short-story writer, maker of exquisite handicrafts, and professional musician and dancer. ***Other Maidens*** (a collection of poetry) and ***An Alphabet of Birds*** (short stories) were both published in 2020.

But I must rewind to June 2016 when ***Forage Poetry Journal*** devoted an entire issue to a re-evaluation of the sonnet form, and it was there that I first saw ***Sonetto in Morte di Madonna Laura***. And although I have since become a great admirer of all aspects of Toti's extraordinarily diverse art, it was inevitable that that particular work would be uppermost in my mind when I spoke to her recently.

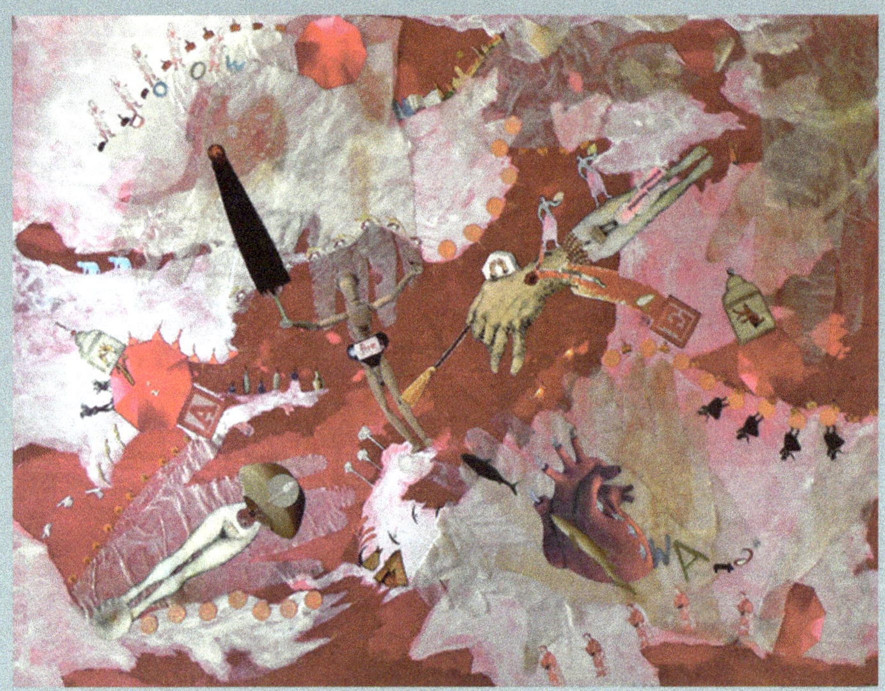

Hand-Made Map, #3

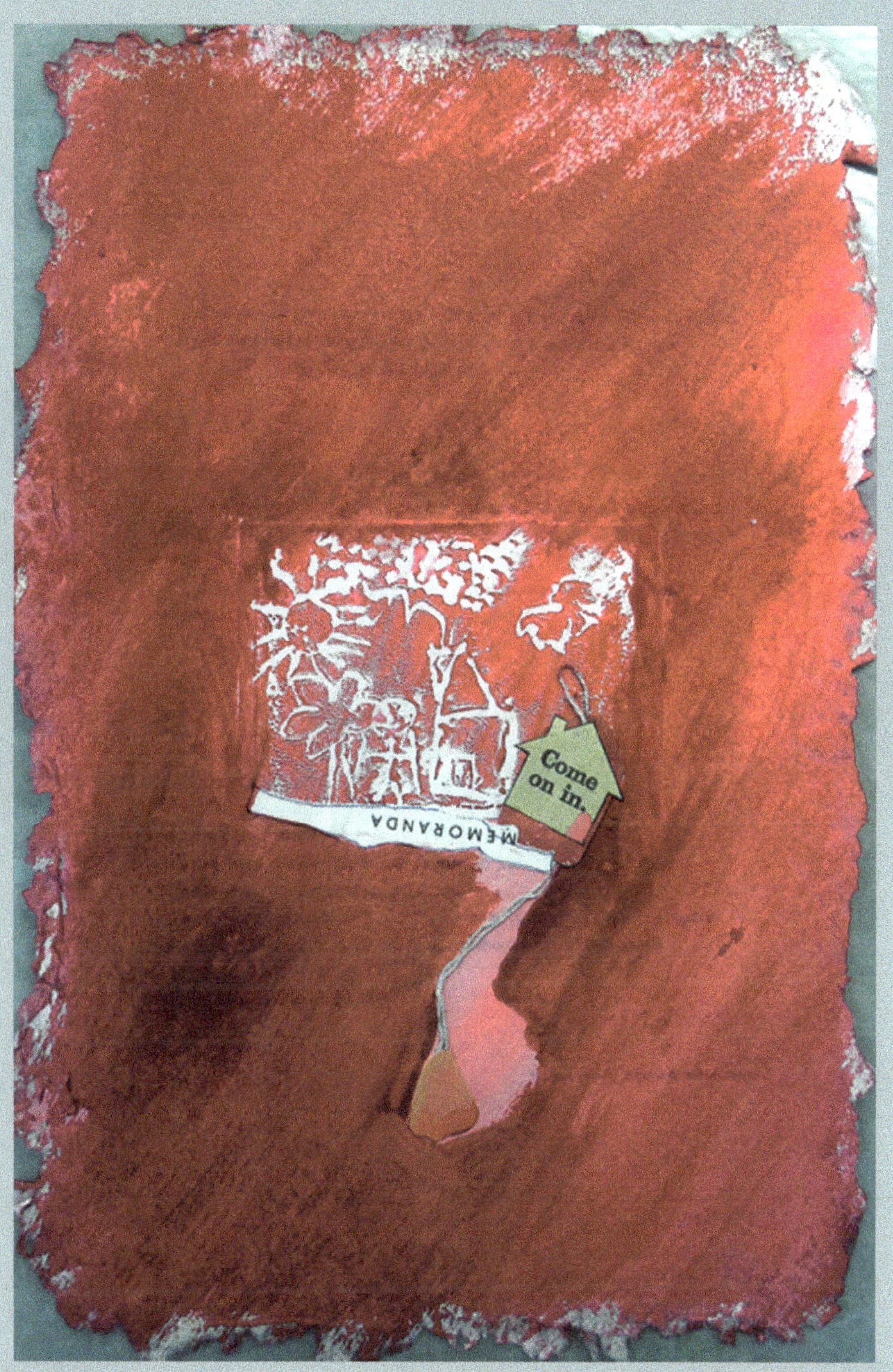

Anatomy, #4

MPH: I want my essay to address the connection between art and writing with reference to people like yourself who are both artists and writers. But writing a poem, publishing a book of poems, or painting a picture is one thing, and it is an important thing, but I am really looking at where the two things collide, where a work of art consists of both words and images. Do you remember the work of yours that I first fell in love with? ***Sonetto in Morte di Madonna Laura***. That is what I'm thinking of—where the divisions between art and literature are blurred or combined or however you want to put it. I want to get inside the mind of artists who blur the distinction between art and literature, between literary and visual forms. And if you have any thoughts on your own approach/aesthetic with respect to combining the two, I would love to hear it.

TO: I am not an artist that specifically and constantly uses the written word as part of her work. Those exist—visual poets, concrete poets, and such. I greatly admire them. I do not include text/words/letters in my work as a rule, though I do it quite often, but when I do, it happens without a conscious intention or a predetermined choice.

An excellent example is the piece you already mentioned. ***Sonetto in Morte di Madonna Laura*** is the title of a famous work by Italian Renaissance poet Francesco Petrarca. I happened to find a few ripped pages of a small and very old edition, and I simply transformed them into a larger object. I had two intentions: first, preserving them, integrating the frail, ripped, yellowing pages into something durable, making a larger, more solid ensemble; and second, extracting their juice, so to speak, see where the handling of those pages, the repeated vision of the words they contained would bring me.

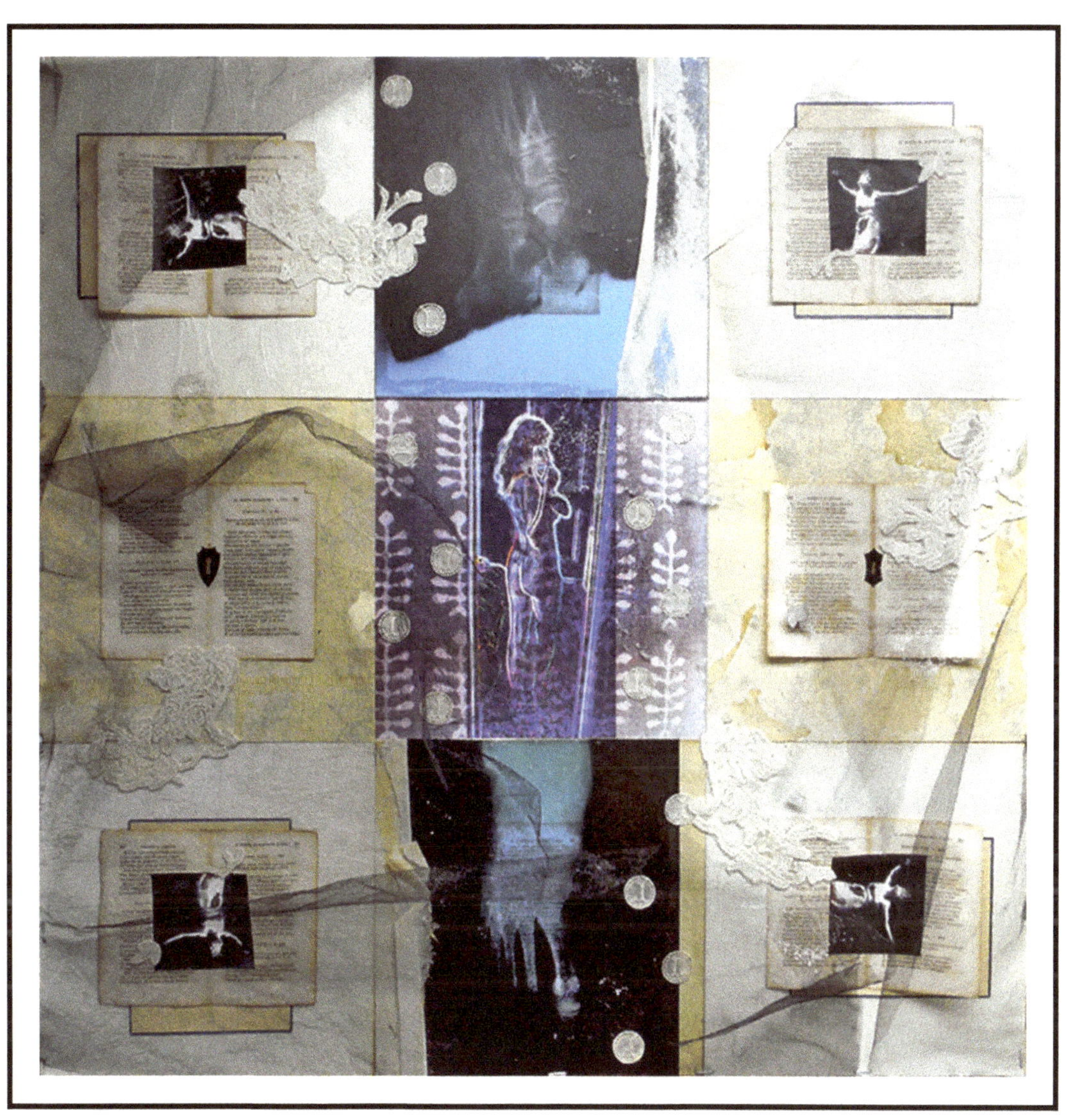

Sonetto in Morte di Madonna Laura

They—the pages and the words I kept reading, some of them rapidly taking the lead, becoming the focus—brought me somewhere indeed, to the central image, as I gradually was fulgurated by the evidence of what had happened to the writer. Only at the moment of Laura's death did Petrarca see the world, and himself. The entire sonnet is the brutality of the revelation that he had lived in a sort of blur, obnubilated by his longing and torment, until she disappeared. But on doing so, in a flash, everything was made visible: the reality that was there, nature, their lives, the possibility, the present, and his own being. Through Laura's death, Petrarca achieved awareness of it all. Therefore, the disappearing woman in the center turns back and takes a picture . . . of him . . . while vanishing, and she gives the picture to him as a gift of the proof of his own existence. And his sonnet is, probably, the acknowledgment of the gift received. So the central image was engendered by the text, no doubt, as it layered itself on the surface.

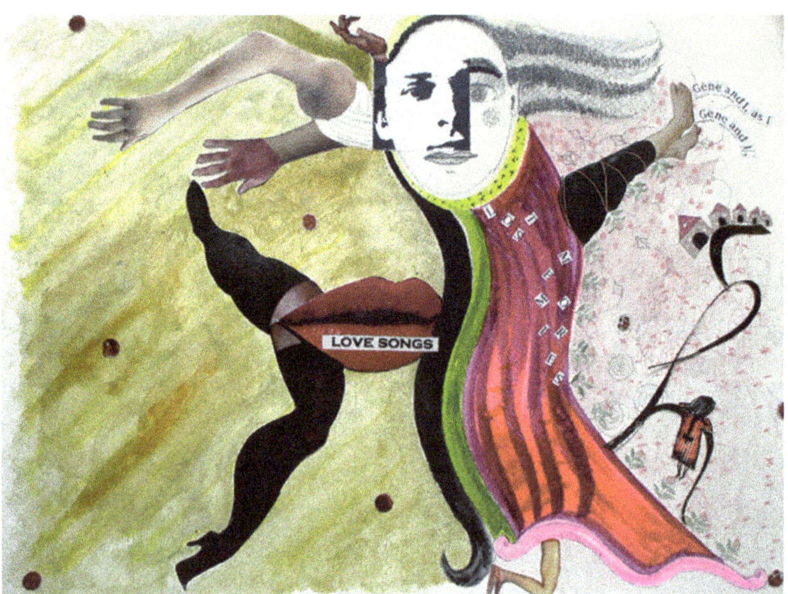

Unamasloveletter #2

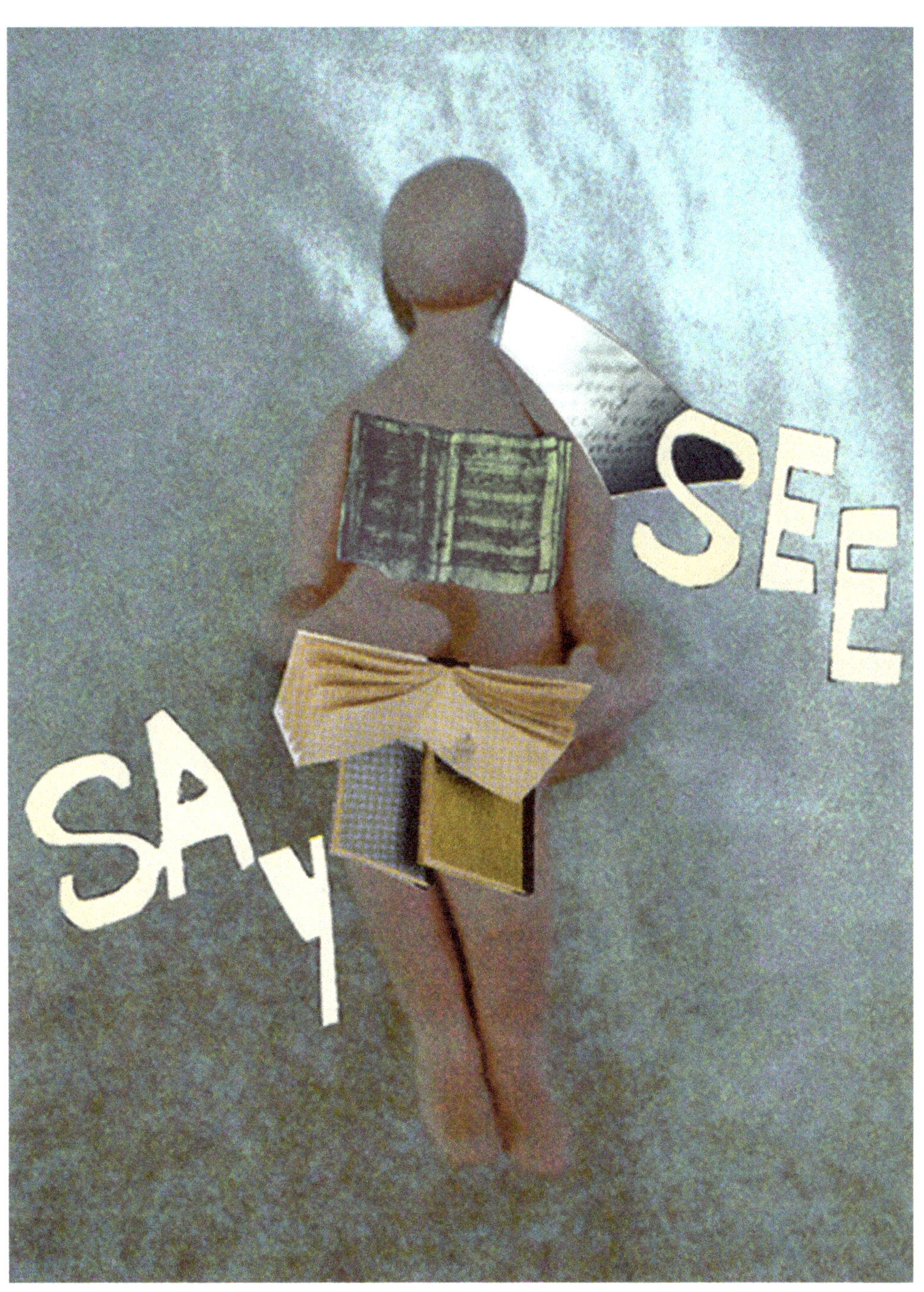

Self-portrait (obscureselves)

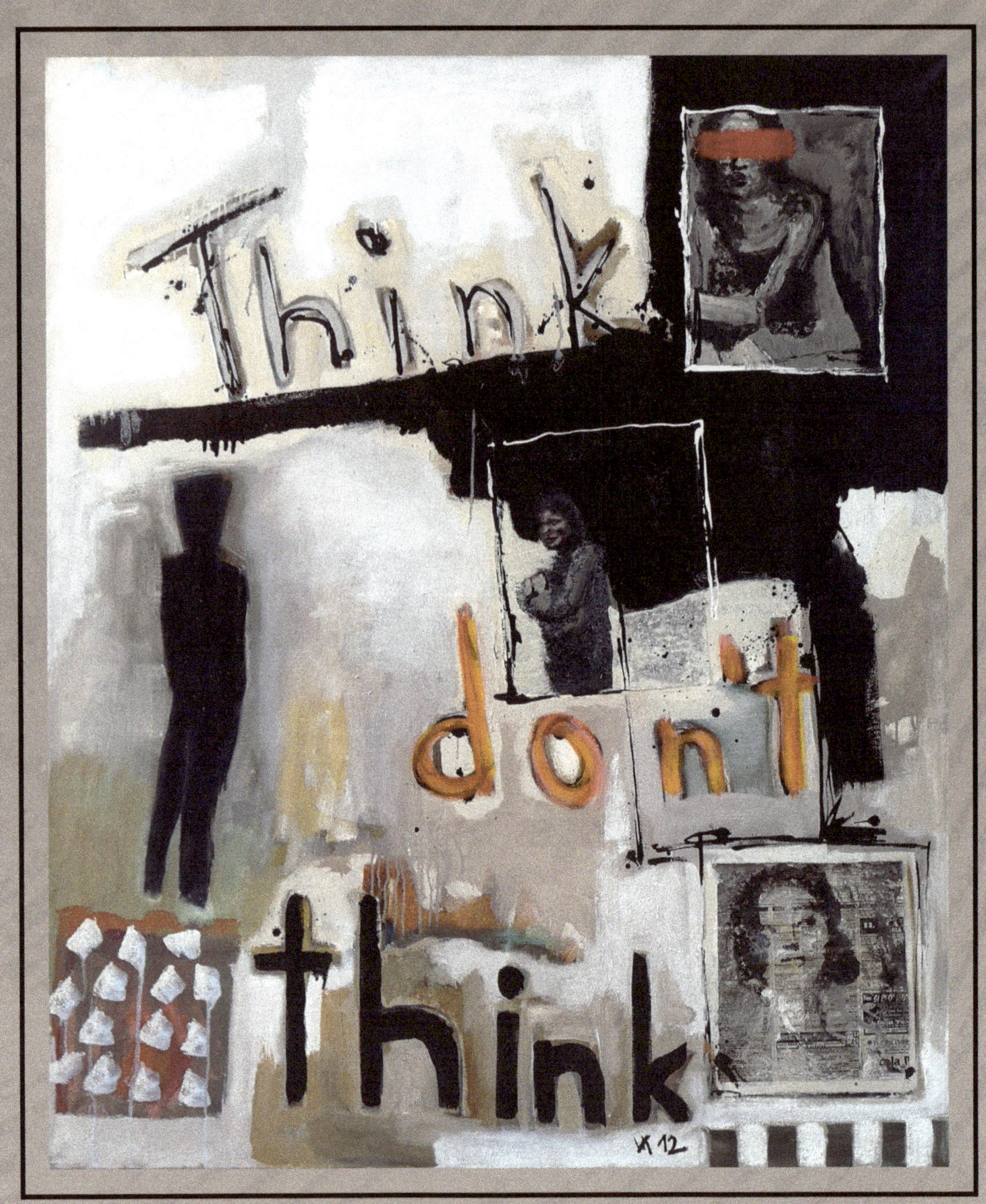

think don't think

Volker Klein

Volker Klein was born in Dortmund, Germany, in 1950 but has lived in Rome for the past forty years. His canvases are beautiful, multi-textured combinations of paint and collage, characterized by sparing use of color and unexpected juxtapositions of seemingly random images and fragments of text. He has given many solo exhibitions in Italy and has also been part of collective showings in Madrid and New York. In addition to being a painter, he is a professional musician; he and his Italian wife, Mimma Santarsiero, formed the six-piece folk band Auriko in 2003, with Mimma as frontwoman and lead vocalist and Volker as principal arranger and player of the cantabile flute. Although they have toured Italy and France and appeared on TV, they are most often found playing in small clubs in Rome.

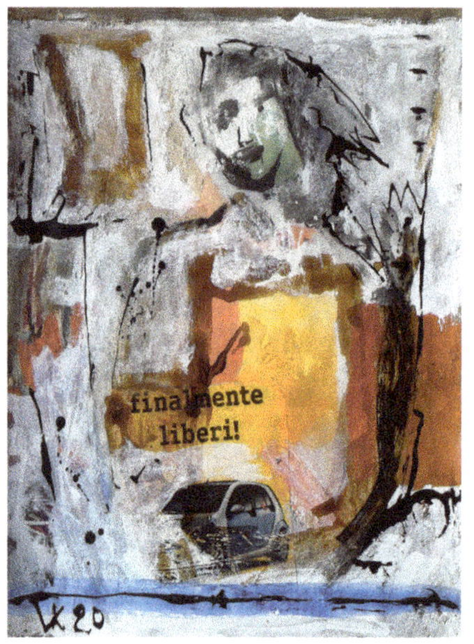

finalmente liberi!

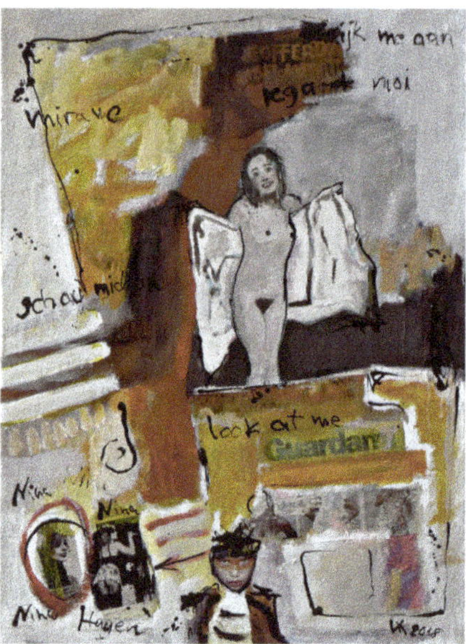

guardami

MPH: Very often the words you use on the canvas are the title of the painting. I like this idea. When and why did you develop it? Sometimes the words are painted like handwriting (***in a bar by the river***) and other times like text print (***finalmente liberi!***). Is this just personal preference at the time, or is there a deeper meaning?

Why the truncated title of ***dea in bici***? It's very intriguing. Is that simply the reason?

What do the other words in ***guardami*** signify? Who is Nina?

In ***la venditrice di limo*** some text is on the surface and some is half-obliterated by the paint. What is the artistic (or perhaps intellectual) purpose of presenting the text in these different ways?

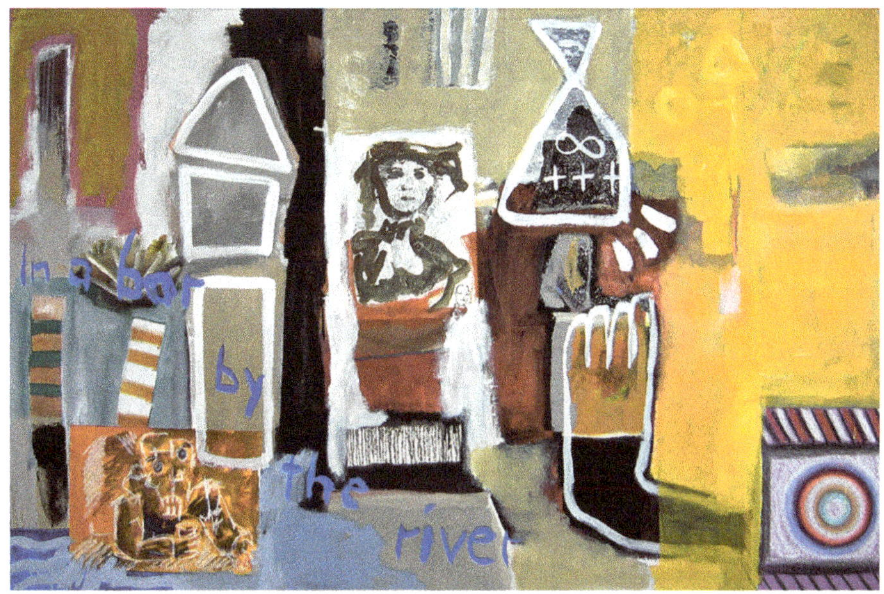

in a bar by the river

What is the aesthetic function of the newspaper in ***think don't think***?

And finally, what kind of paints, brushes, canvases, other materials do you use?

VK: I had to think a lot about your questions, and I also had to observe myself at work to understand why I use writing in painting. Unfortunately, my English is not very good, and I have to resort to Google for help with translating. To answer your questions:

I don't write the title in the picture!!! It is the opposite. The writing appears while I work by association of ideas in the painting and then, since I always have a bit of difficulty finding a more original title, I use this writing as a title. I don't lack ideas when I paint, but when I have to find a title, often nothing comes to my mind.

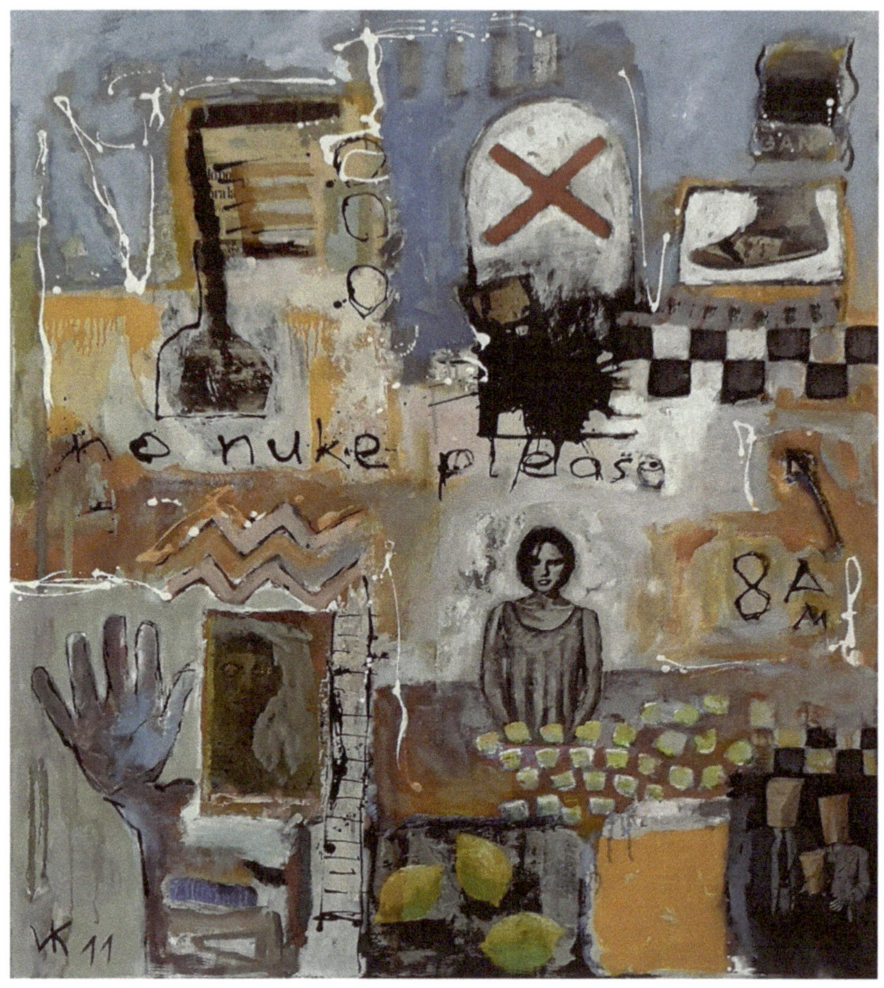

la venditrice di limo

The title ***la venditrice di limoni*** has a different function. I wanted to give a very clear political message with the words "no nuke please" and "8 AM," the time of the explosion of the atomic bomb on Hiroshima. But since I don't really like messages in art that are too explicit, I wanted, with the title, to direct attention to the girl who, with her eyes, asks not to use nuclear power anymore. The other writings in the painting do not have much meaning; therefore, they are veiled.

The choice to write the words by hand or brush is a pictorial decision. ***in a bar by the river*** is written in blue because we needed blue in that place. Otherwise, the picture didn't work. Very similar is the use of the newspaper in ***think don't think***. I like it in the same way that Cubists such as Georges Braque, Juan Gris, and others liked it. Just beautiful and nothing more.

Dea in bici is not truncated. In everyday Italian, instead of bicycle, we say *bici*. Rather, why goddess? Because there is Zeus in the form of a bull watching her. You can see that bicycles are used in my Olympus. It's just a hint of humor that is often found in my paintings as well as in my character.

This kind of humor is also found in my Bob Ross quotes. If you don't know Bob Ross, you MUST watch him on YouTube. Bob Ross did a TV show, ***The Joy of Painting***, for many years and taught the use of oil colors in landscape painting. In every show he said the same sentences. To clean the brushes: "Beat the devil out of it." To paint trees: "Think about shape and form," "bring it all together," or "there are no errors in painting, there are only happy accidents."

The words in ***guardami*** all mean "look at me" in English, French, Spanish, Dutch, and German. I made the painting on the occasion of my exhibition in Rome entitled ***Eros in the Paintings of Volker Klein***. That painting is about exhibitionism, and Nina Hagen, a German rock singer, was always an exhibitionist during her shows. At the bottom left of the painting is a photo of her in a miniskirt.

As for my painting techniques, I have been developing them for decades, and of course I have my secrets.

Alexander Christoph Sterzel

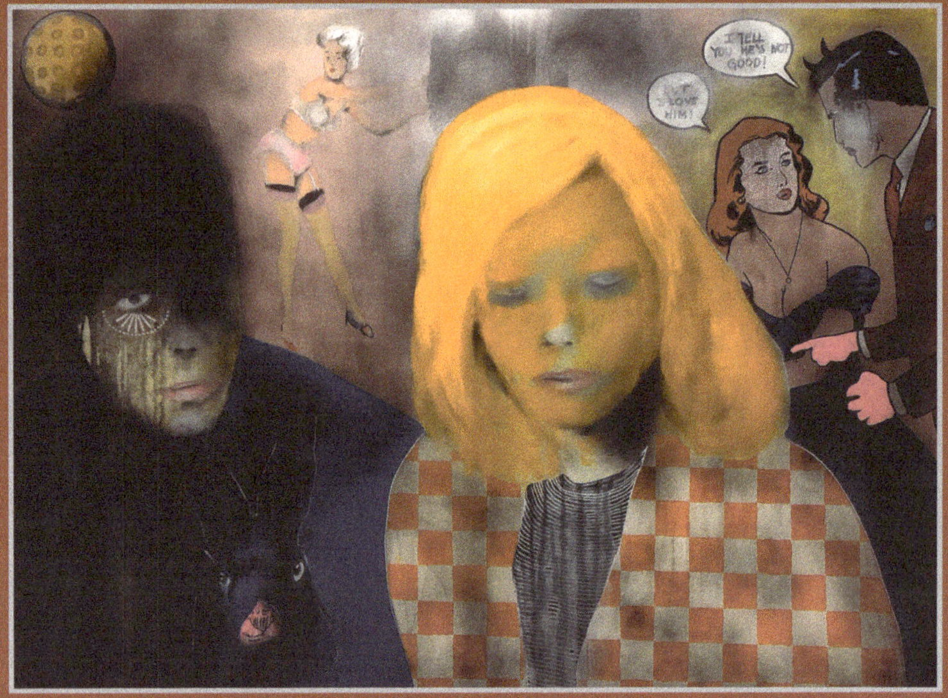

Bonnie and Clyde or Dr. Jekyll and Mrs. Hyde

Born in Ludwigsburg, Germany, in 1967, Alexander Christoph Sterzel now lives in nearby Stuttgart and has worked in a wide variety of artistic fields—including music, theatre, and film—throughout his career. However, it is as a painter that he has particularly made a name for himself, with exhibitions in Paris, London, and New York, as well as Germany, Poland and Italy.

One of Sterzel's favorite stylistic devices is anachronism: people, figures, characters, or pieces of text from the most varied of genres and epochs are connected to one another, leading to their own communication as imposed by the artist.

In this way, Sterzel creates a "pseudo-reality" in his pictures based on his use of independent stories that combine to form an expanded puzzle. It is through surrealism that he has found the appropriate artistic medium to articulate himself, but although analogies to the style of Max Ernst are inevitable, the references to pop art and comic books are no less important. In short, Alexander Sterzel invites us into a fluid surreal world where things come to be and inevitably pass away again. His recently published book, ***Faked Diagnosis I. & II.***, provides an excellent introduction to his work.

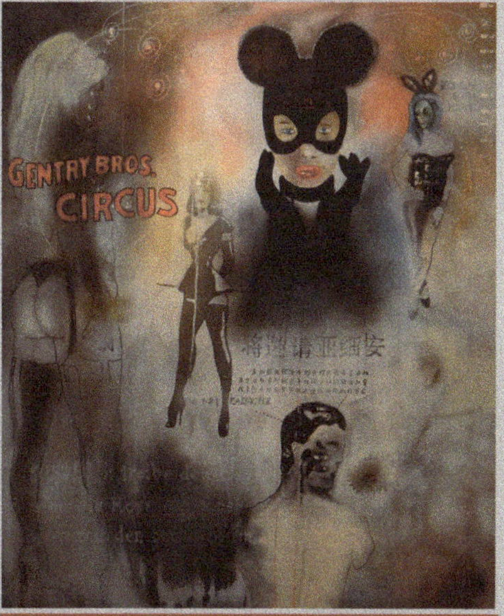

The Big POW Show

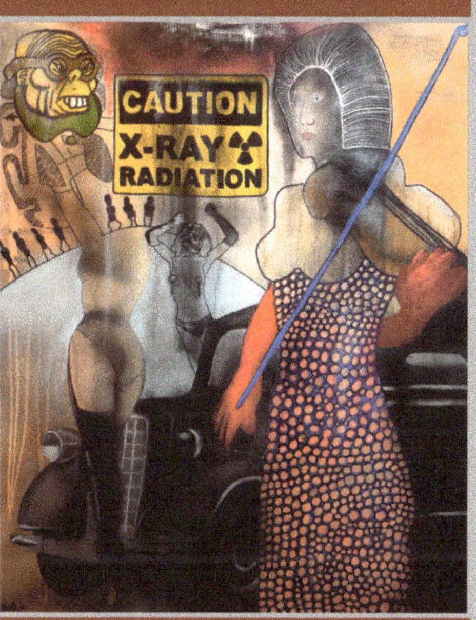

Violin Concerto of Devastation, No.1 in A Minor

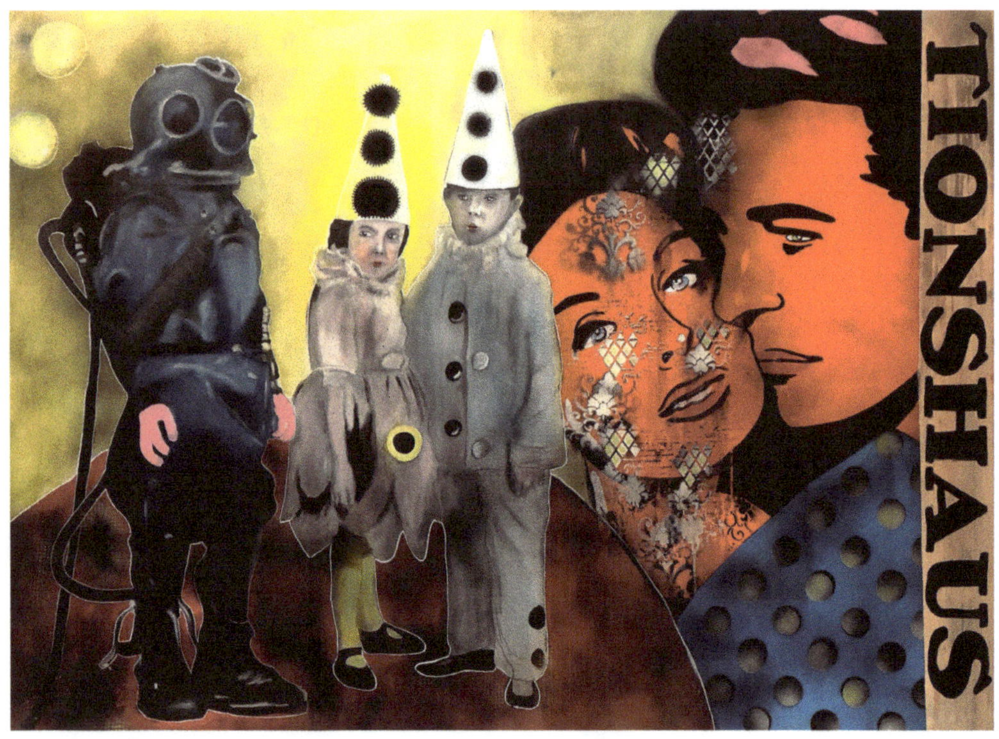

The Forgotten Experiment

MPH: I am interested in where words and images collide in contemporary painting, the aesthetics of incorporating some form of text into a work of pictorial art, and the fundamental relationship between words and images in the work as a whole.

What is your own personal aesthetic in this respect? I assume (perhaps wrongly) that the images come first and the words (or even mathematical formulae) are added later. Are those words chosen primarily for their actual meaning, or is an equally important factor the look of them, over and above their literal value?

What makes you decide whether the words you use are in English or German? In your wonderful painting ***The Big POW Show***, you have not only those two languages but also Chinese characters. Why?

Finally (for now!) some of your most striking paintings (for example, ***The Calypso Cabaret Show*** or ***In Love We Trust***) very conspicuously do not have a textual element. How do you decide whether a piece needs or does not need a piece of written text to be complete?

ACS: Your questions are very interesting. I worry I can't answer all of them. Not because I don't want to, but because one part of my working is building up by intuitiveness. And who can really answer this? Anyway, I will try.

You are right: I always start with a picture. Never with words or text. But when the picture develops, sometimes I have poetry in my mind. It could be that the picture would be modified. But the poetry in mind is still the same. Then it is time for a break. This can be one day or one month or one year.

One day the work goes on. Meanwhile, I forget the lyrics, but I don't worry. The subconscious is now like a little helping hand. It could be that I have overpainted the picture more than one time. If my instinct tells me that it is time to install words right now, I do it. Sometimes the words have nothing to do with the picture anymore, or the words help me to find the way to finish the artwork. However, it is a very long process till I really can finish the work.

Then there are two ways to use written words. First, because of the meaning of them, or second, because the typography used as a written picture doesn't matter to the meaning. To explain more easily: It could be I'm painting a sun and you find the words: this is the sun. Or I'm painting a sun and you can read: sweet danger moments.

This is the problem that Ludwig Wittgenstein explained. We (human beings) have all the same words, but every person has another memory associated with this term. So this is the reason why people never will understand each other 100 percent.

So, what to do if you have no more words for articulation? You use paintings. Pictures. That's why Instagram is so successful. Everybody in the world will understand pictures that people post, even if everybody in the world has other associations with them. And here is the point where I also use words, lyrics, poetry to complete the picture for better understanding. But the words may be distorted now because the meaning of the picture has changed. So sometimes I think it is OK to paint without words inside. Hmmm, not easy in English to describe! At least I discovered this way for my speech in art more than thirty years ago.

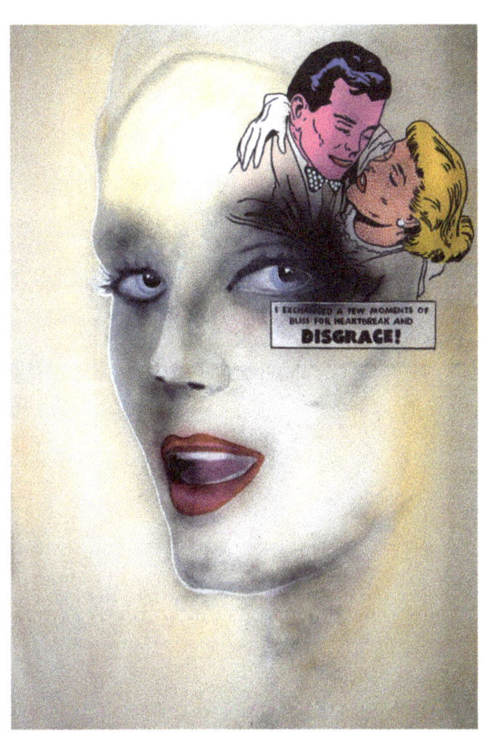

I Exchanged a Few Moments of Bliss for Heartbreak and Disgrace

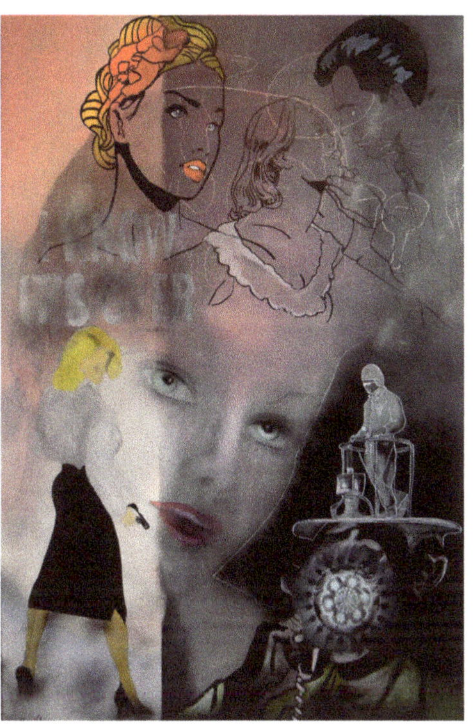

Monkey Business or I know It's Over

Ruben Dominguez Leon

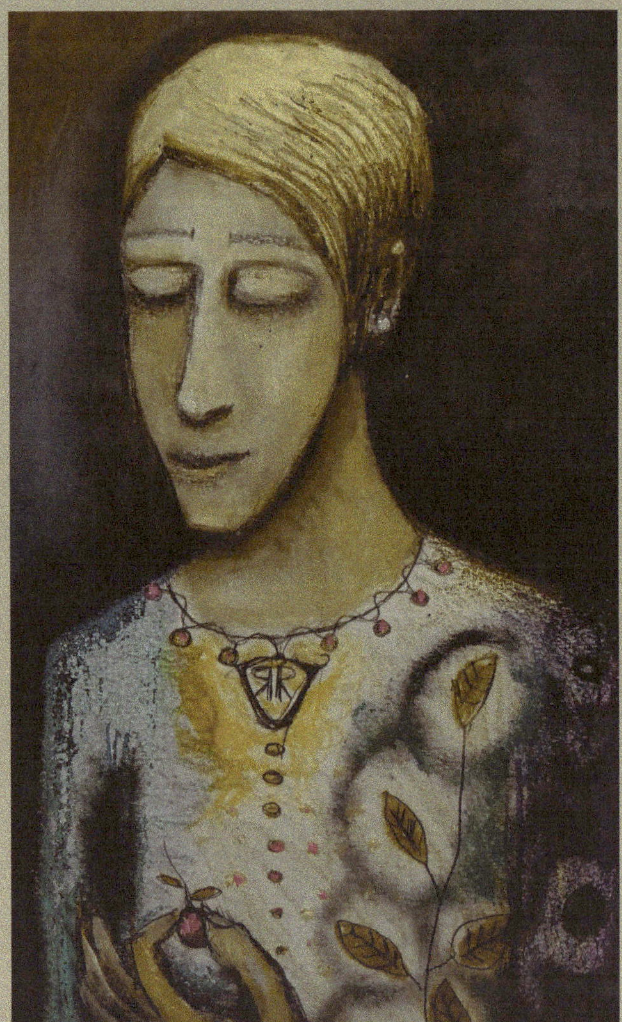

Locked in My Head

Born in Culiacan Rosales, capital city of Sinaloa estado in northwest Mexico, Ruben Domínguez Léon is one of the most striking and distinctive painters of the modern era, creating an extraordinary dreamworld that combines breathtaking imagination with superb technique.

When he was twelve years old, he started writing and illustrating a kind of diary that he called ***The Book of Yoshern***, for which he created an original semi-hieroglyphic language. Since then, he has reached a worldwide audience, holding exhibitions in Moscow, Japan, Argentina, and the United States, as well as many European countries, including Holland, France, Italy, Sweden, and Spain. A brief but excellent introduction to his work can be gained by watching ***Ruben Domínguez Léon—Obras*** on YouTube.

MPH: I am interested in investigating where words and images combine in contemporary painting, the aesthetics of incorporating some form of text into a work of pictorial art, and the fundamental relationship between words and images in the work as a whole. What is your own personal aesthetic in this respect?

Your style is immediately distinctive. What painters or personal life experiences do you believe have contributed to your style, and are there any painters who incorporate text into their canvases who you would say have influenced your own art?

Finally, what materials do you use? I mean, what kinds of paint, brushes, canvases?

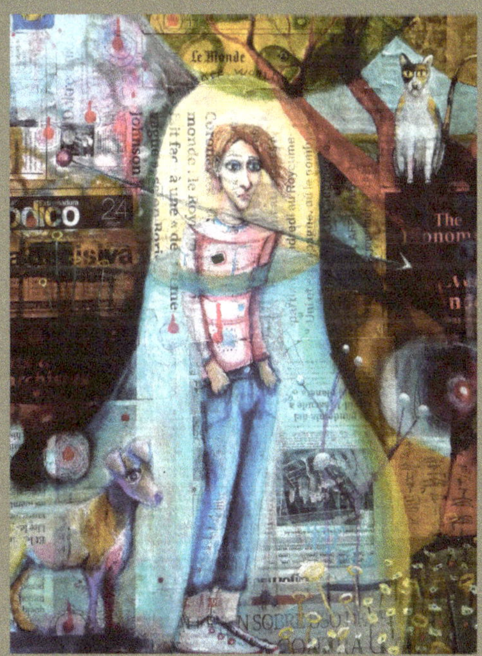

Uncertainty and Isolation in an Imaginary Bubble

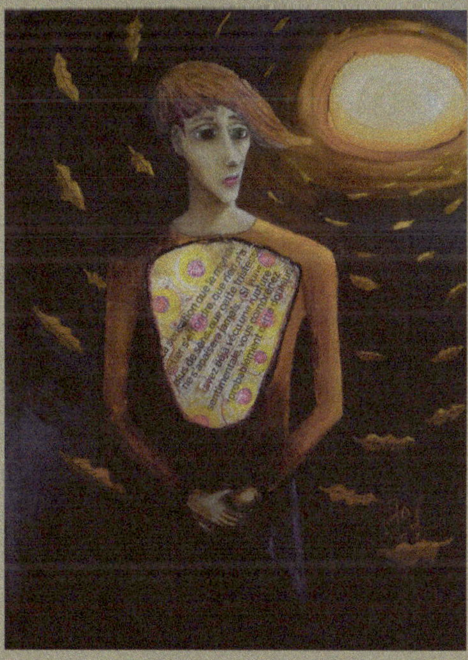

Hope Beyond the Abyss

RDL: I started drawing at the age of eight, and my style has evolved in different stages of my life. Some of my paintings reflect that lonely childhood in a desert place in northern Mexico near the border where a group of Spanish adventurers and exiled Maronite Lebanese arrived—my ancestors. But a fortuitous event made my curiosity explode when a reproduction of ***The Garden of Earthly Delights*** (Hieronymus Bosch, c. 1500) came into my hands. It was like a spell, and since then I have been captivated by many artists. As I have matured, I have moved away from the predominant influence of surrealism. Sure, some elements of surrealism can still be found, but these have been adapted to the way I paint now.

Disappointments and hopes in a different world, the desire to explore new audiovisual fields, the use of art as a mirror in which to reflect our humanity . . . these are some of the engines that drive my search and nourish my works.

The idea of accompanying drawings and paintings with complete sentences or just words began as a teenager. Enchanted by the mystery of ancient civilizations, especially the Egyptian, I invented a kind of alphabet based on symbols with which I accompanied my drawings of that time. There are still some small hidden inscriptions lying around in my current paintings. As I have matured my style, I have incorporated some words in different languages; some are poems, others are simple phrases that come to mind automatically; other times the phrases have a meaning linked to the image in such a way that the text by itself has an aesthetic value; some are symbols that represent a feeling or an entire idea meditated in those long hours working alone. Lately, I have painted a series of images about newspaper clippings from around the world with negative news, the political upheaval, the anti-fascist riots, the climate rarefied by a pandemic that has revealed the fragility of our society. Some images are dramatic and others of complete serenity, as if I was trying to cover the unpleasant reality with colors.

I generally use oils and acrylics on canvas, but lately I have painted on paper and other surfaces and I also use all kinds of pencils and powders in order to experiment.

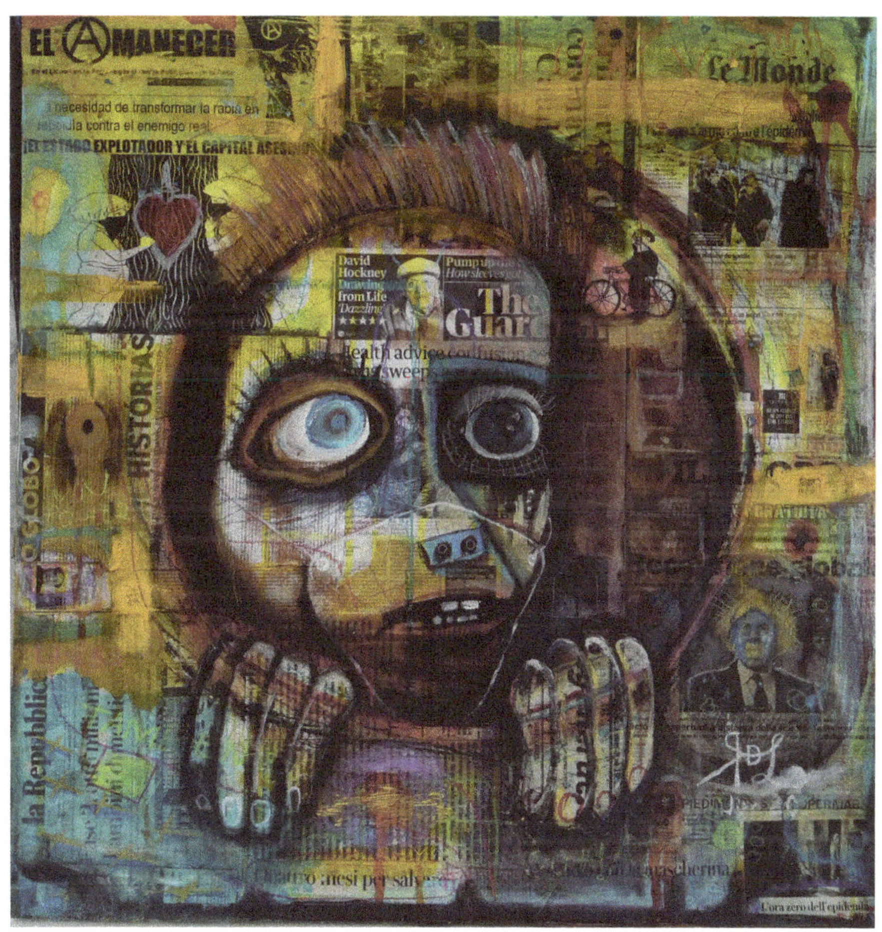

Survive in a Time of Collective Madness

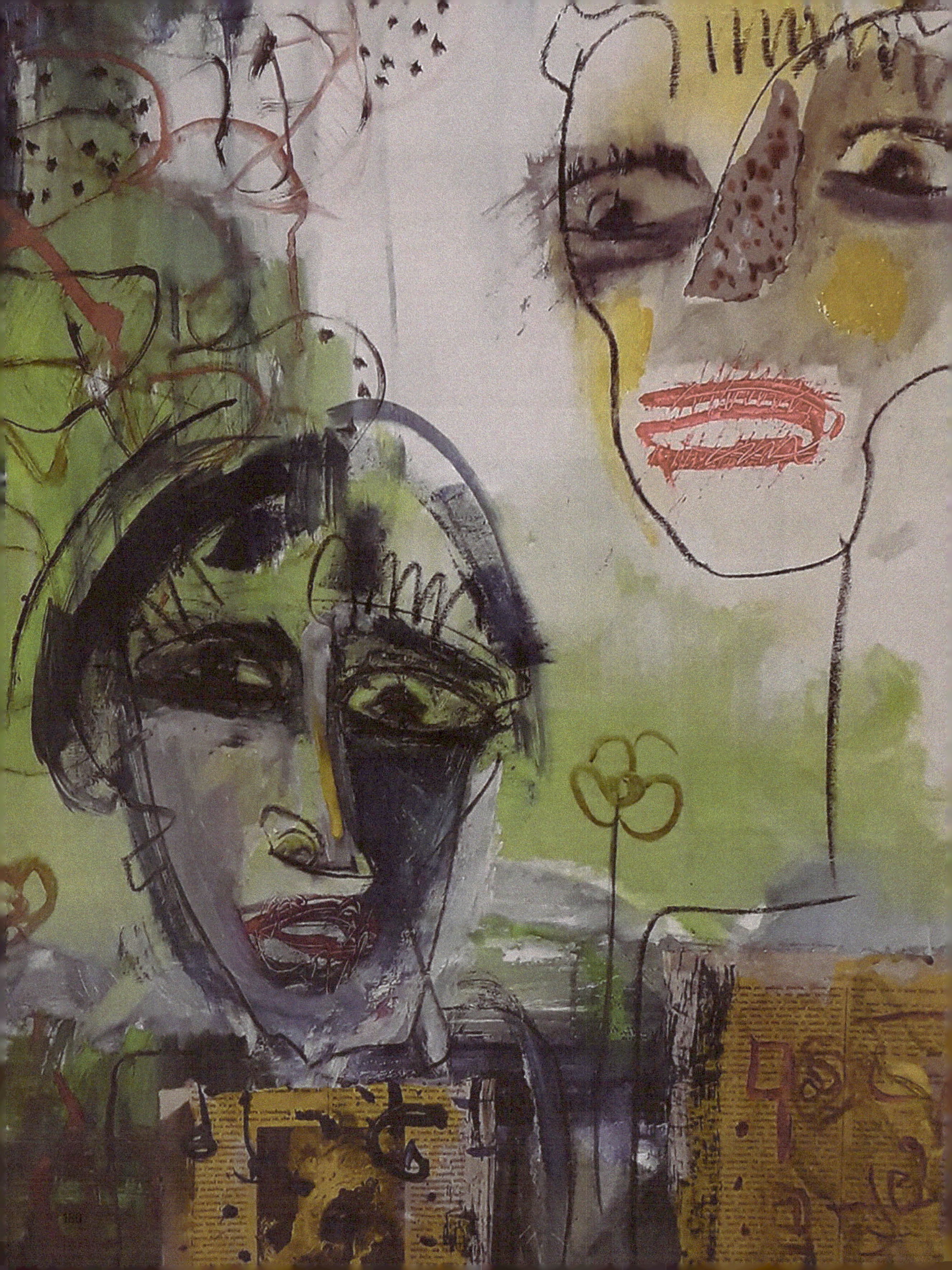

Erika Capobianco

Erika Capobianco was born in Rome in 1961. She now lives in Aprilia, a city in the province of Lazio in central Italy. Nearly all of her paintings are highly stylized, often satirical portraits, characterized by flamboyant brushstrokes, seemingly random collage, and an unerring sense of color and composition. Capobianco tries to pass emotions from the unconscious directly to the canvas, without filtering.

She did not attend any academy or painting course, so her style is spontaneous. Until a few years ago, she did not know there were artists with a similar style and confesses that she was even ashamed to show her own paintings. Since then her work has been featured in exhibitions in Italy, and she has had solo shows in Rome and Milan, the latter at the house/museum of the great modern Italian poet Alda Merini. It is a telling point that she prefers to buy her brushes in hardware stores rather than in artists' supply shops and frequently uses pieces of reclaimed cardboard as a base for her works.

MPH: You use scraps of newspaper as part of your paintings—a kind of collage. What do you think is the connection between writing and painting in your work?

EC: I often insert in my paintings pieces of paper from things I use in everyday life—like leaflets of anxiolytics, food wrappers, things found by chance on the street, etc. *È un modo per portare la vita nella mia pittura.* It is a way to bring life into my paintings. Since I also love to write, sometimes I start a painting by writing verses on the white canvas that I then cover with layers of color, signs, etc. Even if invisible to the eye of the beholder, I like to think that the vibrations or the concepts are buried there and remain part of the final work.

MPH: ***Omaggio a Lindsay Kemp*** has words written on the surface of the image, and the painting you gave me a few years ago has a visible cutting from an Italian newspaper. What is the relationship between the words and the actual painting in these two works? How and why do you choose handwritten words for one painting and printed words for another? What is your aesthetic behind the choice?

EC: I was lucky enough to know Kemp in the eighties when I was very young. He came to Rome to represent his show ***Flowers***, which I saw several times. He impressed me a lot and left a mark on my youthful imagination.

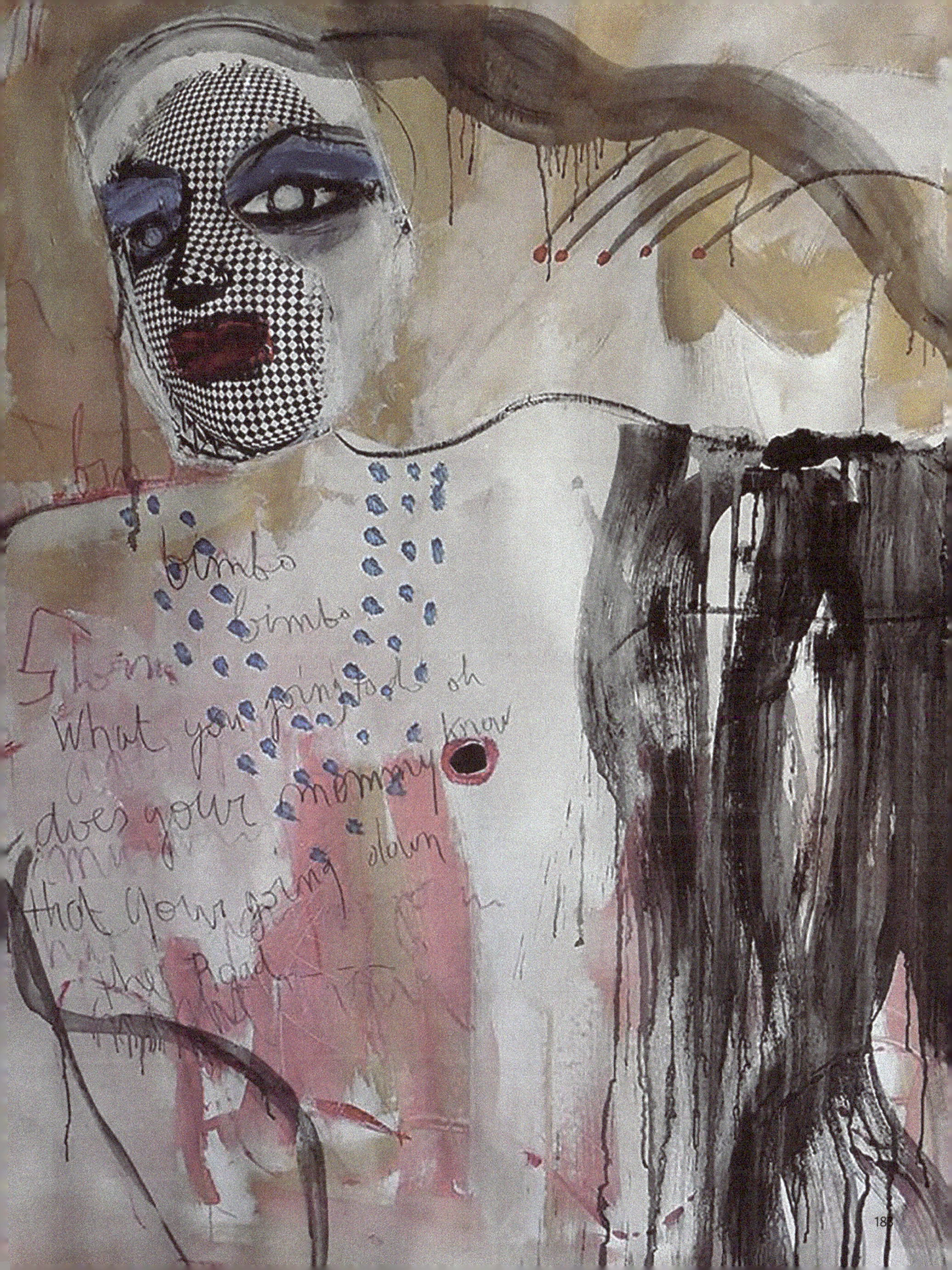
bimbo
bimbo
What you
know
does your mommy
down
that your going
the Road

One evening after a show while in a taxi on the way to a restaurant to eat, he put his head on my shoulder and hummed a song from his childhood in England. I just remember that he went *bimbo bimbo what you go to do,* or something like that.

Some time ago, almost forty years later, that song with his voice came to my ears while I was sleeping. I woke up and wrote *bimbo bimbo* on a piece of paper that I had on the bedside table so as not to forget, and I fell asleep again. *Al mattino ho aperto internet e ho letto la notizia: morto Lindsay Kemp.* In the morning I read the news that Kemp had died. I saw the note I had left on the bedside table, and I did this work to pay homage to a special being.

The work on paper that I gave you is actually the portrait of a severe and grim teacher that I had in school. This teacher, and others, made us hate culture instead of loving it. Putting a piece of newspaper in her face is meant to evoke the many and often useless notions that the teachers gave us.

But I also need the collage simply to give body and movement to the images. *Spesso io faccio senza troppo pensare.* Often I do it without thinking too much.

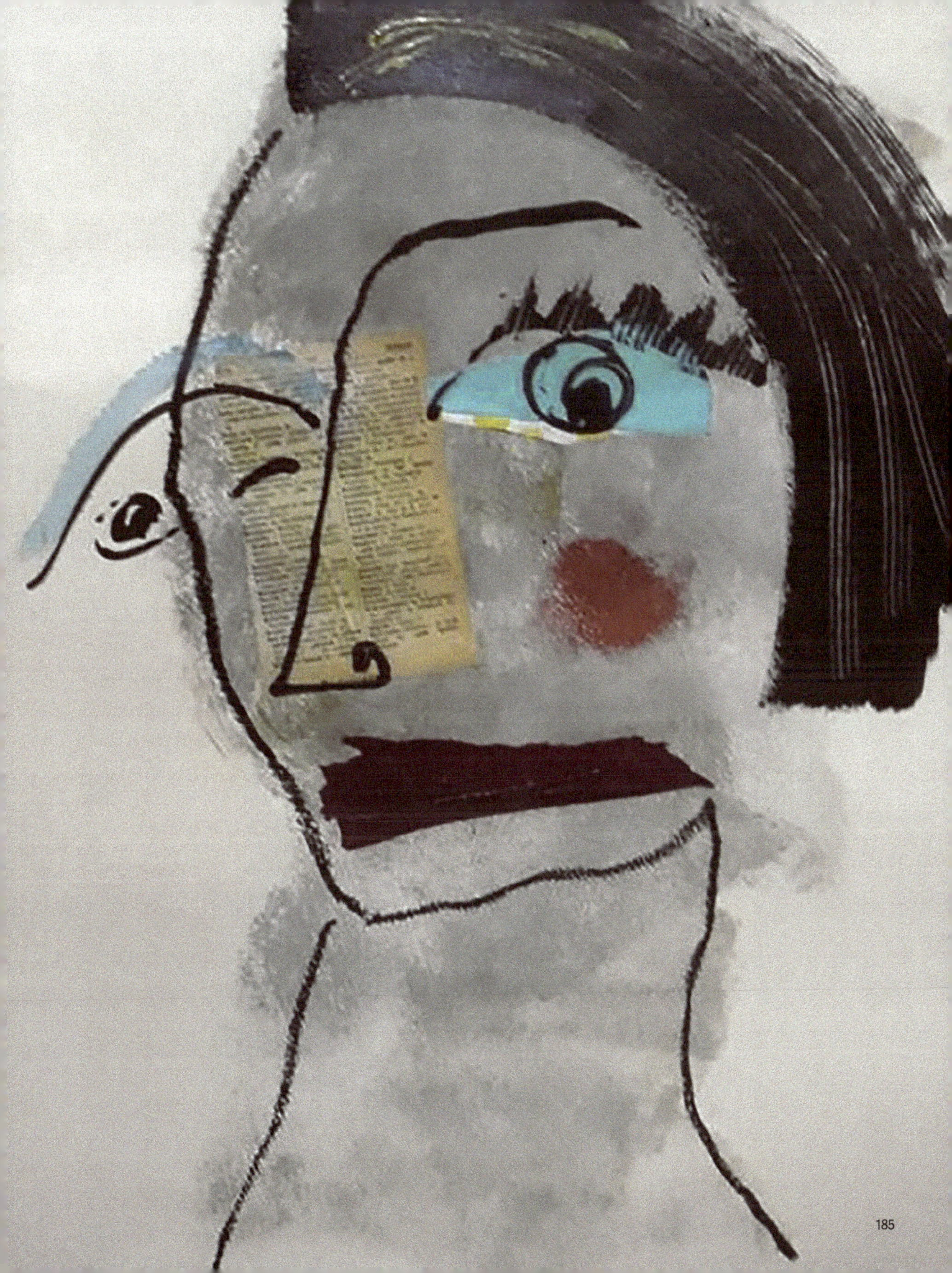

The Future
remains to be seen

Ideally, this article would have been printed out, cut up into strips of text, pasted onto canvases six feet high and four feet wide, spattered with random splashes of paint, and exhibited in the stairwells of Chinese apartment blocks, in waterfront bars in San Francisco, or suspended from the sides of cargo vessels carrying apes and ivory through the Suez Canal. And maybe not even printed—maybe reconstructed with letters an inch high cut from fashion ads in, say, *Vogue* or *Harper's Bazaar* and stuck to a series of vast canvases as if to create some sort of wildly visual but readable collage.

From Cubism onwards, artists who have used words have frequently added them on with no more thought to their meaning than if they were dabs of color or swishes of paint; the literary aspect is entirely subservient to the visual; they are intended to be looked at, not to be read. It would be interesting to see the focus reversed.

If I had been writing this article thirty-odd years ago, I would almost certainly have included a section on graffiti. Jean-Michel Basquiat influenced a generation, and the pioneering photography of Martha Cooper and Henry Chalfant gave permanence and artistic prestige to subway art—an art form that has always intrinsically combined images with words. Who could have predicted what would happen next? If Martha Cooper made graffiti acceptable to the white middle class, then Banksy has reduced it to the level of the white middle class, a petite-bourgeoisie sideshow lacking any artistic merit and exhibiting all the danger of a temporary tattoo. Ironically, if graffiti has any contemporary relevance, it is demonstrated here, in the illustrations accompanying this article. The free expression we see in much of the most striking contemporary art owes more than it sometimes cares to admit to those illustrations of subterranean Chicago and New York from the 1970s and '80s. And as for the future—well, that remains to be seen. No artist in any medium ever predicted an aesthetic future; the Picassos, the Stravinskys, the James Joyces merely created a new present in reaction to a worn-out past, and for all his avant-garde genius I can guarantee you that Picasso never predicted Matthew Barney or Ai Weiwei. The future, as I say, remains to be seen. But one prediction I would like to make is this: that no history of early twenty-first-century art will be complete without specific reference to the five artists I have featured in this article. Their work, their wonderfully inventive combination of text and image, is of today and for tomorrow. It is impossible to do more. ꝏ

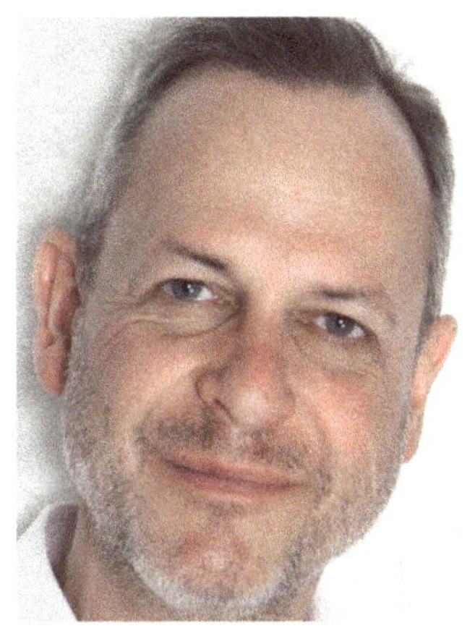

Born in London, Michael Paul Hogan is a poet, journalist, literary essayist, and fiction writer whose work has appeared extensively in the USA, UK, India, and China. His collected poems, ***American Voodoo***, was published by **Bluechrome** in the UK in 2008, and again, with Chinese translations, by **Foreign Languages Press** in Beijing in 2011. Venues at which he has read his poetry include **The Poetry Café** and **The Keats House** in London, and **The Rondo Theatre** in Bath. He was also a guest speaker at the **Ahmedabad International Literature Festival** in 2021. As a journalist he has been Features Writer and Columnist for ***Island Life*** in Key West, Florida, Theatre Critic for ***The Bristol Evening Post*** in the UK, and Features Writer & Features Editor for ***Dalian Today*** in northeast China, while his short stories have appeared in a number of well-respected literary journals, including ***Big Bridge*** (California), ***Adelaide Literary Magazine*** (New York), ***The Oddville Press*** (London), and ***The Blue Nib*** (Ireland). Brought up in England and Wales, he has lived in Key West, India, Sumatra, Java, Thailand, and China, and to support himself during periods of working on experimental poetry and prose has variously sought employment as a commercial fisherman, house painter, bartender, day laborer, radio announcer, and market stall trader. He is married to Yan Xiang Shu, the former ballet dancer and translator of his poetry into Chinese.

www.ingramcontent.com/pod-product-compliance
Lightning Source LLC
LaVergne TN
LVHW060623110826
845147LV00015B/919

* 9 7 8 1 9 5 6 0 5 6 8 7 7 *